New Technology and Manufacturing Management

WILEY SERIES

NEW TECHNOLOGIES AND WORK

Series Editor: **Bernhard Wilpert** *Technische Universität Berlin*

NEW TECHNOLOGY AND HUMAN ERROR

Edited by Jens Rasmussen, Keith Duncan and Jacques Leplat

THE MEANING OF WORK AND TECHNOLOGICAL OPTIONS

*Edited by Véronique de Keyser, Thoralf Qvale, Bernhard Wilpert
and S. Antonio Ruiz Quintanilla*

DEVELOPING SKILLS WITH INFORMATION TECHNOLOGY

Edited by Lisanne Bainbridge and S. Antonio Ruiz Quintanilla

NEW TECHNOLOGY AND MANUFACTURING MANAGEMENT
Strategic Choices for Flexible Production Systems

Edited by Malcolm Warner, Werner Wobbe and Peter Brödner

Further titles in preparation

New Technology and Manufacturing Management

Strategic Choices for Flexible Production Systems

Edited
by

Malcolm Warner, **Werner Wobbe** and **Peter Brödner**

JOHN WILEY & SONS

Chichester · New York · Brisbane · Toronto · Singapore

in association with the Commission of the European Communities

Publication arrangements by
Commission of the European Communities,
Directorate-General Telecommunications, Information Industries and Innovation, Scientific and
Technical Communications Service, Luxembourg

© 1990 ESC–EEC–EAEC, EUR 11938EN, Brussels–Luxembourg

LEGAL NOTICE

Published 1990 by John Wiley & Sons Ltd.
Baffins Lane, Chichester, West Sussex PO19 1UD, UK

Other Wiley Editorial Offices

John Wiley & Sons, Inc., 605 Third Avenue,
New York, NY 10158-0012, USA

Jacaranda Wiley Ltd, G.P.O. Box 859, Brisbane,
Queensland 4001, Australia

John Wiley & Sons (Canada) Ltd, 22 Worcester Road,
Rexdale, Ontario M9W 1L1, Canada

John Wiley & Sons (SEA) Pte Ltd, 37 Jalan Pemimpin 05-04,
Block B, Union Industrial Building, Singapore 2057

Library of Congress Cataloging-in-Publication Data:

New technology and manufacturing management : strategic choices for
flexible production systems / edited by Malcolm Warner, Werner
Wobbe, and Peter Brödner.
    p.   cm.—(New technologies and work)
Includes bibliographical references.
ISBN 0 471 92454 7
1. Manufactures—Technological innovations—Management.
2. Flexible manufacturing systems—Management.   I. Warner, Malcolm.
II. Wobbe, Werner.   III. Brödner, Peter.   IV. Series.
HD 9720.5.N48   1990   89-70549
658.5'1—dc20   CIP

British Library Cataloguing in Publication Data:

New technology and manufacturing management : strategic
choices for flexible production systems.
1. Manufacturing industries. Automation
I. Warner, Malcolm   II. Wobbe, Werner   III. Brödner, P.
(Peter)   IV. Series
670.42'7

ISBN 0 471 92454 7

Typeset by Acorn Bookwork, Salisbury, Wiltshire
Printed in Great Britain by Biddles Ltd, Guildford, Surrey

Contents

Section 1: Overview and 'Predicted Trends' Towards the 'Flexible Factory'

Section 2: Conditions Which Make Flexible Production Work

Section 3: Selected European Perspectives

Section 4: Strategic Management Applications

Advisory Board

Contributors

John Bessant

Department of Business Management, Brighton Polytechnic, Moulsecoomb, Brighton BN2 4AT, UK.

Rob Bilderbeek

Centre for Technology and Policy Studies TNO, PO Box 541, NL-7300 AM Apeldoorn, The Netherlands.

Peter Brödner

Institut Arbeit und Technik, Florastrasse 9, D–4650, Gelsenkirchen 1, FRG.

Hans-Jörg Bullinger

Fraunhofer Institut für Arbeitswirtschaft und Organisation, Postfach 80 04 69, Nobelstrasse 12, D-7000 Stuttgart 80 (Vaihingen), FRG.

Adrian Campbell

School of Public Policy, University of Birmingham, Birmingham B15 2TT, UK.

J. Martin Corbett

School of Industrial and Business Studies, University of Warwick, Coventry CV4 7AL, UK.

Alain d'Iribarne

Centre National de la Recherche Scientifique, 15 Quai Anatole, 75700 Paris, France.

Jutta Fix-Sterz

Fraunhofer Institut für Systemtechnik und Innovationsforschung (ISI), Breslauer Strasse 48, D-7500 Karlsruhe 1, FRG.

William Haywood

Department of Business Management, Brighton Polytechnic, Moulsecoomb, Brighton BN2 4AT, UK.

Peer Hull Kristensen   Institute of Economic Planning, Roskilde Uni-
                            versity Centre, PO Box 260, DK-4000 Roskilde,
                            Denmark.

Gunter Lay   Fraunhofer Institut für Systemtechnik und
                            Innovationsforschung (ISI), Breslauer Strasse
                            48, D-7500 Karlsruhe 1, FRG.

Martin Lockett   Oxford Institute of Information Management,
                            Templeton College, Oxford OX11 5NY, UK.

Rainer Schultz-Wild   Institut für Sozialwissenschaftliche Forschung
                            eV (ISF), Jakob-Klar-Strasse 9, D-8000 Munich
                            40, FRG.

Michael Schumann   SOFI–Soziologisches Forschungsinstitut Göttin-
                            gen eV, Friedländer Weg 31, D-3400 Göttingen,
                            FRG.

Nigel Slack   Department of Manufacturing Systems, Brunel:
                            The University of West London, Uxbridge,
                            Middlesex UB8 3PH, UK.

Arndt Sorge   Department of Business Administration,
                            University of Limburg, F EW-BE, PO Box 616,
                            NL-6200 Maastricht, The Netherlands.

Malcolm Warner   Department of Engineering, Management
                            Studies Group, University of Cambridge, Mill
                            Lane, Cambridge CB2 1RX, UK.

Jürgen Wengel   Fraunhofer Institut für Systemtechnik und
                            Innovationsforschung (ISI), Breslauer Strasse
                            48, D-7500 Karlsruhe 1, FRG.

Werner Wobbe   Commission of the European Communities, DG
                            XII–MONITOR Programme–FAST, 200 rue de
                            la Loi, B-1049 Brussels, Belgium.

Foreword

DO WE NEED MORE AND BETTER TECHNOLOGY OR MORE AND BETTER HUMAN AND ORGANISATIONAL INNOVATION?

It is rather widely spread 'conventional wisdom' to consider that what an open, competitive economy and a successful innovative firm needs is more and better technology at the right time. Be it car manufacturing, new telecommunication systems, new financial services, people attribute a decisive role to the introduction of new technology.

FAST studies suggest that you can design the best hardware, have the best equipment, and conceive the best software in the world, and yet still not be certain of eliminating cases of low efficiency, small productivity increases, major 'technological' failures.

What the economy and the firm need is more and better human and organisational innovation. This calls for a qualitative jump in the understanding of how humans interact with technology and, above all, in the design of increasingly complex techno-organisational systems.

Most of the current inefficiencies, failures and accidents in advanced automated production systems and telematic based service operations are due to system design approaches which do not sufficiently take into account interactions between the human, organisational and technical elements.

We do not need 'management of technology' alone—we need 'ORGWARE' (a fully complementary and integrated dimension with hardware and software), that is, the combination of theoretical sciences (cognitive, information, human and social) and applied knowledge and expertise which enables the monitoring and management of complex interactions between the technical, human and organisational elements of the system.

With the failure to integrate human and organisation elements at the design stage, it should be no surprise to witness in ten to fifteen years increasing breakdowns and accidents, both in production and services activities. This book offers what it considers to be a viable alternative—human flexible production.

Riccardo Petrella[1]
April, 1989

[1]Dr Riccardo Petrella is Head of the FAST Programme of the Commission of the European Communities, Brussels. FAST stands for Forecasting and Assessment in Science and Technology.

Series Preface

This volume is part of a publication series emerging from an international interdisciplinary study group on 'New Technologies and Work (NeTWork)'. NeTWork is sponsored jointly by the Werner-Reimers-Foundation (Bad Homburg, Federal Republic of Germany) and the Maison des Sciences de l'Homme (Paris). The NeTWork study group[1] has set itself the task of scrutinising the most important problem domains posed by the introduction and spread of new technologies in work settings. This problem focus requires interdisciplinary cooperation. The usual mode of operating is to identify an important problem area within the NeTWork scope, to attempt to prestructure it, and then to invite original contributions from European researchers or research teams actively involved in relevant analytic or developmental work. A specific workshop serves to cross-fertilise the different approaches and to help to integrate more fully the individual contributions. Three volumes of NeTWork activities have so far appeared in the Wiley Series 'New Technologies and Work'[2].

Bernhard Wilpert

[1]Members (1988) are: Prof. Dr L. Bainbridge, UK; Dr A. Borseix, France; Prof. Dr P. Drenth, Netherlands; Prof. Dr K. Duncan, UK; Dr J. Evans, UK; Prof. Dr V. de Keyser, Belgium; Prof. Dr U. Kleinbeck, FRG; Prof. Dr J. Leplat, France; Prof. Dr M. de Montmollin, France; Prof. Dr O. Pastré, France; Prof. Dr F. Rapp, FRG; Prof. Dr J. Rasmussen, Denmark; Prof. Dr J.-D. Reynaud, France; Prof. Dr R. Roe, Netherlands; Dr S. A. Ruiz Quintanilla, FRG; Prof. Dr T. Qvale, Norway; Prof. Dr B. Wilpert, FRG.

[2]J. Rasmusen, K. Duncan and J. Leplat (eds): *New Technology and Human Error*, 1986

V. de Keyser, T. Qvale, B. Wilpert and S. A. Ruiz Quintanilla (eds): *The Meaning of Work and Technological Options*, 1988

L. Bainbridge and S. A. Ruiz Quintanilla (eds): *Developing Skills with Information Technology*, 1989.

Series Preface

Edmund A. Spiers

Preface

In this volume we hope to present an alternative view to the technology-centred approach which dominates many of the endeavours in the field, and to contrast it with a human-centred one. The latter will emphasise competence and skills as opposed to hardware. It will underline the social choices which are available, thus playing down the deterministic approach of many of the 'technology' theorists. We hope to show the variety of possibilities available in the manufacturing area, by pointing to ongoing, concrete examples across Europe, from the North Sea down to the Mediterranean. Taken together, we hope, the chapters present a 'European' perspective on a humanistic application of the new manufacturing technology, which is socially acceptable and managerially viable.

The volume is divided into four sections. In Section 1 we present an overview and discussion of predicted trends towards the 'flexible factory'. Chapter 1 outlines the main themes to be treated, how they arose and why they are important. Some basic conceptual notions are introduced in Chapter 2 (Bullinger) apropos the future of the factory and the factory of the future. In the next chapter (Slack), we are taken further into the notion of manufacturing flexibility, as seen by practising managers. After this, changing concepts of work and qualifications are discussed by Schumann (Chapter 4). Then, to complete this section, the newly required qualifications and skill requirements are dealt with by d'Iribarne (Chapter 5).

Chapter 6 introduces Section 2, on conditions which make flexible production possible. Haywood and Bessant deal here with the organisation and integration of production factors needed for flexible manufacturing systems. Next we turn to a discussion of process-related skills (Schultz-Wild) in Chapter 7. In Chapter 8, Brödner looks at 'technocentric' versus 'anthropocentric' designs. In Chapter 9, Corbett analyses the problem of how to select designs for human–machine interfaces. Finally, in this section, Lay looks at ongoing advanced manufacturing technology in the workplace and asks what are the strategic options available in the development of CIM systems.

In Section 3, we present selected European perspectives of the 'state of the art', as exemplified in recent research based on technical and organisational change in different countries. This account covers selected countries in the Community. In Chapter 11, Sorge presents a broad perspective on work and vocational training across the board. This description and analysis is followed by Kristensen's account of flexible manufacturing developments in Denmark (Chapter 12). The German case is then covered by Fix-Sterz and colleagues (Chapter 13). Bilderbeek in Chapter 14 looks at the state of manufacturing in the Netherlands. Last, in this section, Wobbe presents a European view of advanced manufacturing in the US, based on extensive visits to sites developing the newest production technology.

In the concluding section of the book, we turn to strategic management implications of the topic. To start, Lockett, in Chapter 16, focuses on the implementation of information technology by management in a manufacturing firm. Campbell and Warner then end the volume with a discussion of the management roles and structures needed to handle the new manufacturing technology.

Having started with the 'future of the factory' issue, we feel we have introduced enough technological and social evidence in the various chapters to lead us to specific pointers to the 'factory of the future', what it will look like, how it can be more effectively managed and how best 'people' will be given priority over 'machines' in it.

To sum up, we admit our penchant towards the human-centred approach in this interdisciplinary contribution to the debate as to how to deal with the application of the new technology. We have, in developing the approach, drawn on a variety of theoretical perspectives and practical approaches, ranging from experts in industrial psychology and sociology, to those working in the forefront of manufacturing systems and management studies. We hope we have usefully integrated both knowledge and experience in a way which is at the same time interesting for the academic audience as well as the broader practitioner community, namely, for teachers and researchers, for policy-makers and for industrial managers. The reader must now read on, and draw his or her own conclusions from the materials presented. We hope that both we and the other contributors to the chapters have made a truly persuasive case.

Malcolm Warner
Werner Wobbe
Peter Brödner

Acknowledgements

We, the Editors of this volume, wish to thank all those concerned with making this book a viable proposition. First, the contributors for their intellectual and other energies in writing their respective chapters. Next, the various support staff without whom we would have been lost, especially Ms Christine Boulstridge and Ms Jo Grantham. We would like to thank all the colleagues who commented on and reviewed various chapters and offered advice. We also found the support of our host institutions impeccable. The FAST Programme of the Commission of European Communities especially must be mentioned, and CEDEFOP, amongst the other Community institutions. Next we must acknowledge the agreement of publishers and journals for permissions to quote from or reproduce materials, particularly the Journals of General Management, Human Systems Management, Manufacturing Systems, and Vocational Training.

Last but not least, we must thank Professor Bernhard Wilpert, the Editor of the series and the Wiley editorial staff, most notably Ms Wendy Hudlass and Mr Michael Coombs, for all their tireless work in bringing the final printed product into the light of day.

Abbreviations

AGV	Automated guided vehicle
AI	Artificial intelligence
CAD	Computer aided design
CAI	Computer aided industry
CAE	Computer assisted engineering
CAM	Computer assisted manufacturing
CAP	Computer aided planning
CAQ	Computer aided quality
CEDEFOP	European Centre for Vocational Training
CEO	Chief Executive Office
CHIM	Computer and human integrated manufacturing
CIM	Computer integrated manufacturing
CNC	Computer numerical control
DNC	Direct numerical control
EDP	Electronic data processing
FRG	Federal Republic of Germany
FAST	Forecasting and assessment of science and technology
FMC	Flexible manufacturing cells
IGES	Initial graphics exchange specification
IKBS	Intelligent knowledge-based systems
IR	Industrial robots
JIT	Just in time
MAP	Manufacturing automated protocol
MIS	Management information system
MRP	Materials requirement planning
PC	Personal computer
PIS	Personnel information system
PPC	Production planning and control
PSC	Production scheduling and control
R & D	Research and development
TOP	Technical office protocol
TQC	Total quality control

Section 1

Overview and 'Predicted Trends' Towards the 'Flexible Factory'

1. Introduction

Werner Wobbe

Commission of the European Communities, Brussels

This book deals with the 'future of the factory', although much talk is made rather about the 'factory of the future'. Does transposing just two words really change the meaning? We are convinced that the key point of our argument is based on the significance of this change in the wording.

To start with the most common understanding: The debate about the 'factory of the future' rests on technologically based, advanced new systems which are highly automated and computer integrated. It technically covers new ways of carrying out business, engineering and manufacturing tasks, known in its abbreviated form as CIM: computer integrated manufacturing. In the tradition of this debate, we consider the aspects of organisation, human resources and management from the viewpoint of how they will best adapt to the technological potential.

We criticise this technologically dominated view of production systems for being too narrow and for thus misdirecting discussion at the point of departure when discussing manufacturing matters. We would therefore prefer to start the debate about the 'future of the factory' from a fresh consideration of what kind of products and what types of manufacturing might be demanded, and what manufacturing means should be considered in making a strategic choice.

Although we are dealing with technical aspects, it is the organisational and human resource aspects which are considered the basic determinants in future manufacturing. We shall argue that these are the key strategic resources and that technology design has to adapt to this given potential. We hope that it will become evident that the perception of a factory made for manufacturing goods from a technical angle is a very particular 'culturally' biased view. We will make clear that this point of view is detrimental to European manufacturing by putting forward the idea that management has to be open to different choices and that the superior ones are particular manufacturing concepts which take into account human labour capabilities

New Technology and Manufacturing Management   Edited by M. Warner, W. Wobbe and P. Brödner
Published 1990 by John Wiley & Sons Ltd

and the potential of skill-oriented organisation. We shall also explain more clearly the so-called 'anthropocentric technologies' and 'computer and human integrated manufacturing'.

If we were to assess manufacturing concepts applied today within and outside Europe, we could conclude that even today we are governed by production imperatives distilled from 'mass production' rules which are highly efficient only to certain markets and cultural traditions: these imperatives are applied to other kinds of machinery, the logic of factory design, work organisation, required or non-required skills. The fitting together of all these into the clockwork of a big machine called the factory has been the leading concept for management and has evidently been the basis for economic success for a long time.

This technocentric view of manufacturing management is now manifest in the CIM factory. It will still continue to operate under the same rules as the traditional mass production concept, but with less personnel, computer based organisation, and therefore, to a certain extent, more but restricted flexibility than previously offered by the old automation technologies.

Flexibility has therefore become a magic word associated with new information technologies. Robots, computer numerical control (CNC) machines and more recently, knowledge-based systems are the principal symbols of a flexible technology. Does this imply a new generation of machines and equipment suited to changing markets; markets driven by flexible technology?

Further promises involving 'high-tech' flexibility, computer integration and large scale automation have yet to prove themselves. Do they really facilitate manufacturing or are they detrimental to flexible, adaptable and market responsive manufacturing? These critical questions have forced people to think about manufacturing images, strategies and choices. We shall argue that flexible manufacturing is more necessary than before. However, the means for this are not to be found in technology, division of labour and automation as has been perceived by designers educated in the principles of mass production, but rather in skill-oriented organisation.

DEMAND FOR FLEXIBILITY TO SHAPE UP TRADITIONAL INDUSTRIES AND MANUFACTURING MODES

Since the 1970s we can observe increasing changes in the world market position in specialised sectors of industries. Competition has also changed its character. The rise of the Pacific Rim is exemplary, along with newly industrialised countries and threshold countries such as Brazil. Extensive use of labour and assembly line mass production of electrical engineering, cars, shipbuilding, clocks, consumer electronics, plastics, etc., have recently been established in these areas. There seems to be no doubt that the trend towards the transfer of cost-intensive and simple, that is, technologically well-known, production processes will continue and that opportunities for the future, particularly for European industry are only to be found in:

— complex, quality products manufactured to consumer specification,
— quality consumer services, and
— flexible, time reliable manufacturing.

The orientation of production strategies and concepts towards a growing variety of customer requirements, its strategic potential towards quick adaptation for manufacturing factors as well as changing world markets need some explanation in the context of different traditions of manufacturing at world level: the US, Japan and Europe.

The three competing regions of the world differ markedly in their industrial structures. The differences in productivity, product mix, production processes, available skills and industrial relations can be described as follows.

In *North America* huge and fast expanding domestic markets led to the development of an extremely sophisticated form of mass production, due largely to the rapid process of industrialisation in the North-East. This was accompanied by the emergence of a very efficient engineering and machine-tool industry producing high-performance capital goods. As most of the workers were unskilled or at least unaccustomed to working with metal (many were Southern Blacks and European immigrants), but with minds of their own, a great effort had to be made to gain and retain control over production and to ensure that work was done properly and on time.

It was thus necessity rather than chance that gave rise to Taylorism and Fordism in the US. They became widespread in this region and eventually the dominant production paradigm of the industrial world. In recent years, however, the picture has changed considerably. The decline of productivity shows that for a variety of reasons a process of de-industrialisation is under way: while the service sector is growing, the industrial sector is becoming less competitive. Cars, computer chips, machinery, machine tools and tape recorders are familiar examples of this trend.

South-East Asia, economically dominated by Japan, began its industrial rise much later. It did not play a part in global competition until the period of reconstruction following the Second World War. Initially, only Japan was able to compete in world markets, but in recent years it has been joined by such newly industrialising countries as South Korea and Taiwan, which have adopted similar development patterns. The industrialisation process in this region was again based on the principles of mass production and stimulated by comparatively large domestic markets. But it developed within a different industrial structure, one that was adapted to local industrial relations. The enormous, advanced, multisectoral companies of this region attacked their well-established rivals in Europe and the US with carefully targeted campaigns. As a rule, they had two advantages: lower costs and more productive manufacturing processes, the organisation of work being based on a far more limited division of labour and a highly skilled workforce, although economies of scale were exploited wherever possible (e.g. cameras, cars, low-cost, standard NC lathes and machining centres). Recently, however, their success appears to have lost momentum, as the underlying economics of production begin to conflict with the demands made by competition in stagnating markets.

Although industrial structures, skill profiles and labour relations vary widely in *Western Europe*, some generalisations are none the less possible. The evolution of its industrial core (i.e. the UK, the Federal Republic of Germany, northern Italy, Sweden and Switzerland) followed a different production paradigm. As this region's industrial rise owed more to the manufacture of capital goods than of consumer goods, production to order and in small batches dominated from the outset (Germany's industrial rise, for example, was based on engineering, including machine tools, and the chemical industry: even today the capital goods sector accounts, at about 25%, for a far larger proportion of total industrial production than the huge car industry, with its 17% share.) With markets stopping at national frontiers, the core of European industry thus developed a specific ability to adapt its products to the requirements of their users ('tailor-made machinery') and accordingly installed flexible manufacturing processes, whose productivity lay roughly halfway between that of its US and Japanese counterparts. This European industrial evolution was accompanied—regardless of all national differences—by the emergence of a more or less highly skilled workforce and industrial evolution was accompanied—regardless of all national differences—by the emergence of a more or less highly skilled workforce and

If the specific strengths and weaknesses of the industrial structures in these economic regions are considered in terms of future market requirements, Japanese industry seems likely to be much more competitive than US industry. The far more limited division of labour, combined with a more highly skilled labour force, is keeping the growth of productivity comparatively high and also making it easier for Japanese industry to cope with rapid innovatory processes. This trend is true at least of high volume production, with its growing economies of scale, provided that this type of manufacturing meets market requirements. On the other hand, Japan's industrial system has relatively limited experience of highly flexible manufacturing to order, even its machine-tool industry being no exception.

In this respect, the European industrial core, or at least those parts which have long experience of a flexible product system and skilled workforce to match, might even fare better. If the tendency for world markets to stagnate persists and cut-throat competition therefore dominates, Europe's position is likely to become comparatively even more favourable, while the industrial system of the US will probably continue to become less competent owing to mismanagement of technology and waste of human resources.

However, this potential superiority can be converted into genuine competitive advantages only if decision-makers at all levels become aware of this situation and realise that they must adjust future manufacturing processes, the organisation of work and the skills of the workforce to the specific requirements for flexible manufacturing.

Instead of simply imitating Japan, or what might be even more detrimental, carrying on in the American business and manufacturing tradition, it is vital that Europe adheres to its own manufacturing roots by further developing its own manufacturing technologies, specific organisation, industrial relations and its vocational traditions. Therefore, we can conclude that manufacturing of the future in Europe is at a crossroads.

SOCIO-ECONOMIC CRISIS IN EUROPE AND UNAWARENESS OF ITS MANUFACTURING POTENTIAL

The debate about new production concepts and the future of manufacturing is not only fuelled by the idea of new automation technologies. It also represents an indication of the crisis in traditional economic thinking. The reasoning behind economies of scale and adequate mass production concepts has never previously been seriously challenged. However, new socio-economic trends, the growing service sector and competition from the Far East have raised uncertainty in well-established patterns of economic behaviour.

We would like to reflect for a few moments on the understanding on which production systems are based and to which societal needs they should respond before we outline certain configurations and strategic choices.

Pressurised to reduce costs, business firms have changed their operation modes towards greater flexibility. Outsourcing and subcontracting have therefore become a strategic variant. In particular, the arrangements between the bulk of the various subcontractors and the organisation to tie the whole product in with the original equipment manufacturers have claimed the most attention. 'Just-in-time' concepts for stock reduction and new logistic concepts have attempted to make production organisation more responsive and flexible at the highest level.

This has, of course, challenged the contractual status of work and work time arrangements, as well as work and factory organisation in general. The reaction capacity of companies towards rapidly changing consumer demands is important not only for technical reasons. While the traditional mass production was based on a hierarchical and bureaucratic factory organisation with a high division of labour and specialisation, frequently with low-skilled workers, a flexible and organic organisational structure is now required with the capacity to adapt, as a precondition for rapid changes in production.

Hence, one of the most decisive social changes concerning industrial and technological policies, as well as future innovations in the field of technology, organisation, work and employment, is referred to as the 'end of Fordism'. In very broad terms, Fordism describes an organisation of industrial society based on the concepts of Henry Ford in the mass production of automobiles, extensive division of labour, specialised production engineering, concentration of production in large plants. Because of its wide employment and economic success, this organisation of work and factories had as a consequence a societal impact: high wages, mass buying power and consumption, quasi-bureaucratic, life-time employment contracts in big industry, welfare state measures in all areas of life. 'Fordism' was therefore in keeping with the ideal of social progress until the 1970s, and up to that time the future was seen as an extension of these developments.

The Fordist type of mass production and factory organisation was so prevalent that *awareness* about different types of production modes was minimal and is only now being newly developed. The term 'flexible specialisation' (see Chapter 6, for example) describes other principles of manufacturing organisation and is opening up avenues of thinking about how complex manufacturing systems work with new modes.

The manufacturing mode of flexible specialisation particularly aims at sophisticated quality products and consumer specific variants. Its advantages lie less in price competitiveness but more in quality. The manufacturing of these kinds of products has to be organised in a different way to that of mass products. These factories are based on skilled workers, low division of labour, intensive development inputs and an intelligent adaptable organisation. Flexible specialisation works in small production units and therefore offers a perspective for small and medium-sized enterprises (SMEs). It offers a future oriented perspective to small enterprises. No longer are SMEs seen as historical, obsolete factories which have either to expand into 'Fordist factories' or remain as artisanal shops. On the contrary, they might now be well suited to the birth of a new manufacturing landscape in Europe—in so far as they can exploit their skilled workforce together with flexible organisation modes and adapt new flexible manufacturing technologies to their needs, as well as being able to develop new products.

CULTURAL DIFFERENCES AND OPPORTUNITIES

As already mentioned, the different production concepts of Fordism and flexible specialisation are based on different types of factory and work organisation and different uses of skilled or unskilled labour. This point is of the highest importance for future development because these social or so-called human factors are decisive to the success of anticipated changes and developments. Also, the kind of technology used is based on the social organisation or, to put it another way, is conceived for the kind of social organisation the designers have in mind. In most cases, this organisation is the traditional one that designers have been educated to accept as the 'natural' one.

This point leads us to certain comments about the cultural attitudes in different countries and the problems arising from adopting production organisations and concepts which come from particular cultures.

Just as Fordism swept over from the US with its positive and negative social consequences and features, so has the concept of CIM. As long as CIM is understood as a concept of a high level of automation suitable for various production items (production variants), it has a specific cultural connotation which has its roots in the background from which it stemmed, and one should be aware of why this concept, in its technical sense, is pushed very hard in the US. It is useful to assess whether this is applicable under the same conditions in Europe.

That there is a crisis in US manufacturing is evident, for example, from the trade deficit, the extremely low productivity growth, and the low percentage of the entire workforce engaged in manufacturing. These factors have mobilised the public authorities to heavily fund research and development in the CIM area, because this is seen as the response to fierce price competition by mass producing with automated systems. Also, two of the strengths of US manufacturing are its software capacity and white-collar engineering expertise, both of which are essential inputs. However, the logic behind this reasoning is based on certain cultural prejudices and social foundations. Education and further training of blue-collar workers in the US are not as elaborated as that of engineers. There is a general view that only white-collar workers can organise the manufacturing well and that blue-collar workers just supply their manual labour. If they become too expensive, manufacturing has to be transferred to a cheaper location. Also, the military sector, which heavily funds factory automation or sponsors it indirectly via the manufacture of missiles and aeroplanes, is of the philosophy that one has to use automated equipment, and soldiers, like blue-collar workers, have to be the button-pushers. Hierarchy and white-collar supremacy in the US have created, in consequence, a situation whereby society is not willing to explore an industrial production mode based on the experience and competence of the shop floor in charge of quality products. The aim has been the production of robust, but cheap mass products.

In this context, the history of the NC machine is well known. The development of an initial playback controller for shop-floor programming has been stopped, because the intention was to have planning and control in the office and to gain control over the shop floor. This kind of attitude and thinking has been repeated also with other kinds of computer aided technologies, namely control and scheduling systems, computer aided design (CAD) systems and so on. New automation technologies in the US are conceived as a replacement of man's ability and not as an aid in manufacturing tasks. This aim is explicit to CIM and its different elements as developed in the US.

Technocentrism

The problems arising from such entrenched traditions for flexible specialisation manufacturing patterns are evident. As stated above, technology design is a social attitude, which for the most part is not explicit. It presents a conflict of interest which is not under debate, in so far as it is rooted in a coherent culture where one group, in this case the white-collar workers, is overwhelmingly dominant, and able to assert that this technology is the most rational one for solving manufacturing problems. The more software specialists and engineers who have not been educated in fields other than their own discipline gain ground in highly automated systems, the more this particular point of view becomes an unchallenged consensus. Although white-collar practitioners in factories, and also foremen, point out that technical systems do not work adequately, the green-desk engineers will offer the more sophisticated technical solution instead of trying to understand the manufacturing problems caused by organisation and 'human interfaces'. This kind of reasoning is implicit in the education of engineers. The more people are educated in informatics and a mathematical perception of reality the more these kinds of problems will be accelerated as they move up through the corporation.

We call this dominance of purely technological thinking 'technocentrism'. It is the engineering approach which follows the logic of technology to solve manufacturing problems of which only a part is technology and which judges human work as a marginal or disappearing element in the production process. Because this element cannot logically be calculated, the aim is to replace it by technology.

'ANTHROPOCENTRIC TECHNOLOGIES' AND COMPUTER AND HUMAN INTEGRATED MANUFACTURING'

Because of the problems the technocentric approach has caused in previous years, attention is now being paid to the voices of the shop-floor practitioners who are sceptical of big technical systems due to breakdowns and inefficiency. The solutions are seen mainly in organisation and mechanisms which allow for the better adaptation of man to technical systems. Evidently, this only offers a half-way solution to the problems.

If it is considered that small-batch production, steadily changing complex products and customer specification are not suited to a Fordist type of manufacturing organisation and cannot be based on a hierarchical organisation and a high division of work, new basic manufacturing principles have to be sought. As we have tried to point out—the cornerstone of flexible manufacturing in this context is therefore not technology: it is human based organisation and skilled shop-floor personnel aided by a specific technology. The *organisation* has to adapt to quickly changing manufactured products. It has to be organic and responsive. 'Flexible specialisation' inevitably needs qualified personnel, and hence requires production technology which takes account of human competence, the operators. In other words, it is only when the technologies allow the development of human capabilities and skills that they become optimally productive. We call it *anthropocentric technology* if the tacit knowledge and skills are a fundamental aspect of interaction with man–machine interfaces. The design of the machine has to allow for control by the use of various skilled actions and strategies of man. The calculation abilities of the machine have to be limited to decision support functions, such as the simulation of alternative strategies. Humans should not just be relegated to monitoring and error recovery tasks.

Owing to the potential of new information and communication technologies, it is now possible to take account of human skills in the production development of technology. The leading principle of technology design should be the flexible, adaptable organisation of production, rather than full technological automation. The necessary integration of a production process should be based on a framework of computer aid allowing autonomous decentralised human decisions. This approach is not the same as belatedly compensating for the limitation of the old rigid technologies through organisational measures.

Research and development for industrial application should, therefore, in future pay much more attention to the human aspects and new organisation approaches. Technologies should be such as to assist man to achieve his practical ends, rather than treating him as a servant of technology. Such an approach demands the development of *computer and human integrated systems* (CHIS), and promises to be a much more fruitful approach in generating productive, robust and controllable technologies than a purely technical one. Not the computer, but the 'computer aided craftsman' will emerge as the new model.

In the early phase of the development of information technology, there might have been some good reason to go for the determination of human actions by algorithms and automation of human actions. The modest performance of information technologies in its early stages had led to this development. In the meantime, however, the limitations have become clear. The large technological potential of today enables the information and communication technologies to be developed as instruments for aiding man in his work and education. However, this requires a change in engineering philosophies. We are confronted with the option of either imposing on society the traditional thinking on automation with a preference for technical logic, or we accept that decision-making and control is given to the person who is familiar with the particular issue and is assisted by processing aids in the form of technical instruments adapted to human skills for effective decision-taking and action. The catastrophes of complex systems clearly demonstrate the unreliability of the first option. Risks, for example, can no longer be minimised through more automation, but rather through complex system planning which takes human decision-making into consideration. The ability of European economies to compete and to adapt will be put to the test over the next decade by ideas on computer and human integrated manufacturing systems.

The above reflections are to a great extent the conclusions drawn from an exercise of the European Commission FAST Programme (Forecasting and Assessment in Science and Technology), which has organised research, workshops, a major conference, and a working group on future production issues. It has profited from the national programmes of the member countries such as, for example, experiences from the German 'Projektträger Fertigungstechnik', and British and Danish/Swedish discussion in this field. The exercise has attempted to explore to what extent the factory of the future can be interpreted as the future of the factory and the strategic choices to be highlighted. It was carried out in cooperation with CEDEFOP, the European Centre for Vocational Training.

From this attempt to bring together European discussions on future manufacturing patterns, three important results have emerged. As A. d'Iribarne has described (see Chapter 5), researchers from all European member countries have first challenged the idea that all factories in a vast range of manufacturing industries would soon be built to the same model of comprehensive computer integration at all levels of production. Second, it was doubtful that technology integrated flexibility would reach its aim, and therefore a model of decentralised organisational flexibility was favoured. Last, the new thinking gave a new approach towards the organisation of labour, changing patterns of skills and new training needs associated with new technological developments.

It is evident that there are no easy solutions to the questions posed, particularly as regards a coherent European perspective. Socio-economic differences, as well as organisational cultures, industrial relations and the distribution of industries and SMEs vary to a great extent. The starting point and the traditional perceptions have to be confronted. We have started with this process.

After long and fruitful discussions, the Editors have selected papers from more than one hundred contributions related to this context. The papers have been arranged either to respond to the conceptual question of new production systems, or to give an overview on the state of the art of flexible manufacturing in the European countries concerned. In the case of a country report, we have accepted this as a contribution to the perception of state-of-the-art flexible manufacturing, not wishing to make a distinction between a new technical point of view or a strategic one for new production systems as a whole.

The conceptual contributions reflect most of all the common base of certain factors viewed from different angles; factors such as the human potential, technology, organisation, vocational training, SMEs, and so on. They are supposed to fit like a kind of mosaic to the picture of a 'renouvellement' of production concepts in Europe.

Address for correspondence:

Werner Wobbe: Commission of the European Communities, DGXII–Monitor Programme–FAST, 200 Rue de la Loi, B-1049 Brussels, Belgium.

2. Integrated Technical Concepts: Towards the Fully Automated Factory

Hans-Jörg Bullinger

Fraunhofer Institut für Arbeitswirtschaft und Organisation, Stuttgart

SUMMARY

This chapter provides an overview on the state of the art of different automation technologies, the implementation and trends. The author points out that the new technologies are marching ahead in all parts of the enterprise, but he does not believe that we will see the 'unmanned factory' in the next 20 years. He takes a 'holistic' view of planning factory structures, including not only machines but also man, information, materials and energy, with a prominent emphasis on work and systems design for specific man–machine relationships.

INTRODUCTION

The headlong development of information technology has led to a technological breakthrough which will have a greater influence on manufacturing companies than any other previous innovation. Alongside technology, economic and social changes must be regarded as critical influencing factors which will determine the nature and the speed of the forthcoming changes. Even where technical feasibility exists, they will have a decisive influence on whether the factory of the future is a factory without people, and thus an automatic factory. A more realistic approach, however, would be to adopt the view that the factory of the more immediate future, apart from a few exceptions, will be an automated factory, that is, a factory in which fewer people will work and greater productivity will be achieved than is now the case.

The development of industrial production can be described in terms of three major, far-reaching structural changes. The first, which began at the end of the eighteenth century, is characterised by the substitution of machines for human muscle power. The age of power engineering started with the

New Technology and Manufacturing Management   Edited by M. Warner, W. Wobbe and P. Brödner
Published 1990 by John Wiley & Sons Ltd

invention of the steam engine. The start of the second great industrial revolution was at the end of the nineteenth century. The harnessing of electricity, combined with inventions relating to its application (e.g. electric motors), led to the decentralisation of driving power. The basis was created for the mechanisation of working cycles. This step was the start of the age of mechanisation. We are currently in the midst of the age of automation, which started in about 1950 with the introduction of electronic data processing. This third industrial development phase is characterised above all by the dramatic development of information technology over recent years. It will have a decisive effect on the future of the factory, and thus on the factory of the future.

THE FACTORY OF THE FUTURE—THE CHALLENGE FACING COMPANIES TODAY

Practically all industrial companies consider that they are faced by increasingly fierce national and international competition. Growing competition not only results in considerable downward pressure on prices, and thus in the need to reduce costs by measures of the most diverse kind—automation representing only one possibility in this context. To at least an identical extent, the demands of customers are leading to what is to all intents and purposes an explosive growth in the range of different models available, to small-batch sizes, to short delivery times, to fluctuating numbers of items, and to increased demands on the quality of the product and the level of customer service. From the point of view of technological development, this trend is reinforced by shorter product-service lives, by shorter lead-times for product and process innovation, and by developments in the field of microelectronics which can only be described as dramatic.

Apart from these factors, the organisation of work within the companies is influenced by changing fundamental conditions derived from, for example, legislation, collective agreements or standards. Social developments in the form of a higher level of education, or increased affluence, lead to the wish for more attractive workplaces and more flexible working time models. Increasing environmental awareness results in the demand to learn from the negative effects of an undiscriminating approach to the use of natural resources, and in so doing to give greater prominence to aspects of environmental protection as part of the plans.

In view of these social and economic changes, which are illustrated above only in broad terms, product and process innovations will play a critical part in the success of our companies. They will only be able to gain an advantage over the competition if they are in a position to react at a high level to the requirements of the market by producing innovative products at the most advantageous cost possible. This will frequently involve the use of new, flexible production processes.

We may use the example of trends in the machine-tool manufacturing sector to illustrate the consequences of new market requirements. What is regarded by the machine manufacturer primarily as a product innovation will be reflected as a process innovation in other branches of industry which utilise machine tools.

Entire sectors of industry, as well as companies, will not remain viable in the future if they have not mastered the above task. This trend has been illustrated by developments in the past, such as the problems of the clock and watch industry in Germany, or the steel industry in the US. The challenge facing companies is accordingly to identify and overcome any existing weaknesses in the area of product and process innovation. In so doing, they will lessen the effect of two areas of risk which can lead to a reduction in competitiveness: these are the strategic risk associated with markets and products, and the operational risk in the area of production engineering (Bullinger *et al.*, 1985, 1986).

ELEMENTS OF THE FACTORY OF THE FUTURE—CURRENT SITUATION AND FUTURE TRENDS

From the 'isolated approach' to computer integrated manufacturing (CIM)

The hardware and software systems previously planned and implemented with regard to the use of computers in the central, functional areas of production have been of an isolated nature. The various computer systems used for designing and for the preparation of drawings (CAD), for the processing of parts lists, for the formulation of working plans, and for numerical control (NC) programming (CAP) and production control (CAM) operate with specific sets of data, whereas the exchange of data takes place by means of non-machine-readable input–output media.

The reasons for such an isolated approach can be appreciated first and foremost from the following:

— No proven and standardised CIM concepts have as yet been offered in the marketplace.
— The financial cost of purchase, individual development and implementation measüres, is high.
— There is a lack of modular concepts by means of which the investment cost can be spread over a period of time, experience of the new technology can be gained, and the primary rationalisation reserves can quickly be exhausted in subsidiary production functions.

— Reluctance on the part of users faced with the complex problems presented by far-reaching and comprehensive changes in existing organisational structures, and with considerable uncertainty relating to planning.
— A lack of know-how concerning the selection, adaptation and introduction of integrated solutions on the part of the potential system user.
— Departmental egoism and acceptance problems.
— A lack of processes enabling the profitability of integrated concepts to be demonstrated.

The disadvantages associated with the isolated approach can be appreciated in particular from the following points:

— Multiple storage of identical sets of basic data.
— Manual multiple entry of identical data at the interfaces of the computer systems.
— Costly and non-simultaneous updating of the sets of data, with the result that the sets of data are frequently not identical.
— Manual recording and retrieval of data at operative level (for example, production, stores, transport).
— A lack of clarity and lengthy throughput times when processing jobs.

One significant feature of the factory of the future is that these deficiencies of the isolated approach are overcome by an integrated concept for information processing. A characteristic feature of computer integration is linked program modules, which are able to gain local access to a common database. On-line interfaces are also provided for the feedback of data from production, which is made possible by an operating data recording system. In a further stage of expansion it is possible for the functions of computer aided quality assurance (CAQ) and maintenance to be executed with computer assistance, and to be integrated into the computer integrated manufacturing (CIM) system. A management information system (MIS) and a personnel information system (PIS) can also participate in the centrally recorded and stored production data. The software structure corresponds to a computer hierarchy on the hardware side.

Integration in the above sense not only involves compatibility and a corresponding configuration of the interfaces, but also imposes the need for communication. A fundamental prerequisite for communication is the linking of the computers through suitable networks. In order to keep abreast of developments in computers and in networks, it is also necessary for data management to be developed further. Hierarchical database management systems are being replaced increasingly by relational databases. The problem of semantic database management systems is already the subject of intensive research.

Development of manufacturing engineering in component manufacture and assembly

Component manufacture has been characterised in recent years by increasing automation, involving the gradual transfer of the machining of replacement parts, the handling of workpieces and tools, and the transport of workpieces and tools from human operators to machines. Flexible, automated component manufacture involves the use of

— flexible production cells for the single-stage machining of various workpieces, with automatic workpiece and tool changing and storage arrangements for workpieces and tools, in order to permit limited automatic operation;
— flexible production systems for the multi-stage machining of various workpieces with integrated machining, material flow and information systems and external interlinking, in order to permit any desired production sequence to be achieved on the machining units; and
— flexible production lines for the multi-stage machining of various workpieces with integrated machining, material flow and information systems and internal interlinking for cycled workpiece transport.

The flexible production systems represent for the time being the final development stage for flexible production automation. Until now they have been applied almost exclusively to the cutting of prismatic workpieces in small- and medium-sized batches. A number of systems for the machining of rotating and sheet metal components are planned and are in use in a number of scattered cases. In view of their higher flexibility with regard to products and numbers compared with transfer lines, flexible production systems will be increasingly encountered in the future in series production (Warnecke, 1984).

In spite of the fact that considerable potential for rationalisation is associated with the use of flexible production systems, many users are disappointed during operation of the system. A confidential survey conducted amongst about 40 system users in Europe, Japan and the US resulted in the admission by more than 80% of the chief executives or managing directors that their high expectations had not been met, and that it had been necessary to revise the data used for the profitability calculations (Ingersoll Engineers, 1985). In addition to the unexpectedly high planning and acquisition costs, the systems do not as a general rule possess the necessary flexibility to do justice to the changing spectrum of components. The failures can be attributed first and foremost to an insufficient level of detail at the planning stage.

The most common planning defects were:

— A lack of management involvement.

— Inadequate project management; in particular poor cooperation between planners, suppliers and plant operators.
— Incorrect definition of the performance requirements expected of the system in respect of flexibility, interfaces between components and the system as a whole, and profitability.
— Inadequate planning of hardware and software components.
— Lack of integration of the system into the operating environment.
— Insufficient information, involvement and training of the personnel involved in production.

The profitablity of many flexible production systems can only be guaranteed if they remain capable of being applied beyond the product spectrum existing at any given time. The shortening of the throughput and delivery times achieved through these systems should be offset outside the limits of the system. The costs for the systems must be lowered, and the planning and implementation phases shortened, through the further standardisation of the interfaces in the material flow and information flow, and through the availability of finished software modules capable of being linked to a single control system.

Measures which increase productivity are not the only way to increase the profitability of the production facilities used in component production. It is also possible to increase the utilisation of the plants. Nevertheless, a third shift presents major problems of a technical nature. The production facilities must be capable of dealing with their own supply and disposal requirements and of monitoring themselves.

By comparison with component production, only a very few flexible automated systems have been installed in assembly plant. The opportunities for their use will increase, however, if greater attention is paid to the rules for a product design which takes account of assembly (e.g. modular construction, linear jointing movements, and individual components which take account of handling), and if assembly equipment with improved sensors and perfected peripheral devices (e.g. grippers, workpiece holders and component supply devices) is made available. The range of future assembly systems will be characterised essentially by the following features:

— Personnel-intensive assembly systems.
— 'Hybrid' assembly systems with manual and automatic workplaces.
— Flexible automated assembly systems.

By way of summary, therefore, if the requirements relating to assembly (e.g. shorter product life-cycles, and smaller numbers of each type and variant) are compared with the actual situation in present-day assembly systems, the following becomes clear:

— Companies with predominantly manual assembly systems must increase their productivity through the integration of flexible, automated equipment, but without losing flexibility.

— Companies with inflexible, automated assembly systems will be compelled to increase their flexibility through the use of flexible assembly systems.

In addition to the automation of assembly, the manner in which work is organised as a contribution to rationalisation will retain its significance to assembly:

— Approximately 50% of all products are not suited to automation over the next few years, due to the very small numbers produced. Nevertheless, the assembly systems for these products will have to be adapted to meet the modified requirements.

— Approximately 60% of assembly work does not lend itself to automation without restructuring of the assembly system, because of the cycle times involved.

— Appropriate work structuring measures will have to be taken in order to arrive at a division of work which takes due account of humans and machines, since many assembly processes do not lend themselves economically to automation to the fullest extent.

Industrial robots are being used increasingly, both in component production and in assembly, for workpiece handling and for machining operations. The areas of application for industrial robots in the Federal Republic of Germany are mainly spot welding, painting and, increasingly, track welding and loading and discharging at machines. The highest rates of growth for industrial robots are predicted in the area of assembly technology.

INCREASED JOB SATISFACTION—AN AIM FOR THE FUTURE TOO

The situation of employees in production companies is also changing alongside the changes which are taking place in production engineering (CNC, IR) and the use of computer systems in design and work preparation (CAD, CAP, CAM). Each problem area has its optimistic and pessimistic viewpoint. There is no doubt that the greatest significance attaches to the questions of the future work content and work tasks for humans, and to the conditions under which human work is performed. A large number of factors are involved (e.g. skills, wages, health and personality development), which determine the quality of human work. A distinction must, however, be made between the effects of the new technologies on the organisation of work and on employees.

A generalised summary involves the risk of inadmissible generalisations and misunderstandings, since the peripheral conditions relating to statements of a summary nature cannot be illustrated to a satisfactory extent. Nevertheless, the following observations are permissible on the basis of a study carried out at the Fraunhofer Institut für Arbeitswirtschaft und Organisation (Bullinger *et al.*, 1986):

— Technological change, which is often referred to as a revolution, takes place slowly. The degree of automation and integration is not as far advanced, by a good margin, as to permit many a futuristic notion of the future, such as the paper-less flow of information and the 'man-less' shift, to become reality. As a general rule, conventional and new technology are encountered side by side, frequently at an individual workplace (e.g. that of the designer). The disadvantages, as well as the advantages resulting from the application of technology, are thus diminished.

— A decline in the skills of large groups of workers, which was expected by many people, has not yet occurred. A change is taking place instead in the skills required, which must be dealt with by training measures. A trend towards a decline in skills is emerging in very few groups of workers (e.g. draughtsmen, foremen).

— The progressive sub-division of work in many of the areas in which technology is being applied (e.g. machine operators, foremen) is balanced by areas in which work is expanding (e.g. designers, control of robot production lines).

— There is a move away from physical and towards psychological and mental forms of stress.

— Disadvantages to the workers, such as loss of earnings, transfers or dismissals, are prevented or diminished, not least by resort to works committees.

— From the point of view of the national economy, the use of the new technologies naturally leads to a loss of jobs. In those businesses which are directly affected by the use of technology, the release of personnel is compensated as a rule by omitting to fill vacant positions and by transfers, etc.

— Little resentment of technology is to be found amongst the workers and on the works committees. An amazing lack of interest in the possible consequences of the use of technology is, in fact, often encountered.

— Many of the effects resulting from the use of technology (e.g. career opportunities, lowering of the age structure) are only observed in the introductory phase.

The effects of the use of technology on the problem areas are dependent to a very high degree upon:

— how the technology is used, and which type of technology is used; and
— the organisational conditions under which the technology is used.

Two of the disciplines within the field of ergonomics, namely ergonomic work design and the organisation of work, can be applied to these fundamental factors connected with the application of technology—how technology is used and the organisational conditions. By the application of these methods, and by taking account of their formal rules, it will also be possible to have a high degree of job satisfaction in the factory of the future.

Ergonomic work design

By the assumption of repetitive and physically stressful activities, and by permitting human operatives to distance themselves from the production process, the use of automatic means of production makes a recognised contribution to the relief of physical stress and to the increase of safety at work. However, the use of new information and communication technology also places increased demands on the sensory organs and on the degree of vigilance, as well as on the ability to devise complex procedural strategies (thinking, combining, deciding) so that it is possible to speak of a shift of emphasis from physical to mental forms of stress. New means of production to a certain extent conceal previously unknown risks of accident, and new materials and fuels themselves lead to as yet unresearched environmental effects. As a part of the current technological breakthrough, ergonomics has also retained its rank with regard to work design in the field of production. There has admittedly been a change in the task facing it.

Alongside the traditional working areas, such as determining the tolerance limits for physical effects from the environment or bodily strength, the discipline of ergonomics is also being presented with new investigative and design challenges. In line with technological change, man is being provided with increasingly powerful tools with which to process information as an aid to performing his work. The human work equipment interfaces must be correctly designed both for the user and for the task concerned. Accordingly ergonomics does not only limit itself to the hardware, but also concerns itself with the software, which has such a critical part to play in determining the content of the work. The expression 'software ergonomics' has been coined for this new problem. Software ergonomics sees its primary tasks as being the ergonomically correct and efficient design of human–computer communication, on the basis of the cognitive and aesthesiophysiological capacities of humans, and the gaining of acceptance for these new 'tools' by the user. Software ergonomics thus sees the following as its main tasks:

— The analysis of work, and the establishment and structuring of the necessary information for humans;

— Dialogue design (e.g. command set, menu structure and user guidance);
— Design of the information display on screen (e.g. background image), and of the information input (e.g. command coding).

It is possible to distinguish between corrective and conceptual applications of ergonomics, rules governing ergonomic design are already finding their way with work design (Bullinger and Traut, 1985). In the case of conceptual ergonomics, rules governing ergonomic design are already finding their way into the planning phase of work systems. Corrective ergonomics consists of searching for and eliminating points of ergonomic weakness in existing work systems. The consideration of ergonomic requirements at the appropriate point in the planning phase is of great importance, in particular with regard to future complex and highly mechanised work systems, since the implementation of corrective measures at a subsequent stage leads to high costs and as a rule achieves only partial success due to the restricted scope for design changes.

The organisation of work

The primary objective of the measures relating to the organisation of work will be to create integrated job contents, through job enlargement and enrichment, in order to provide employees with an opportunity to develop their personalities through a balanced variety of demands, cooperation requirements, and autonomy. An employee's job content is characterised by:

— the skills required;
— the division of labour;
— the scope for action and decision-making.

The central factor is constituted by the skills required, which are shaped to a high degree by the division of labour practised and by the existing scope of the worker for action and decision-making. There is accordingly no justification for considering the three factors individually.

In conjunction with the application of new technology, it is necessary to discover and test new forms of work organisation in order to permit humans to be involved in the production process in a way which gives them job satisfaction. We may allocate the advantages and disadvantages to the characteristic features of new work organisation concepts as follows:

— little vertical and horizontal division of labour;
— a high degree of separation of man and machine; and
— teamwork.

On the basis of the following examples:

— programming of the workplace for CNC machines,
— 'production islands' in component production,
— residual work associated with the use of industrial robots,

it is proposed to discuss the opportunities for job enlargement and enrichment in the area of automated production.

Programming of the workplace for CNC machines

The characteristic feature of NC technology is that the detailed knowledge of the workshop personnel (machine operators and foremen) relating to the manufacture of the product can be transferred in its entirety into the technical office. This fact is true both for planning and arranging activities, and for the complete control commands for the machine. These tasks are taken over in the technical office by the NC programmer, the work planner and the production control engineer.

In conjunction with the introduction of NC machines, it was essential to transfer the NC programming function into the technical office, since there was no decentralised intelligence available at the machine enabling the program to be accessed. This aspect was regarded as a major disadvantage, apart from the associated decline in the skills of the machine operators, with the result that the penetration by NC technology only occurred in conjunction with the introduction of CNC machines. The CNC machine again offers the machine operator an opportunity to influence the NC program and the program sequence even as far as programming the machine tool itself. Whether or not use can be made of these new opportunities afforded by CNC machines will depend on the organisation and utilisation of NC technology.

The types of utilisation were identified in a study conducted by the Fraunhofer Institut für Arbeitswirtschaft und Organisation. It emerged that the machine operators in 94% of cases, in addition to the more simple operations such as 'charging/unloading/clamping' and 'operating'/monitoring/trouble-shooting', also involved themselves with setting up the machine and making corrections to and optimisation of the NC program, at least in cooperation with foremen, section leaders, fitters and NC programmers. Depending on the particular case study, setting up occupies between 5% and 20% of the working time, and NC program correction and optimisation between 5% and 10%. Workplace programming was performed on only a single machine in the area of tool manufacture.

In spite of the fact that a restriction of the activities of machine operators to the areas of 'charging/loading/clamping' and 'operating/monitoring/trouble-shooting' was envisaged in only 4% of the investigated cases of use, the results indicate that they were unable in practice to perform workshop programming. When questioned, the production managers concerned indicated the following reasons for this:

— Stopping the machine during NC programming, since CNC control does not permit programming to take place during machine running time, or because the machine operator would be overtaxed by the need to supervise the production process and to carry out NC programming simultaneously.
— Complex products which impose high demands on NC programming, with which only specialists are able to cope.
— Adoption of geometry data from the CAD system for use in NC programming.
— The need for standardisation and for clear documentation for the NC programs.

'Production islands' in component production

The concept of production islands has done away with the strict division of labour between the direct (workpiece machining and control) and the indirect functions, and is aimed at achieving the integrated processing of all functions by a single group of employees. The procedure which is adopted in this case is based on the following approach:

1. The grouping together of workpieces with identical machining characteristics into production families. Where the various parts of the production family belong largely to a single product group (e.g. an engine), this will make order processing more comprehensible.
2. The grouping together on a spatial and organisational basis of the means necessary for the production of, as far as possible, a single production family. The means of production are frequently made up of one or more 'master machines' (e.g. a machining centre), for which a high rate of utilisation is aimed at, together with a number of 'subordinate machines' for residual machining work (e.g. burr removal) and quality control.
3. The transfer of the direct functions and, wherever possible, a large number of the indirect functions involved in the production of the production family to an autonomous working group. The working group is then responsible independently for the allocation of tasks to the employees, taking into account their skills and under the guidance of a group leader.

Using this approach as its starting point, the Committee for Economic Production (Ausschuss für Wirtschaftliche Fertigung, AWF) has proposed the following definition for the concept of the production island:

The purpose of the production island is to produce product components or end products as completely as possible from given starting materials. The necessary means of production are grouped together in spatial and organizational terms within the production island. The field of activity of the group employed there bears the following characteristic features:
— largely autonomous control of the working and cooperation processes, associated with planning, decision-making and control functions within specified basic conditions; and
— the abandonment of an excessively rigid division of labour and, in consequence thereof, the broadening of the scope of possible activities for the individual (AWF, 1984).

Depending on the conditions and objectives which are specific to the particular operation, the production islands will in practice take on their own individual character. They will then not only be characterised by the specification of the range of workpieces, the group of employees and the means of production, but will also differ in particular with regard to the following criteria:

— The extent of the adoption of indirect functions, such as production control, work planning including the preparation of work plans and NC programming, quality control, the supply and management of tools and apparatus, maintenance, materials supply, transport, and the planning of personnel requirements and deployment, by the production island.
— The allocation of the functions of the production island humans and machines and the division of labour between the employees in the working group. Every effort should be made to ensure that every employee is competent to perform every task in the production island, and that he actually performs each one in turn with his workmates. Appropriate training measures will be necessary in order to be able to deal with the extended range of tasks.
— The degree of autonomy enjoyed by the team of workers in the production island, with regard to personnel management. It is possible in this respect for traditional company management structures to be adopted, or for self-determination by the group to be aimed at, by giving members of the group the authority to issue instructions together with certain powers and responsibilities.

The following objectives are pursued through the flexible production organisation offered by production islands:

— High flexibility with regard to the numbers of individual workpieces, capacity utilisation, product changes, product replacement, the number of different types of product and personnel deployment.

— Reduction of production times, with an associated lowering of the level of tied-up capital.
— Fostering of motivation and personal responsibility amongst the workers through integrated job contents with considerable scope for action and decision-taking.
— Increase in the degree of utilisation of the means of production.
— Increase in product quality.
— A high return on investment with short amortisation times.

Residual work associated with the use of industrial robots

It is an accepted fact that the industrial robot has often led to the elimination of physical stresses and to greater safety at work. In many cses, however, humans have been used as stop-gaps in order to perform those functions which could not be automated for economic or technical reasons. To be asked to perform such residual activities exclusively leads to one-sided strain and monotony. The industrial robot is also accused of curtailing the employee's freedom when it comes to space, time and methods. Communication and cooperation are suppressed or become superfluous. Residual activities which are reduced simply to handling tasks lead to a lowering of the skill levels required and to a reduction in wages.

The measures proposed by the Arbeitsorganisation zur Bildung ganzheitlicher Arbeitsinhalte (Work Organization for the Formulation of Integrated Job Contents) can be summarised to produce the following organisational guidelines, using the example of the application of industrial robots (Bullinger, 1985):

— Separation of cycles via buffers.
— Job enlargement through exchanging work stations and taking over preceding and subsequent functions (e.g. materials preparation, control, finishing operations and assembly).
— Job enrichment through taking over functions which are associated with and which prepare for production (e.g. materials supply, setting-up, maintenance and programming).
— Separation of automated and manual functions through block formation.
— Group work.

It must be recognised that these organisational guidelines have a mutual effect on and reinforce one another. It is accordingly essential for the free exchange of work stations to be achieved in combination with group work. Block formation will only make all its advantages available if the automated and manual working areas are separated by buffers.

The successful application of the organisational guidelines listed above is determined to a critical degree by the specification of the system limits in conjunction with the organisation of work. If the scope for planning is too narrow, the result will be the loss of opportunities for finding solutions to problems both of work organisation and of a technical nature, which can bring an improvement both in working conditions and in profitability. The widening of the system limits in this respect should not be restricted to the preceding and subsequent, directly productive functions, but should also take account of the indirectly productive functions, which are associated with preparation for production and which accompany production. This will permit the total utilisation of the opportunities available for the formation of integrated job contents.

The aim of block formation is to take residual workplaces between automated work stations and in single-station systems and group them with manual work areas. The coordination of isolated workplaces between automated work stations can frequently be achieved, therefore, only through the automation of the residual activities, through changes to the working cycle, or through changes in the product. These manual work areas should, if the opportunities for job enlargement, job enrichment and group work are to be fully utilised, be separated by buffers from automated work areas.

Through the application of the principles of job enlargement and job enrichment, it should be possible to provide integrated job contents with greater scope for action and with an increased level of skills for the workers.

REQUIREMENTS IN RESPECT OF SYSTEM PLANNING

The increasing complexity of production systems, the interdisciplinary character of the system solutions, the shortening of the planning phases, and the increased needs of the workforce all impose new demands on system planning. The following premises are the basis of the changing planning process:

— Global planning.
— Interdisciplinary teamwork (project management).
— Extended target system.
— Strengthening of the conceptional phase.

Planning is concentrated at present on the technology of the production systems. One of the basic premises of the planning process, however, is the global consideration of the data from, and requirements of, departments external to the planning function. This in turn affects the composition of the planning team, in which experienced employees from a variety of specialist areas are brought together. This teamwork demands a greater capacity for cooperation. Old-established functional divisions are broken up in this way.

The adoption of future-oriented forms of working is associated with the need to develop, through interdisciplinary cooperation, new models for the planning, management and operation of such working structures.

It is essential to take into account an extended system of objectives during the planning phase, in view of the increase, in the context of the new technologies, in the number of factors which cannot be quantified in monetary terms or can be quantified only with considerable difficulty. This is the case, for example, with objectives such as increasing flexibility in terms of adaptability and quantities, the shortening of delivery times, the speeding-up of the flow of information, or the improvement of working conditions. The traditional processes used for the calculation of profitability are not adequate for the purpose of evaluating these criteria. They must be supplemented by methods which permit the evaluation of factors which are difficult to quantify.

New production systems require an increase in capital expenditure as a general rule. The capital tied up in the fixed assets must be utilised intensively. This is hampered by incomplete information and inadequate planning methods during the conceptional phase. By emphasising this need, the aim should be to endeavour, by concentrating more on the planning phase, to guarantee an efficient operating system from the very start and to avoid adjustments, so that the profit threshold can be reached at an earlier stage in spite of the higher cost of planning.

CONCLUDING REMARKS

In spite of all the uncertainties which are associated with any look into the future, the route leading to the factory of the future has already been mapped out. The essential steps along this road have been set out in the foregoing. The aim of the individual measures is to achieve an integrated system of humans, means of production, information, materials and energy. The chance of achieving this aim is presented in particular by developments in the field of information technology. In order to take advantage of the available chances, it will be necessary for workers at all levels of the companies concerned to adopt a more flexible approach to processes of adaptation. The development of technology and, more particularly, the planning process relating to the application of technology, should not be left to the technologists alone.

Address for correspondence:

Fraunhofer Institut für Arbeitswirtschaft und Organisation, Postfach 80 04 69, Nobelstrasse 12, D-7000 Stuttgart 80 (Vaihingen), FRG.

REFERENCES

AWF (1984) Flexible Fertigungsorganisation am Beispiel von Fertigungsinseln. (Flexible production organization, using the example of production islands). Ausschuss für Wirtschaftliche Fertigung e.V., Eschborn.

Bullinger, H.-J. (1985) Anforderungen des Technologietrends an Forschung und Praxis (Research and practical requirements of the technological trend). In H.-J. Bullinger (ed.), Menschen—Arbeit—Neue Technologien. Berlin: Springer-Verlag.

Bullinger, H.-J., Lorenz, D., and Traut, L. (1986). Influence of the new technologies on work organization and employees in production. In *Proceedings of the 3rd International Conference on Human Factors in Manufacturing*. Stratford-upon-Avon: IFS.

Bullinger, H.-J., and Traut, L. (1985) Möglichkeiten und Chancen einer konzeptiven Ergonomie (Opportunities and chances for conceptual ergonomics). *Die Umschau*, 5, 288–92.

Bullinger, H.-J., Warnecke, H.-J., and Lentes, H.-P. (1985) Toward the factory of the future. In H.-J. Bullinger *et al.* (eds), *Toward the Factory of the Future. Proceedings of the 8th International Conference of Production Research*. Berlin: Springer-Verlag.

Ingersoll Engineers (1985) *Flexible Fertigungssysteme* (Flexible manufacturing systems). Berlin: Springer-Verlag.

Lorenz, D., and Traut, L. (1985). Einfluss neuer Technologien auf die Arbeitsorganisation und Arbeitnehmer im Produktionsbetrieb (Influence of new technologies on work organization and employees in production companies). Dublin: European Foundation for the Improvement of Living and Working Conditions.

Warnecke, H.-J. (1984). Die Fabrik 2009—Entwicklungen in der Produktionstechnik. (The factory in the year 2009—Developments in production engineering). *Technische Rundschau*, 76, 144–55.

3. Flexibility as Managers See It

Nigel Slack

Department of Manufacturing Systems, Brunel: The University of West London

SUMMARY

Flexibility is now a fashionable manufacturing virtue. Customers are demanding faster response and a wider variety of updated products, and competitors are achieving levels of performance well above what was considered feasible a few years ago. Flexibility, above all other measures of manufacturing performance, is cited as a solution. More flexibility in manufacturing operations, it is held, means more ability to move with customer needs, respond to competitive pressures and be closer to the market.

INTRODUCTION

There are many reasons why managers are coming to regard manufacturing flexibility as increasingly important. First, industrial managers have been coping with some of the most turbulent trading conditions for many years. Large fluctuations in demand, suppliers struggling with their own problems, and increasingly effective competitors, have all highlighted the need to adapt and respond to a less predictable environment. Second, this period of unstable trading conditions has roughly coincided with advances in process technology of such proportion that the potential of technology has outstripped our ability to use it to its full advantage or even understand its potential fully. In addition, the same technological advances which have influenced process technology have also started to influence product technology, shortening product life-cycles, and contributing further to general trading turbulence. Third, managers are being told constantly that flexibility is important. Developments such as robotics and flexible manufacturing systems are being actively promoted as contributing to flexibility, and the debate which these developments have provoked has, to some extent, shifted the legitimate focus of manufacturing away from an exclusive preoccupation with cost and

New Technology and Manufacturing Management   Edited by M. Warner, W. Wobbe and P. Brödner
Published 1990 by John Wiley & Sons Ltd

productivity towards a broader concept of 'overall manufacturing competitiveness'. This widens the scope of manufacturing objectives to include unit cost, quality, delivery lead time, delivery dependability and, with increasing emphasis, flexibility.

There is some evidence that these pressures are having an effect, especially in the more advanced manufacturing nations. One survey (De Meyer, 1986) reports that an emergent trend is the emphasis which some of the more advanced manufacturers place on enhancing their flexibility. More especially, they seem to be concerned with attempting to overcome the trade-off between flexibility and cost-efficiency. Indeed, he goes as far as suggesting that whereas the period 1975–85 can be called the era where manufacturers discovered that quality and cost-efficiency were not necessarily opposing objectives, the period 1985–95 could well be the era in which manufacturers draw similar conclusions about the relationships between flexibility and cost-efficiency. In particular, Japanese manufacturers are reported as leading in this change of view.

One explanation for Japanese manufacturers being further down the road towards cost-effective flexible manufacture is, according to De Meyer, that Japanese manufacturers' present performance in terms of quality gives them sufficient lead over American and European competitors to concentrate their efforts on the trade-offs between flexibility and cost. This view is reinforced by the most common 'action plans' which the Japanese respondents in the survey seem to be pursuing. These include the introduction of flexible manufacturing systems, the reduction of lead time in own production, the development of new processes for new products, the reduction of set-up times and giving workers a broader range of tasks.

Thus, as the paradigms of manufacturing change (Ferdous, 1985) to encompass a broader, interrelated and refocused view, and as 'economies of scope' seem to replace the more traditional scale economies, then versatile, adaptable, flexible, manufacturing systems are seen to contribute directly to overall company competitiveness. Yet for all its new-found popularity, flexibility seems to be the least understood of manufacturing objectives; even consensus on the very word is elusive, as flexibility is used by different managers to mean different things under different circumstances. To argue that increased manufacturing flexibility is, at least, part of the answer to increased market turbulence and competitiveness seems intuitively reasonable. It certainly seems to have helped those companies who have implemented successfully some of the new (and in many ways more flexible) manufacturing technologies (Bessant and Haywood, 1985). But, as yet, the whole issue of manufacturing flexibility, in its broadest sense, poses as many questions as it seems to provide solutions.

If manufacturing management is unclear as to why flexibility is important (or indeed what alternative there is to being flexible) how can any sensible justification for the necessary changes in manufacturing structure or infra-structure be made? If they are unclear about what type of flexibility is important, how can they concentrate their efforts on ensuring that manufacturing contributes to competitiveness in the best possible way? If they do not know how much flexibility is needed, how can the effects of any proposed change be usefully evaluated?

More specific questions include:

— What types of flexibility are important for different modes of competition?
— How much manufacturing flexibility is justified under differing conditions?
— What alternatives to total manufacturing flexibility are worth considering?
— How can manufacturing resources be developed in order to contribute to alternative types of flexibility?

and perhaps the most important point,

— How should a manufacturing organisation best approach developing a policy on manufacturing flexiblity which clarifies its needs and capabilities?

The remainder of this chapter:

(a) briefly examines how these questions have been treated in the sparse, but growing, literature on manufacturing flexibility;
(b) describes and presents observations from a study of 10 manufacturing organisations and the attitudes of their managements towards flexibility;
(c) presents a conceptual framework in the form of a hierarchy, which relates the various elements of manufacturing flexibility.

THE MANUFACTURING FLEXIBLITY LITERATURE

Interest in the position of flexibility within the range of operations objectives derives from the move away from regarding productivity as the dominating criterion of operations effectiveness. This move can include flexibility in an extended set of manufacturing objectives also including delivery lead time, quality, delivery reliability and productivity. Of the attempts to link each objective in the set in a coherent conceptual framework, Wild's (1980) is the most useful vis-à-vis the position of flexibility. Although flexibility is not treated explicitly in this framework, it does identify one objective, 'reliability', as a qualification to be applied to a more fundamental attribute of operation. In this formulation the operations system objectives include absolute levels of product specification, cost and delivery but also reliable specification, reliable costs and reliable delivery. Production management will have more influence on this reliability dimension, according to Wild, than on setting absolute levels of each objective.

A similar use may be made of flexibility in which it is used as a qualification to be applied to other objectives. This analysis derived five basic types of flexibility, new product flexibility, product mix flexibility, quality flexibility, volume flexibility and delivery flexibility, all contained within a framework of customer service manufacturing objectives. Gerwin (1983) derives a somewhat different typology of flexibility by again examining manufacturing objectives. His set is as follows:

(a) Mix flexibility.
(b) Parts flexibility.
(c) Routing flexibility.
(d) Design change flexibility.
(e) Volume flexibility.

Earlier typologies had concentrated on the intrinsic attributes and capabilities of manufacturing systems. So Mandelbaum (1978), reported in Buzacott (1982), starts by defining flexibility as 'the ability to respond effectively to changing circumstances', and then distinguishes between two basic flexibility characteristics of systems:

(a) 'Action flexibility'—'the capacity for taking new action to meet new circumstances', in other words leaving as many future courses of action open to be exploited should the need arise.
(b) 'State flexibility'—'the capacity to continue functioning effectively despite the change . . . (it has) . . . built-in absorbency, robustness or tolerance to change' (Buzacott, 1982, p. 10).

Buzacott (1982) further refines this typology in the context of flexible manufacturing systems, by distinguishing between two types of state flexibility.

(a) 'Job flexibility'—'the ability of the system to cope with changes in the jobs to be processed by the system'.
(b) 'Machine flexibility'—'the ability of the system to cope with changes and disturbances at the machining and work stations . . .' which make up the manufacturing system.

Much of the literature on flexibility typologies is reviewed in Alder (1985). He suggests that manufacturing is entering a period of flexibility where automation revolutionises management priorities as it can reduce the cost and penalties. Alder summarises a 'managerial' view of flexibility by comparing it to rigidities or stabilities. Stability, he says, is a fundamental value while flexibility is difficult to manage and, by the nature of things, more costly. Indeed, flexibility only becomes meaningful in the context of stabilities.

Partly it is with this 'central managerial question' in mind that the following empirical research project was framed.

MANAGERS' PERCEPTIONS OF MANUFACTURING FLEXIBILITY—A STUDY

An investigation, performed between June 1985 and October 1986, collected data on how managers view the flexibility of their manufacturing systems. The study was not intended to be a comprehensive survey, rather it was intended to provide an empirical basis for the development of a framework useful for the analysis of broad manufacturing flexibility. More especially, it had the objective of developing propositions relating to a number of issues, namely:

(a) Was flexibility regarded as intrinsically desirable under all or most circumstances, or was it viewed as an attribute of the production system, useful only under certain circumstances.
(b) Where flexibility was regarded as important, why it was so regarded.
(c) What types of flexibility were recognised, and which were seen as being important.
(d) How was the desirable degree of flexibility articulated, assessed or informally judged.
(e) How (if at all) flexibility was formally evaluated, for example for capital budgeting purposes.

The companies and the managers

Ten manufacturing organisations were studied in the investigation. Three of these were in the process/mass production area, three were mass/batch producers of consumer durables, one a large batch producer of industrial products and three were batch/jobbing producers of industrial products. Depending on the company's management structure and the availability of key executives, several managers in each company were interviewed. In all cases the manufacturing director, works manager, or whoever bore overall responsibility for the manufacturing function, was interviewed. Also interviewed, where possible, were other managers in the broad manufacturing area, for example engineering, production control, industrial engineering and quality control. In addition, senior managers outside the manufacturing area were questioned in all of the companies visited. Usually these included the chief executive officer (CEO) and the marketing director and, in six of the companies, either the purchasing or personnel managers, or both.

The interviews were conducted on an informal basis, although the same topics were raised, usually in a similar sequence, in all cases. These roughly correspond with the previously described research objectives. In all but two of the organisations some of the interviewees were given notice of the subject of the discussion and the type of questions which would be raised.

Given such a small sample and a wide spread of companies, and given the relatively loose methodology of the investigation, conclusions cannot be regarded as definitive. What did emerge were several generalisations about how managers seem to view manufacturing flexibility. These can be summarised in the form of 10 'observations' which will be used later to develop a conceptual framework which links many of the issues contained within the field of manufacturing flexibility.

The results—ten observations on manufacturing flexibility

Observation 1—'Managers had a partial rather than a comprehensive view of manufacturing flexibility'

There was a tendency amongst most managers to restrict their view of flexibility in two ways. First, most managers focused more on flexibility as it applied to the individual resources of manufacture as opposed to the flexibility of the production system as a whole.

Using Buzacott's distinction, they focused on 'machine' rather than 'system' flexibility (Buzacott, 1982). This tendency was especially marked amongst managers in the production function below director level, where there seemed to be little voluntary discussion of how resource flexibility contributed to the overall performance of the manufacturing function. The managers who were least likely to discuss flexibility exclusively at the individual resource level were those in the marketing area (and to a slightly lesser extent the CEOs) who often actively sought system flexibility as a solution to unpredictable market conditions.

Second, not only was perception frequently limited to the resource level but it often focused exclusively on one particular resource. So 'flexibility' was synonymous with 'machine flexibility' or alternatively 'labour flexibility' in many managers' vocabulary.

Observation 2—'Different types of manufacturing are concerned with the flexibility of different resources'

Across all companies there as a tendency to concentrate on flexibility at the resource rather than the system level. Amongst the companies studied this tendency was most marked in the jobbing/batch manufacturers for whom 'flexibility' equated with 'machine flexibility', and for process manufacturers where 'flexibility' usually meant 'labour flexibility'. Companies in the batch/ mass production areas seemed to concentrate either on machine flexibility or alternatively both machine and labour flexibility. In only one company (in the mass/batch class) was the issue of infrastructural (using Hayes and Wheelwright's (1984) classification) flexibility raised, this in relation to the ability of the company's production control system to reschedule production at short notice.

Observation 3—'At the total manufacturing system level, managers identify four main types of flexibility'

When managers volunteered views on system flexibility or when discussion was thus guided, four distinct types of flexibility emerged as important.

Product flexibility. The ability to introduce and manufacture novel products, or to modify existing ones.

Mix flexibility. The ability to change the range of products being made by the manufacturing system within a given time period.

Volume flexibility. The ability to change the level of aggregated output.

Delivery flexibility. The ability to change planned or assumed delivery dates.

Observation 4—'Volume flexibility and delivery flexibility have some degree of interchangeability determined by the type of manufacturing system'

All the studied companies were concerned with mix flexibility and product flexibility, but volume and delivery flexibility seemed to be interchangeable to some extent. Process and mass producers were more concerned with volume flexibility, whereas batch and especially jobbing companies were more concerned with delivery flexibility. The various functional managers' interest in the types of flexibility was intuitively predictable; product engineers focused on product flexibility, process and industrial engineers on mix flexibility, and production controllers on volume and/or delivery flexibility. Marketing, purchasing and general managers were interested in all four types.

Observation 5—'Managers seek to limit the need to be flexible'

Managers questioned in the study did not usually regard flexibility as something to be promoted indiscriminately throughout the production system. In fact, they seemed to try and reduce the need for flexibility by using one or more of three broad strategies: controlling the external stance, controlling the internal need generally, and confining the internal need to a limited part of the manufacturing system. In more detail, these three 'flexibility avoidance' strategies can be described as follows.

(a) Moving the company's (external) market stance towards competing on a non-flexible basis, involved, for example, adopting strict limits on product range, attempting to stabilise demand fluctuations or discouraging frequent production modifications.
(b) Reducing the overall (internal) need for flexibility throughout the organisation involved, for example, adopting modular product design principles or making for stock rather than following demand variations.
(c) Confining the need for flexibility to selected parts of the manufacturing system usually involved matching market segmentation with segmentation of the production system, often to restrict wide product range to a limited part of the manufacturing system.

Observation 6—'Managers accept that the word flexibility is used in two senses—to mean range and to mean response'

After initial discussions with most of the managers interviewed the distinction between range and response flexibility was introduced.

There was widespread support in the organisations studied for the differentiation between these two distinct dimensions of flexibility. One dimension involves the range of states a production system can adopt. So one production system is more flexible than another if it can exhibit a wider *range* of states or behaviours; for example, make a greater variety of products, manufacture at different output levels or delivery lead times, and so on. However, the range of states a production system can adopt does not totally describe its flexibility. The ease with which it moves from one state to another, in terms of cost, time or organisational disruption, is also important. A production system which moves quickly, smoothly and cheaply from one state to another should be considered more flexible than a system which can only achieve the same change at great cost and/or organisational disruption. Both cost and time can be regarded as the 'friction' elements of flexibility which constrain the response of the system. They are the manifestations of the difficulty of making a change.

Observation 7—'Differentiating between range and response flexibility to articulate their flexibility needs'

At this stage the two dimensions of flexibility were formally defined as:

Range flexibility. The total envelope of capability or range of states which the production system or resource is capable of achieving.

Response flexibility. The ease (in terms of cost, time, or both) with which changes can be made within the capability envelope.

It became clear that failure to distinguish between range and response flexibility seemed to be a major cause of confusion between managers in the same organisation. For example, in one of the sample companies a new flexible machining centre was installed which considerably enhanced the production function's response flexibility (giving major benefits in terms of shorter throughput times, lower work in progress etc.) but which actually reduced the range of (different sized) products which the company could produce. Not surprisingly the marketing manager could not understand why the new 'flexible' technology seemed less flexible (in terms of range flexibility) than the old jobbing shop which it had replaced.

Observation 8—'Response flexibility is of more immediate concern to most managers than range flexibility'

There was in most organisations a distinct tendency to view response and range flexibility as short-term and long-term problems, respectively. In other words the most pressing issues of flexibility improvement which could reasonably be resolved in the short term were nearly always concerned with improving response, i.e. the time or (more rarely) cost of making changes. So, for example, immediate flexibility problems included machine change-over times, new product lead times, purchasing lead times, time to make volume changes, and so on. Issues of range flexibility, on the other hand, were usually regarded as being long-term in nature and involved extra or improved resources. For example, the range of products or parts capable of being produced in the manufacturing system is usually determined by the capabilities of the technology and labour resources in the system. Changing the possible range of products therefore means changing or adding to these resources in a longer-term sense than improving response.

Observation 9—'Managers see flexibility not as an end in itself but as a means to other ends'

Surprisingly the interviews seemed to indicate that managers see little intrinsic merit in flexibility *per se*; rather they want to be flexible in order to improve some other aspect of production. In other words the justification for enhancing flexibility was usually instrumental, and indeed often expressed in terms of other attributes of production performance. Companies did not see themselves as selling flexibility directly, they considered themselves to be selling what a flexible manufacturing function can give. This was usually:

— Better product *availability*, i.e. shorter delivery lead time or a wider or customised product range.
— More *dependable* delivery, i.e. processing the part or product on schedule even in the face of unreliable supply or uncertain process reliability.
— Increased *productivity*, i.e. better utilisation of process technology, labour or material resources.

So, flexibility was often judged in terms of how it enhanced other measures of manufacturing performance, usually some aspect of dependability, productivity and availability.

Which of these was regarded as being most important by individual managers was governed partly by the received competitive position of the company, but also seemed to be strongly influenced by functional responsibility.

Managers on the *supply side* of companies such as purchasing managers (suppliers of material) and personnel managers (suppliers of labour) had a tendency to stress flexibility as an answer to dependability problems. For example, in-house manufacturing capability (mix flexibility) helps to overcome slow vendor response, transferability of labour between departments (labour flexibility) helps cope with temporary skill shortages, and so on.

Manufacturing managers, at the heart of the material chain, were more likely to see flexibility as contributing to overall productivity. Manufacturing systems which were flexible were seen as overcoming such problems as long machine change-over times, excessive work in progress, fluctuating demand between product groups and so on, all of which adversely affected resource utilisation and therefore manufacturing cost.

Sales and marketing managers on the *demand side* of the company seemed to focus on flexibility as a solution to problems of availability. The major advantages of a flexible manufacturing function were seen as reducing delivery lead times, reducing new product information lead times, the ability to offer customisation, and so on.

It should be stressed that there was not an exclusive preoccupation by any class of manager on dependability, productivity, or availability alone. Most managers cited all three justifications, but in perceived importance, the focus was as described.

Observation 10—'The types and dimensions of flexibility which most concern manufacturing organisations are determined by variety and uncertainty'

Leaving the most speculative observation until last, this final point is presented with less empirical support from the study. However, as well as an intuitive attraction, the idea does have some support from the research data and was not directly contradicted in any of the sample companies.

In searching for some predictor of which types of flexibility were of interest to the companies in the sample it seemed that two factors more than any other were at the root of the need to be flexible. These two factors were (a) the variety of products, processes and activities with which the system has to cope, and (b) the ability of the system to predict the demands on it, i.e. the degree of uncertainty under which it operates.

In the short term, *variety* in manufacturing operations increases the need to change the mix of products loaded on the system (mix flexibility—response) and the need to readjust due dates since there are many different due dates (delivery flexibility—response). In the long term the likely product design turbulence increases the need to be able to introduce a wide range of new products (product flexibility—range).

High levels of *uncertainty* in the market mean that in the short term, emphasis will be placed on responding to unexpected changes in demand (volume flexibility—response), introducing new or modified products at short notice (product flexibility—response) and rearranging due dates (delivery flexibility—response). Longer term, the likelihood of continued market uncertainty will prompt concern over the limits to how much or how little needs to be produced (volume flexibility—range), what can be produced using current technology and labour (mix flexibility—range) and by how much orders can be expedited (delivery flexibility—range).

Concurrent high levels, both of variety and uncertainty, will presumably result in the whole field of flexibility types being relevant.

A FLEXIBILITY FRAMEWORK

It would be useful to link some of these ideas together. After all, one suspects that behind much of the perceived confusion surrounding manufacturing flexibility is the lack of any model or framework which links the various aspects and types of flexibility discussed above. In an attempt to provide a suitable framework, a flexibility hierarchy is presented which can be used to clarify the contribution and role of flexibility in overall manufacturing strategy.

Any useful framework should be able to clarify the relationships between those elements which, taken together, form the decision set of manufacturing flexibility. These elements should include:

(a) The inherent flexibility of the production resources themselves, both structural (process technology and labour) and infrastructural resources (supplying and controlling systems).
(b) The general tasks or decision areas which manufacturing management need to define the flexibility of the whole manufacturing system.

(c) The two 'dimensions' of flexibility, range flexibility and response flexibility.
(d) The overall objectives of the manufacturing function.
(e) The competitive performance of the whole company.

Each of these will be treated in turn.

Resource flexibility

Much of the literature in professional journals and, as we have seen, management interest, centres around the flexibility of the production resources themselves. Here we shall again use the useful distinction between structural and infrastructural resources (Hayes and Wheelwright, 1984).

Structural flexibility includes:

(a) *Flexible technology*—machines and linkages between machines which are capable of a wide range of processes and routings and/or whose capability can be changed rapidly when change is required; and:
(b) *Flexible labour*—which could mean either skill flexibility (within departments, between departments, or between direct and indirect labour), and/or the ability to adjust the number of people employed.

Infrastructural flexibility includes:

(a) *Flexibility by suppliers* to the production system, for example suppliers of materials (purchasing systems), suppliers of people (personnel systems) or suppliers of product information (product design); and:
(b) *Flexibility by controllers* of the production system, for example controllers of volumes/orders, controllers of loading/scheduling, or controllers of quality.

Resource flexibility is fundamental to manufacturing flexibility yet at the same time is far removed from strategic manufacturing flexibility. While no manufacturing organisation can be flexible without flexible resources, flexibility of resources is not itself a legitimate manufacturing objective. Resource flexibility may define a company's capabilities but it should not drive its flexibility objectives.

Manufacturing system flexibility

Nor do the flexibility capabilities of individual resources totally describe the flexibility of the whole manufacturing system. This is more adequately defined in the terms identified previously, namely:

Product flexibility. The ability to introduce and manufacture novel products or to modify existing ones. It is defined by the range of products which the organisation is capable of designing and making, and the time it needs in order to develop the product and its processes into a state where the products are ready to be manufactured on a regular basis. The capabilities of the product engineering and development function and its interface with manufacturing contribute to product flexibility as well as the capabilities of the manufacturing system itself.

Mix flexibility. The ability to change the range of products being made by the manufacturing system. It is defined by the mix of parts or products which the manufacturing system can produce simultaneously or within a given time period and the speed with which it can vary the mix. Thus, if a manufacturing system has many alternative production routings for each part or product (most machines can do most things) then it has a higher mix flexibility than one in which products need to follow a strictly defined process route. Similarly, mix flexibility is high when a manufacturing system can quickly change the mix of products it has loaded on the system.

Volume flexibility. The ability to change the level of aggregated output. It is defined by the extent to which a manufacturing system can vary its output level, for a given product mix, and the lead time it requires to make the change. In practice the constraints on 'varying' output levels apply only to 'increasing' output levels, where the constraints are those of capacity and purchasing lead times. Decreasing output levels is usually easier, the exception being some process industries where output below a minimum level is technically infeasible.

Delivery flexibility. The ability to change planned or assumed delivery dates. It is defined by the extent to which delivery dates can be varied and the ease with which the changes can be made. Again, in practice, the difficult changes are in one direction, i.e. bringing forward delivery dates for some products. Usually this means re-prioritising and re-scheduling orders or batches within the system.

Range and response

All these types of system (as opposed to resource) flexibility have been described in terms of both 'range' and 'response'. It is useful, in practice, always to distinguish between the two distinct dimensions, one which defines the range of states which the system is capable of adopting, and one which indicates the time the system takes to move between states.

Manufacturing performance

Flexibility, we have inferred from the study, is unlike other manufacturing objectives. Whereas performance criteria such as productivity, quality, availability and delivery reliability are all direct links into the marketplace—companies sell products directly on these criteria—flexibility is attractive not directly in its own right but for what it contributes to other performance criteria. So a manufacturing company may attract customers by the cost of its products, or their quality, or the speed of delivery, or promises to keep to the quoted delivery date; but it would not compete explicitly on its ability to be flexible. More likely it would emphasise the attributes which flexibility can give. These were identified as:

— Dependability: flexibility enables unexpected disturbances to the system to be accommodated more easily which, therefore, maintains system reliability.
— Productivity: flexibility allows better utilisation of resources and therefore lower manufacturing costs.
— Availability: flexibility gives better responsiveness to the market in terms of product range and/or delivery lead time.

A flexibility hierarchy

There is a logical link between these different levels of analysis. Structural and infrastructural resources determine the degree of flexibility (measured in terms of both range and response) of the four types of manufacturing flexibility at the task level—new product flexibility, mix flexibility, volume flexibility and delivery flexibility. Enhanced flexibility in these four areas gives better production performance in terms of availability, dependability and productivity. Improved production performance in turn increases overall company competitiveness.

In fact, the idea of the hierarchy is presented not to assess the effect of enhanced production resources on company competitiveness by working up through the four levels. Rather it helps to define guidelines for the development of appropriately flexible production resources by working down through the levels. In other words, a company's chosen competitive position should define the desired levels of availability, dependability and productivity. This will indicate the necessary range and response characteristics for the four types of flexibility which in turn will set goals for the development of appropriately flexible resources.

This hierarchical structuring of the issues raised in the empirical study is presented with two uses in mind. The first is to provide a background structure, simple, but sufficiently comprehensive to include most or all of the aspects of flexibility debated in the academic literature, scattered through the professional journals and widely misused through the hyperbole of some sales literature. More important though is the need for an underpinning structure to support a procedure to assess the flexibility needs, capabilities and change proposals at the company or business unit level (for example, see Chapters 6, 12, 13 and 14).

CONCLUDING REMARKS

Managers' views on manufacturing flexibility seem to be influenced by their functional responsibilities and partly by their organisational position. However, most managers have only a partial view of their company's flexibility needs. Rarely do they consider all the facets of manufacturing flexibility, nor do they recognise that all manufacturing structural and infrastructural resources contribute to flexibility.

As regards functional responsibility, managers who supply resources to the manufacturing core of the organisation such as personnel and purchasing managers stress flexibility as a means of coping with unplanned disturbance. A flexible organisation is one which can accommodate such disturbances and thus ensure dependability of supply. Manufacturing managers see flexibility as an aid to greater productivity because flexible resources can be utilised more readily without cost penalties. Managers on the demand side of the organisation see enhanced availability of supply, either by widening the range of what can be made or by shortening supply lead time, as being the main benefit of a flexible manufacturing function.

Address for correspondence:

Department of Manufacturing Systems, Brunel: The University of West London, Uxbridge, Middlesex UB8 3PH, UK.

REFERENCES

Alder, P. (1985) Managing flexibility: a selective review of the challenges of managing the new production technologies potential for flexibility. *A Report to the Organisation for Economic Co-operation and Development*, Stanford University, July.
Bessant, J., and Haywood, B. (1985) The introduction of flexible manufacturing systems as an example of computer integrated manufacturing. Final Report. Innovation Research Group, Brighton Polytechnic, UK.
Buzacott, J. A. (1982) The fundamental principles of flexibility in manufacturing systems, *Proceedings of the 1st International Conference on Flexible Manufacturing Systems* (Brighton). Bedford: IFS Publications.
De Meyer, A. (1986) Flexibility: the next competitive battle. INSEAD Working Paper 86/31.
Ferdous, K. (1985) The shifting paradigms of manufacturing: inventory, quality and now versatility. Fontainebleau, France, INSEAD.
Gerwin, D. (1983) A framework for analysing the flexibility of manufacturing

processes. *School of Business and Administration*, University of Wisconsin, Milwaukee.

Hayes, R., and Wheelwright, S. C. (1984) *Restoring our Competitive Edge*. New York: Wiley.

Mandelbaum, M. (1978) Flexibility in decision making: An exploration and unification. PhD dissertation, Dept of Industrial Engineering, University of Toronto, Canada.

Wild, R. (1980) *Operations Management: A Policy Framework*. Oxford; Pergamon.

4. Changing Concepts of Work and Qualifications

Michael Schumann

SOFI–Soziologisches Forschungsinstitut Göttingen eV, Göttingen

SUMMARY

This chapter focuses on trends in work organisation and new technologies. The first part deals with changes emerging in industrial work and new emerging job profiles. The second part tries to analyse the origins of changes rooted in their social and entrepreneurial contexts. The author concludes that in the 'high-tech' areas and industrial key sectors, new concepts in the use of labour will emerge which focus on 'holistic' job structures because they are more efficient. The older industries and manufacturers (with low skilled labour) will stick to more traditional 'Tayloristic-rationalisation' patterns.

INTRODUCTION

It has never been so difficult as at the present time to look into the future. Or, to put it the other way round: a couple of years ago, the forecasters at least had it easier! Scientific investigation of the current situation in work still offered useful tips to guide us towards the immediate future. The so-called extrapolation of trends, upon which social science bases its prognoses, was already on an unsure footing both methodologically and in content; but in times of relative stability, prudent forecasts were certainly admissible on this basis.

I shall concentrate as a sociologist of work on the following questions:

1. What changes are emerging in industrial work, and what new profiles of work are to be expected?
2. What social and entrepreneurial reasons lie at the root of the forecast changes in industrial work?

New Technology and Manufacturing Management   Edited by M. Warner, W. Wobbe and P. Brödner
Published 1990 by John Wiley & Sons Ltd

Today, in a time of radical change in the shaping of work, a simple extension of what is currently present is totally inadmissible and can lead only to false conclusions being drawn concerning the future. Even if we are not prepared to concur in the already widespread labelling of our time as the beginnings of a new industrial revolution, founded on microelectronics, it cannot be denied that this is a period of upheaval. That, in turn, means that the tried and tested method of using what is typical today to underpin statements about tomorrow is no longer of help, since the present as a mirror for the future offers no reliable information.

What is the sociologist therefore to do when he cannot evade the justified question about the future world of work, but where up to now there is no theory on which pertinent statements can be unambiguously drawn? He is also someone not content with visions, or merely hypothetical constructions of ideas such as are currently fashionable in the approach to scenarios (see Bullinger and Lentes, 1982). Indeed, a forecast of the future cannot entirely avoid a good deal of speculation. We should not attempt to disguise these uncertainties of prognosis with apparent scientific precision, but on the contrary ourselves point to the relative openness of developments. However, I consider that on the other hand we by no means need *only* speculate.

In my attempt to sketch in developmental trends in industrial work, I intend to use investigations undertaken by myself and colleagues at the SOFI institute (Kern and Schumann, 1984, for example) where we have not merely analysed the current work forms but have also looked into planning by firms where today work profiles of tomorrow are actually being *developed*. We have also concentrated on key industries in the Federal Republic of Germany as well as researching into the ongoing industrial situation, and analysing those technical and labour-usage concepts which are now not only being tested and evaluated in firms but have already proved significant for the future. We were also able to check such newly emergent work structures for ourselves and to clarify how far within the firms the models now developed reappear in the general planning of the next few years, are regarded as solutions which can be generally applicable, and are therefore of necessity included as a matter of course in concrete new plans for innovation or projects of organisational change (Brödner, 1985). It was precisely this inclusion of intentions to implement these changes that was for us an important indicator of how serious the firms were about the new work structures, or whether management theories about the workplace of the future were being merely demonstrated.

The new concepts of work design pointing towards the future, and the plausibility of the arguments by firms on why they preferred and promoted the chosen solutions in the context of their declared aims, are the main basis of the assertions which follow.

ONGOING RESEARCH

The principal result of our investigations (Kern and Schumann, 1984) was that at present many firms are rethinking their *work design, training* and *personnel* policies. In search of the most efficient solution, the work policy of these firms no longer gives absolute priority—as was typical in the past—to a significant division of labour. Increasingly often, a work structure producing higher output is seen as lying in functional integration and a comprehensive allocation of tasks. A decrease in the division of labour is developing into a visible innovation in these firms and is a far cry from being nostalgia or impracticable dreaming. Such a change means that the old principle of rationalisation which still characterises many firms has to be justified, no longer unquestionably represents the best solution, and is in the process of losing its monopolising position. The 'myth of progress', which previously served as an excuse for the increasing division of labour and the separation of work tasks, is therefore beginning to seem threadbare.

In these cases, we found the changes of direction which are of great significance for the future of industrial work. After all, these concepts will determine whether in certain industries, such as engineering, professional work will remain available; whether in certain sectors, such as the automobile industry, a 'reprofessionalisation' of production work can be expected; and finally whether in other branches, say the chemical industry, a skilled type of production worker can be re-established. The question therefore is whether skilled work, which during a process stretching over many years has been forced into secondary sectors, can return to the *primary* production area.

I will attempt to outline briefly the type of work, and above all the qualification profile which is beginning to crystallise here. The new concepts of the use of labour have as their aim to collect at least the *core functions* of production work into a single hand; even the professional demarcation lines of quality control and maintenance are not spared here. Some areas of production control and the checking of materials are passed on, according to this concept of the use of labour, to the production worker and there remain for quality control and repairs, only the specialist tasks.

The firms need, for such a concept of the use of labour, a particularly well-qualified worker. What is required is a person who is both manually *and* theoretically competent, both able to diagnose *and* to act effectively; a worker who possesses to an equal degree, metal-cutting and electrical and electronic knowledge of basics. A new kind of skilled production worker is therefore appearing. This new category of worker is not the traditional person trained on the job who achieves the position of machine- or line-operator without formal training, let us say only on the basis of several years' experience. Much of the brainwork has been removed from this workplace in normal running, by steering, regulating and supervising functions taken over by computer systems. But, according to the new concept of use of labour we are invoking, such a workplace is instead allotted new tasks for dealing with exceptional situations. Coping with these tasks requires, much more than previously, a greater theoretical competence than could be obtained only from 'learning by doing'.

A more formalised degree of training thus becomes necessary. Frequently, this is still in the form of training and further education undertaken by the firm. Finally, in fact, this approximates to a reformed kind of skilled worker apprenticeship. At any rate, the new professional image of the industrial or manufacturing mechanic in the metal-cutting field almost certainly has implications for training policy.

The new skilled production worker is also not, as has often been mistakenly assumed up to the present for the phase of automated production technology, the 'pure theoretician'. By this we mean in the final analysis, the *technician or engineer* who deals above all with symbols of the production process and merely processes appropriate information. According to our new findings, empirical knowledge has retained its major importance alongside increased theoretical competence. But the firm still requires, as in previous times, the practical person who first acquired his necessary assurance in action through his daily dealing with machines, with the sequences of the production process and with the materials to be processed. The 'trouble-shooter' who can sniff out problems before they happen and anticipate hiatuses in the sequence of production before they result in disruption is still needed, as well as the manual 'Jack-of-all-trades' and 'bright boy' who can jump in if production breaks down and who can produce a satisfactory improvisation. Using a combination of theoretical know-how, experience and manual dexterity, he must be in a position to compensate for weaknesses in the technical systems by practical action. The qualified industrial worker of the future will therefore by no means be the 'half-educated' quasi-engineer, who in spite of all the changes in his activities remains within the continuous development of manual ability.

This change should, however, not lead us to expect in the new skilled production worker, the return of the traditional craftsman. The craftsman originally represented a type of worker essentially defined by his material— wood, metal, textiles, and so on. Later, his professional image was further defined by the method by which he processed the material—tool maker, mechanic, turner. In this, the traditional craftsman was still master of the work process, had a high work autonomy, and could also in the performance of his work to a great extent escape control from outside.

This description, however, no longer applies in this way to the modern skilled production worker. His work is far less determined by the material and its direct processing. He is integrated into the 'functional logic' of a mechanical system which he has neither devised nor completely comprehended. The worker is in fact no longer really master of the procedure which he is to supervise, optimise and maintain, since the method of functioning of the production system is to a great extent predetermined, by others. It is others too who define the 'gaps' in the system which still require human intervention and determine what part the production man should be allotted in them. This fact makes the control by the firm over the performance of the work extremely strict.

In the same way, his possibilities of responding to output demands by the firm using his own independent economy of work and time are limited. This move, however, means that compared with the traditional craftsman, the new type of worker has lost a considerable amount of autonomy. However, the level of qualification must still be formally estimated at a similar high level, in spite of all the imbalance of content. The new skilled production worker can, however, remain content far less than the traditional craftsman with his once learned knowledge and ability. The intellectual ability to learn permanently and go on learning, that is, being able to cope with the high-grade 'dynamisation' of the production process, is the important specific new demand being made of him.

When we discuss the industrial world of tomorrow, it is important to include the skilled production worker just described. What his work and professional profile will precisely look like, and to what extent he will be used, is a matter which will be determined by the policy discussions of the next few years, including those of the works councils and trade unions. Their position will to a considerable extent be determined by the following factors:

— whether the approach is succcessfully realised on a broad front and not only for a small elite group in the firms, and
— whether a compromise concerning output policy can be found for the new kinds of work.

It has still not been determined *why* a qualification expansion in the task-integrated approach to work is frequently accompanied by a considerable increase in stress. However, no matter which lines of compromise are found here, in the future, qualified, skilled industrial work will be more often found in direct production. We are therefore seeing a tendency towards a 'reprofessionalisation' of production work.

CAUSES OF CHANGE

Why has there been in recent years such a basic change in the work concept? Why are firms now testing concepts of work design which have long been known in the work and social sciences and for which many have been fighting for decades?

In my estimation, these questions can only be answered to any reliable extent if we are careful to avoid simple, one-track patterns of explanation:

— It is also, but not solely, the phase of flexible automation, that is the change in production techniques, which requires a new utilisation of work.
— Similarly, a new product philosophy and market strategy determined by changes in world markets also make greater demands on the production process.
— Further, the increasingly unavoidable realisation that traditional Tayloristic rationalisation is counterproductive and provides an impulse towards new solutions.
— Finally the tendency now becoming visible of a change in values which increases the acceptable level of professional work and requires an appropriate restructuring of work by the firm.

Only when understood as a single 'package' do these technical and economic as well as social and political qualities produce such pressures as makes it advisable (and even sometimes unavoidable) for firms to act along the lines described.

Let us now go into further detail about these four causes.

The 'technology' factory

It should first be stated that work should never be understood only as a subordinate quantity determined by technology. The technical possibilities do not oblige their use without any alternative, nor does the technology actually employed determine work design without any alternative. Work organisation still has its margin for restructuring: this has been and remains valid. It is, however, true that the new technologies in many ways permit the qualified, labour-divisional pattern of work tasks, and in certain areas they even make it advisable.

It is precisely the new technologies, from industrial robots to flexible production systems and digitalised screen steering of processes, which in the first instance represent only a potential for efficient manufacture. In order to employ this potential on the shop floor and above all to guarantee and optimise the now technically feasible flexibility, the traditional work design based on the division of labour is proving increasingly dysfunctional. In the capital-intensive factory, the highest priority must be given to trouble-free runs, continuous full usage and minimised delays. The degree to which the machinery is used becomes the predominant criterion. Defining workplaces as 'comprehensive', in particular with the partial integration of production and maintenance functions, has proved a suitable solution which often then secures technically induced flexibility on the part of labour and may even strengthen it.

But the 'technology' factor also exerts influence from quite another direction. The technical euphoria of the past few years has largely been blown away *vis-à-vis* what is feasible. The inevitable (and for many technicians disappointing) experiences of practical use in firms has shown that even the new technologies cannot work miracles. The sales slogans in the glossy advertising brochures of machine manufacturers often promise far more than can be fulfilled in practice. A reliance on total automation, which claims to work without human labour in the direct production process, appears unrealistic for the foreseeable future. The dream—or nightmare—of the factory without human workers is at present over. However paradoxical it may sound, at the moment when there is the explosion of technical possibilities to replace human functions, there is at the same time an increase in the appreciation of many qualities of human labour.

The mathematical modelling and algorithmisation of production processes remain in many cases incomplete. Besides, technically achieved complete security from disruption is either technically impossible (at least up till now) or totally uneconomic, since with every increase in technical redundancy there emerges also an increase in sources of breakdowns. This state of affairs means that the skilled worker will remain irreplaceable as a source of correction for the still imperfect technology, that is, to offset the remaining deficiencies in theory and control. The worker here helps to plug the gaps, no longer of mechanised but of automated production technology, but with totally different tasks.

Changing world markets

The new concepts must also be understood as the general response of firms to global economic upheavals and the new shape of the international division of labour. We have therefore been able to observe similar developments not only in Germany, but also in France, the US, and elsewhere. We may also interpret them, however, as the strategic reaction of export-oriented industrial countries in the face of the economic crisis which has characterised the past decade. This offensive is intended to be more than merely internal rationalisation leading to competition with low-cost production. In standardised mass production, the fight with 'threshold' countries is already regarded to some extent as lost. Changes in the sales markets make totally new product strategies advisable for many branches, from the mass-produced product to the customised one with a high proportion of precision work and innovation. Advantages in competition are being sought in product superiority, processing quality, and a more exact regard for the needs of the customer, that is, a strategy of diversified, quality production with shortened innovation cycles (see Piore and Sabel, 1984).

This policy, however, means increased flexibility from the production processes. The new technologies enable a move from the logic of mass production, without damaging efficiency. But without an equivalent application of labour and without an increased variability of the workforce, nothing can be achieved. The new concept of work application is an innovative contribution of work policy to the new strategy of firms.

Availability of labour resulting from the 'crisis of employment' of course makes it easier for the firms to experiment with training and application of labour. Thus, from the point of view of the firms, the crisis helps the implementation of the newly required, innovative labour policy.

Obsolescence of Taylorism

'Tayloristic' rationalisation was always more than merely a concept of efficiency. It was at the same time an instrument of control, with the aim of securing production against the 'disruptive worker'. Therefore, the strict control of the worker was based on the detailed prescription of how he was to carry out his work and the centralisation of production knowledge outside the workshop.

Today, however, people increasingly often question whether it is still necessary to practise these policies. Workers are regarded as self-confident representatives of their own interests. Therefore, their output control can without risk be transferred to the systems of production and information technologies. The maintenance of the firm's claim to control the work situation no longer requires the old instruments of power.

In addition, it is becoming increasingly clear that the old Tayloristic methods no longer work in the altered man–machine relationship, especially in the areas of high technology. The necessary human interventions in the production process evade the 'more' or 'less' of the previously standardised, qualifiable application of effort. They are equally unlikely to be achieved by instructions within the 'orders-and-obedience' system or merely by monetary incentives. The best possible fulfilment of duties, for instance in optimising work or preventive checks and interventions, is often only attainable when the worker is given wide freedom in activity and responsibility. In short, from the point of view of output policy, Taylorised control appears increasingly antiquated, and new developments in labour policy more and more appropriate.

Increased demands made by workers of their work

Many investigations during the past years have found that demands made *vis-à-vis* the acceptability of work have increased. We have just completed a survey into the work consciousness of young employees and came to the conclusion that, in general, work has gained greater meaning in the life of young people.

According to our findings, the old contrast of 'working to live' or 'living to work' is today less than ever regarded as offering a correct system of coordinates, in which the actual attitudes of young people towards work can be measured against reality. The majority of young people today are self-assured enough not to accept such a contrast with their own concept of life. They demand in both areas a sensible content as well as satisfaction and do not dream of accepting their absence in exchange for solacing words about the increase in leisure time. Work activity now holds a central position for the majority of young people as the focal point of their lives.

Here the classical orientation towards a career, and interests which are principally materially determined, are on the decrease. It is not career consciousness or dreams of professional success or hopes of 'a lot of money' which are in the foreground of youngsters' thoughts, but an activity with a satisfying content, in which they as persons can participate, where they can find recognition, personal confirmation and the sense of social integration. This applies even though the current employment crisis forces many of them to accept working conditions far below these demands simply because they have to survive.

Even in the medium term, firms should not permit a further gap between work on offer and the kind of work quality which is demanded. When satisfaction in work is being sought, work motivation and the required work output can be expected only if this interest in the work content is satisfied. This development therefore plays into the hands of those who advocate the new concepts of the use of labour.

We are only at the beginning of a process which can be understood as the winning back of 'production-intelligence'. The reasons are as follows:

— the cracks in the technocratic dream of making production totally separate from, and independent of, human labour;
— the new economic necessities of changed internal production conditions and external demand;
— the loss of credibility which the old methods of securing control and compliance in the firm have undergone;
— and finally the change in values which increases the gap between the work system and demands being made of work.

These numerous influences make an expanded use of labour both necessary and possible for the firms. Areas of conflict and long-term processes of change are to be expected. Arguments in the management of firms are taking place between the proponents of different directions rather than between the modernists who want to put through such concepts faster on the one hand and the traditionalists who want to hang on to the old ones, which in their opinion have proved viable, on the other. The most recent decisions on technological policy taken by the German trade union federation point to the fact that the unions want to use the opportunities for improving work along the lines of the new concepts as comprehensively as possible and for as great a number of employees as possible. Such a policy means that it is extremely likely that the appearance of the industrial world of tomorrow will be essentially determined by the above developments.

NEW DEVELOPMENTS AND OPTIONS

The picture outlined thus far emphasises the new developments and options which can definitely be regarded as positive for tomorrow's world of work. It would, however, be totally irresponsible to let this picture stand without pointing to its darker aspects.

First, I would like to emphasise again that the process of automating production does not necessarily free industrial work from the accusations of destructive wear and tear. I see no evidence for this optimism regarding automation. Rather it is true that economic, social, political as well as technical conditions are becoming more and more open to solutions for restructuring in a way which will satisfy demands on the content of work and the interests of employees. Whether and how far these possibilities will be used remains the task of restructuring. Ultimately, the arguments about labour policy which will take place during the next few years will decide this. According to our estimate, relatively easy success could be achieved in the direction of improving work, where all the underlying factors give an impetus in the direction of new concepts of the use of labour. This applies—as has been said—in the first place in the high-technology area of the key industries. Where, however, only one single influence factor points to a change in the traditional concepts of rationalisation, the forecast must be made with greater scepticism.

We therefore do not support the standpoint that the new concept could become *the only* rationalisation pattern for the next decade, and is to be understood as *the* decisive quantity for further development in industrial work. In the important sectors and certainly for large numbers of workers, the *status quo* will be hardly changed at all at first. For their work situation, further traditional rationalisation with greater deskilling will remain a deter-mining factor, for example for many machine operators, assembly workers, and checkers. In these sectors either the urge towards a conceptual change in thinking concerning work policy is not great enough, or else the realisation of the new concepts would be hindered by technical difficulties or perhaps simply by economic considerations. We can only emphasise that it will only be overcome in the foreseeable future by increased efforts to change how labour is used.

In this connection, however, a major problem that could arise as a direct consequence of the new concepts of the use of labour in areas where the integration approach, for economic or technical reasons, does not group all functions together at one workplace, is that the unqualified tasks remaining could even be re-created as distinct positions at the lowest level. A typical example is loading jobs on an automated welding line for preliminary assembly of car bodies in the automobile industry. Often the firms define them as special workplaces which are marked by particularly strong one-sidedness of content and lack of operator qualifications and which also produce great physical and mental stress.

This polarisation of labour utilisation is sufficiently familiar to us from past cases, and the problems it contains for the employment groups involved are becoming increasingly urgent. The possiblities present previously for working one's way up will in addition become practically impossible in the altered structures. Not only is the formalisation of the qualification preconditions in the way, but also those work units are now lost which made more demanding activities possible due to spatial nearness, conversations about work and informal substitution in jobs.

In accordance with the new concepts, the poles are now becoming established in sectors which make the position within the firm of those who have been functionally excluded both permanent and inescapable. It is true that mostly 'gap-filling' jobs are concerned which still exist in conditions of incomplete mechanisation but which will most likely be eliminated in the next stage of technical change, but this should not make us blind to the fact that because of it there will first arise (or threaten to arise) new problem areas during the foreseeable future. Any discussion of tomorrow's world of work must not ignore these facts.

CONCLUDING REMARKS

In the contemporary social structure, which has emerged from long-term unemployment and the lack of certificated training, the trend towards an overall social division—very favourable conditions and expectations for the majority, bad jobs and unemployment for the minorities—has been strengthened. The prevention of this state of affairs is the task of a robust *training and work design* policy. In this way, the changing conditions can be understood and utilised as new political challenges.

Address for correspondence:

SOFI–Soziologisches Forschungsinstitut Göttingen eV, Griedlander Weg 31, D-3400 Göttingen, FRG.

REFERENCES

Brödner, P. (1985), *Fabrik 2000—Alternative Entwicklungstade in die Zukunft der Fabrik*, Berlin: Sigma.

Bullinger, H. J., and Lentes, H. P. (1982) The future of work. Technological, economic and social change. *International Journal of Production Research*, **20**, 259–96.

Kern, H., and Schumann, M. (1984) *Das Ende der Arbeitsteilung?* Munich: G. H. Beck Verlag.

Piore, M. J., and Sabel, S. F. (1984) *The Second Industrial Divide: Possibilities for Posterity*. New York: Basic Books.

5. Qualification and Skill Requirements

Alain d'Iribarne

Centre National de la Recherche Scientifique, Paris

SUMMARY

The possibility that a dominant 'production model' will arise from technological developments is very slight, due to the social forces which exist at national and enterprise level. However, these changes manifest themselves in more general forms which modify the competence and skill requirements of enterprises. The factory of the future will be very different from the factory of today, likewise the skills of the workers in that workplace.

INTRODUCTION

The major change in industry today is the development of new technologies for data processing. This change is often projected into the future in the notion of 'The Factory of the Year 2000', completely automated, and functioning without human intervention, or almost so. The last survivors, on the one hand, would be the engineers and technicians monitoring such automated systems, and on the other, unskilled workers who keep them supplied with raw materials. In such a vision of the future, the main focus of industrial change will be centred on workshops, i.e. on production. Industrial jobs, their content and the qualifications needed, will be strongly conditioned by the corresponding technology. It is necessary to lose the idea that all factories in the vast range of manufacturing industries will soon be built to the same model: the comprehensive computerised integration of design, machine control, logistics and management, combining computer-aided production management (Bullinger *et al.*, 1986).

The dispute is not that there is a growth in computerised integration, but whether or not it is a universal model, or rapidly becoming the general rule. These arguments are based on the observation that in most European countries computerised systems are still on the whole confined to large

New Technology and Manufacturing Management   Edited by M. Warner, W. Wobbe and P. Brödner
Published 1990 by John Wiley & Sons Ltd

private-sector concerns (Fix-Sterz *et al.*, 1986). Above all, they are based on a desire to define more precisely how these integrated computerised factories can help to achieve a satisfactory solution to the problems of competitiveness faced by different types of concern: not only the need to cut manufacturing costs and production time and improve product quality but also the problem of flexibility (Hollard and Margirier, 1986). As an alternative to the model of integrated technological flexibility, a model based on decentralised organis-tional flexibility can be proposed, which seems far more likely to solve many of the problems of competition (Kristensen, 1986). It is increasingly apparent that factories of the future will opt for various combinations of these two models (d'Iribarne, 1986).

The organisation of labour, the changing pattern of skills and new training needs associated with those technological developments must also change. The question is not to know whether computer technology is leading to 'deskilling' or polarisation of skills (Sorge, 1983). The main concern is to identify policies which promote the acquisition of technologies at low cost and at the same time reduce the risk of a rigid division of labour.

This change in the nature of the debate comes about as a result of progress in research, which has clearly revealed the links between technological developments and the methods of labour organisation associated with those developments within individual countries and companies on the one hand and, on the other, the skills available and the ways of creating those skills through training. For example, it is clear that there is a far less marked division of labour within a highly skilled labour force, and that it adjusts more rapidly to technological change (Haywood, 1986). With this in mind, training and skills acquire an entirely new status. With the emergence of the 'new' factories, training and skills are no longer viewed as aids to adjustment but rather as basic factors that will be part of the architecture of future systems.

Before the skills and training needed in the new factories can be assessed, the levels of analysis and the factors to be taken into account at each level must be defined. In determining the operations entailed in a job, the basic knowledge called for and its psycho-cognitive aspects, consideration must also be given to important factors such as technological developments, organisational models and management practices. When examining jobs and the functions they entail, the main consideration is the organisational model. When, on the other hand, grouping jobs under occupational headings, when determining their classification, occupational category and socio-occupational status and when deciding what training—expressed in terms of general education and specialisation—is required for each one, a far more vital factor will be the form of social organisation prevailing in each European Community member state, in other words at a much broader level than the single workplace, with its own individual background.

KNOWLEDGE AND ABILITIES

Drawbacks of technological specialisation

When people discuss new technology they tend to stress the need to acquire knowledge in the field—in electronics, optics or programming, for example. In practice, however, this knowledge is directly needed by only a few groups of practitioners such as product and production systems designers and maintenance specialists. For others, any one technology is only one part of a complex technical system embracing a number of technologies.

Their problem is how to master the system and meet its technical, economic and social demands. In acquiring a specialist skill, it makes little sense to learn about all the individual technologies on which that skill is based. The knowledge that is acquired about those technologies must be ordered, combined and directly related to the problems to be solved.

More importantly, it is becoming harder to understand the way in which new generation systems function. Nevertheless, people must have frames of reference if they are to cope with the jobs they will be called on to do. This means that technology should be an integral part of everyone's basic education, creating what is often called 'technical mindedness' (d'Iribarne, 1985).

A second approach to the relationship between labour and technology relates to the 'man–machine interface'. The emphasis here is not on the technologies incorporated into equipment but on the development of equipment as 'tools of the trade'. In the computer age, now that it is more and more common for terminals to be interposed between operators and the flow of materials they have to handle, the relationship between people and the products they manufacture is far more abstract and formalised.

The main problem is the form taken by the dialogue between the operatives and the materials being handled via the interface system. Initially, this dialogue was off-line. Then it was conducted on-line, first in the conversational mode and now in the interactive mode. The cognitive demands are fundamentally different: someone working off-line had time to reflect, prepare several alternative solutions and then see which was best; on-line interaction replaces that procedure with a direct set of questions and answers based on different cognitive processes. What is now needed is a combination of reflection (research) and reflex (the ability to take immediate action).

The speed of convergent interaction in solving a problem has become an essential skill. To find a solution, the operator has to draw on what is often a large body of formal pieces of information just at the threshold of perception. Since the solution must be found rapidly, 'patterns' must exist to help the operative interpret signals received and relate them to the problem. This presents trainers with an ever more acute problem of how to provide 'patterns of interpretation' that can be applied to work situations, rather than just knowledge. It is, then, all the more vital to incorporate a basic knowledge of working practices into training right from the outset.

Communicating in isolation

The new systems are 'economical' in direct manpower: fewer people are required on the shop floor, increasing the risk of physical isolation in vast 'hangars'. The desire to alleviate this isolation is part of the reason for organising manpower into teams.

While the work is done in greater physical isolation and offers greater freedom of choice, it is also an integral part of broader and more closely linked information, action and decision networks. This calls for the ability to operate within the bounds of stricter methodological procedures and in a broader production and social space, a space that is intangible and perceived in the abstract.

The abstract conceptual ability needed in computerisation and networking is not confined to the ability to grasp the material demands of a job, a piece of equipment or the technology in that equipment, nor to understanding the work space in relation to the product being handled. The conceptual ability must extend to the ability to adapt to new social spaces calling for a broader range of knowledge.

Operatives and their supervisors are today expected not just to react to events and single incidents but to anticipate them and take action. This broadening of the abilities demanded is radically changing the basic skills needed. Operatives must be capable of analysing and thinking for themselves. In addition to their basic technical knowledge, they must be capable of lateral thinking so that they can apply that knowledge within certain frames of action. They must also possess what, for want of a better term, will be referred to as the 'behavioural and attitudinal qualities' of forethought and commitment to the work they do. These will be determined by their 'social skills', their value systems and, in the final analysis, their education. Thus the new skills expected of workers extend far beyond technological expertise, raising the question of what basic standard of education is required of skilled operatives.

Artificial intelligence versus human intervention

Of greater relevance to the future than the computerised automation of equipment control and the flow of materials is the development of expert systems of artificial intelligence. In its present stage, automation is gradually reducing the need for human intervention in the sense of direct physical action, but is increasing the intellectual effort of monitoring and coordination. This advance is a new step in automation, the aim being to state human physical actions in algorithmic terms, starting with the simplest actions— repetitive tasks that can easily be broken down and defined—and progressing to the most complex actions—unpredictable tasks that depend on 'fluid cognitive processes'.

In the long run, this will have major implications for relations between people and their work, since artificial intelligence will no longer be used merely to solve problems associated with fairly complex physical actions but actually to simulate the cognitive processes themselves. Artificial intelligence will reinforce the development of production process regulating systems that combine those stages in which processes are automatically regulated by closed loops, based on elements which can be modelled directly, with more advanced open-loop stages where the focus is on human skill.

In the latter stage the operative will have recourse to increasingly sophisticated decision-making aids based on structured data. Having to work to ever more precise standards when he acts on decisions as to regulation and the correction of discrepancies, the operative will have to foresee corrections ahead of the self-correcting mechanisms. His role is bound to grow, in that he will intervene in exceptional circumstances even though the processes are in theory structured and standardised. This will be his real job and the foundation of his skills.

To keep pace with new developments in both technology and organisational management methods, management increasingly expects shop-floor workers to be able to verbalise and where possible define the components of the practical expertise they use in their work, as this will help with the incorporation of their expertise into control software. Similarly, management expects its employees to know more about the theoretical side of their work, so that they can acquire a better grasp of how systems function and continually improve their production effectiveness. Operators as a whole are expected to do less routine work but to step in more often to deal with non-routine situations; they are expected to progress from the lower to the higher cognitive processes, handling complex, multi-dimensional and less clearly defined information.

Given this outlook for the future, it is apparent that the debate as to the relative merits of a general education and technological knowledge as a basis for vocational training is meaningless. Technological knowledge is an essential foundation of vocational skills and for using the systems that already exist and are under development. A general education is no less vital in that it enables people to verbalise, break down and define their technical skills and 'see the point' of the work they do. An effective combination of general and technological knowledge is a prerequisite for the acquisition of a sound basic education. There are obvious immediate steps if we are to ensure that a sizeable proportion of the working population today and tomorrow is not excluded from acquiring the basic skills that will be demanded.

Organisational decisions and their effects on jobs

Traditionally the breakdown of a firm has been by its main functions (production, sales, marketing, etc.), each one organised as a more or less autonomous department. Today, there is a change in the way in which those functions are structured. More specifically, the dividing line now tends to be between production planning and commercial marketing on the one hand and, on the other, manufacturing and control or maintenance. There is also a dividing line between those functions as a whole and financial/social management. These developments are a response to the problems of competitiveness already mentioned.

The reason why production planning and commercial marketing have come closer together is the development of what are known in French as 'gap-filling strategies': product differentiation and rapid product turnover, based on the ablity to predict changing tastes in key markets and create the products that will satisfy those tastes at the lowest possible industrial cost. This development calls for quick interaction between departments within a company, not only in routine matters but in defining their individual roles. There must be a considerable overlapping of knowledge between the people responsible for each department. There must also be close cooperation between designers and researchers, since it may well be possible for the design people to make direct use of the researchers' findings in planning product differentiation and changes. This type of interconnection also calls for both organisations and individuals to combine a variety of skills in basic research and production expertise.

Closer links between production and control are created if the twofold aim is to improve the quality of the finished product and cut production costs. Poor quality, as expressed in a high rejection rate and a greater need for quality control resources, costs dear in the long run, both in the factors of production indirectly mobilised. The solution currently being developed is to incorporate quality controls as early in the production process as possible and at every stage thereafter. This step requires a reliable automatic control system, with the operators accepting more responsibility and stepping in at each stage of the process where necessary.

The integration of management functions into every other department stems from the need to cut production costs. The operating criterion is no longer expressed as a technological optimum but as a financial/technological optimum. The criterion applies both to product and system designers and to the managers of human/machine systems. This is why analytical tools such as value analysis are coming into more common use, as well as the simple tools widely used in quality circles such as 'Pareto diagrams'.

With this shift in frontiers, new 'mixed profile interface' functions are replacing the traditional specialisations, a situation that is gaining widespread recognition.

Several approaches to the restructuring of jobs

There is greater uncertainty as to what are the optimal strategies in terms of the organisation of production and the linking of production with maintenance and planning. Starting from the current situation—where the compartmentalised division of labour is the prevailing model and where, at the same time, integrated computerised control is being introduced—how should basic activities be aggregated and basic jobs then restructured?

One approach would be to aggregate jobs horizontally along a production line. Several steps in this line could be grouped together to form a single stage. For example, there could be three such stages; pre-processing, processing and post-processing (combined with packaging). The advantage of this method of restructuring would be to engender a feeling of responsibility among workers for their production line and therefore for the goods they produce.

A second attack would be the cross-aggregation of jobs on two or more production lines, with responsibilities being broken down in phases or stages, depending on the workplace. This solution has the advantage of creating greater uniformity of tasks and skills.

A third approach is to group external services such as maintenance, quality control or planning. The links between these and production are becoming ever closer because of the new market constraints and the need to make optimum use of systems. This is particularly true of maintenance, since the quality of maintenance affects the percentage use of systems and the evenness of production workers' workloads. Start-ups and shutdowns always create an extra workload by comparison with normal operation, as well as production losses. If the third approach is adopted, production workers would take over certain aspects of maintenance as part of their normal work. They would thus perform a more active role in the detection of breakdowns and in routine maintenance work, giving them a greater sense of responsibility for their machines and reducing the rate of wear and damage.

All three strategies have their advantages and disadvantages, and the choice will depend on the practical circumstances, the main problems to be solved, the skills available and workplace configuration. Given the constraints in matching people to their jobs, each one will entail what are bound to be major organisational decisions.

There is even greater uncertainty as to whether the practice of matching one man to one job will continue to vanish. As integrated production systems become more fluid there is a growing tendency to entrust full responsibility for a substantial part of the production process to a team of workers. The team is led by a foreman, but there are no distinctions between its members in the jobs they do, their skills or their trades. The idea is that a team is semi-autonous and self-renewing. Each team, therefore, is homogeneous, organises itself and has multiple skills in that portion of the process for which it is responsible (Cofinneau and Sarraz, 1985).

The approach goes against the grain of French tradition, but it looks very promising provided that it is properly supervised. Labour costs are likely to be high because the job classification of every member of a work unit must be high. Training will also be costly, as money will have to be spent on giving every worker the level of skills for his grade. On the other hand, it promotes greater operational flexibility and adds to the ability to cope with technical and social contingencies, since members of a unit are interchangeable. It also provides scope for a more flexible adjustment of the volume and nature of the work provided.

Through 'learning by doing', members of a team can cope with additional workloads when a process is being started up and stabilised, and the time they start to save thereafter can be reinvested. It can be put to use elsewhere without the reduction in the size of the workforce disrupting the production process. Alternatively the terms of reference of that workforce can be broadened, and the extra time devoted to thinking how to improve the machines. If this approach is taken, it is easier to deal with reductions or changes in the work or the number of teams.

Provided that this approach is properly managed in terms of the team's experience and relations with the hierarchy, a group of people will be formed who are not only competent to do a given job at a given time but are capable of training themselves and others. Working together, they will be able to manufacture products, generate their own skills and pass on those skills to newcomers. It will also reduce the cost of formal training and retraining, while increasing direct production efficiency.

Last, the advantage of this approach is that it alleviates the constraints that the architecture of a computerised control system may impose on the organisation of labour and the role of each individual.

JOB CLASSIFICATIONS, TRAINING AND SOCIETY

Workplace structures in relation to macro-social structures

The division of labour, the organisation of work and the effects on jobs or tasks will depend on employers' decisions as to technology and models of organisation and management. Employers' actions or intentions as regards future developments are, however, swayed by two factors which are sometimes underrated and sometimes overestimated. The first is the internal structure of each workplace, which acts as a brake on any evolution not in line with its past development. The present is a strong constraint, often making it hard to contemplate a future that represents too abrupt a departure and makes too great a demand in terms of change and conflict. The second factor is society and its structures, the framework of reference for people within the workplace which to an extent determines their scope for manoeuvre or the ways they will perform.

These two opposite factors interact and, depending on the circumstances, each one influences or is influenced by the other, sometimes both at once. In combination they serve as benchmarks for the people involved and even create standards.

The significance they bring to the division of labour is not just technical but social as well—status, pay, requirements governing access to jobs and the prospect of joining certain social groups. This explains the differences observed in the structuring of labour from country to country.

On the macro-social level, status, pay and prospects are embodied in rules and procedures laid down by law and negotiated agreement. What form they take in practice, however, depends on the way people within the workplace interpret the law and agreement. For example, companies may be subject to the same collective labour agreement, operate in exactly the same markets, manufacture similar products by comparable methods and be similar in size but still differ considerably in their pay structure, technical organisation, production management, the way they regulate labour relations and how they handle tensions among the employees concerned.

Scope for widely differing choices of skills

Because of this interplay between macro-social norms and the values inherent in each workplace, the question of building up the skills that will be needed in the medium-term future is an open-ended question and a challenge.

This situation is very evident in France in the matter of machine programming. The questions are how to allocate the task among different departments (production, maintenance and methods) and among job categories (shop-floor workers, foremen and engineers), and what is required of someone before he is capable of programming (should he first have had the kind of advanced technological training acquired in a course leading to the Baccalauréat de technicien supérieur (higher technician's diploma) or at an Institut universitaire de technologie (university faculty of technology)?) In some cases, this would be a fairly sharp break with tradition (Maurice *et al.*, 1986).

For example, if the task of production planning is assigned to engineers from the work-study methods department and if the skill is acquired through shop-floor experience plus a slightly higher level of initial training and further in-service training, the equilibrium does not really change, it just evolves. This is not the case if the skill is acquired by direct recourse to young technicians with a higher level of training. In this case, the methods department not only preserves but reinforces its lead, and shop-floor workers lose the opportunity of promotion via the channel carrying the greatest prestige. The equilibrium is severely disrupted.

The equilibrium is also destabilised, although in a different way, if programming is performed within the production department. The effects on the balance of power will depend on whether programming is assigned to supervisors or to shop-floor workers. If it is assigned to the latter, they will move up to a higher grade in the register of factory jobs, as permitted by the revised collective labour agreements for the engineering industry. If the task is assigned to supervisory personnel, their role and status by comparison with the methods department are enhanced and they regain some of the technical prestige they were tending to lose; at the same time, access to skills via shop-floor experience and continuing training would once again make their jobs attractive as a potential channel for promotion for the shop-floor worker. If, on the other hand, programming is made the responsibility of shop-floor workers, and if their job classification is then upgraded and brought in line with that of their supervisors, the position of the latter is weakened: supervisors will lose their edge over those subordinates who have acquired higher status and a skill the supervisors lack. The result would be an even greater disruption of the traditional balance of power in French factories.

Another alternative strategy is to assign programming to the methods department, raise the level of recruitment of workers to those, for example, holding the Baccalauréat de technicien supérieur, and then promote them to supervisory and method posts. It involves creating a new level of shop-floor skills which is in keeping with the French tradition but is out of step with the educational system. It also creates a break further down, as regards access to skilled labour jobs.

CONCLUDING REMARKS

We hope that the examples we have given illustrate the need for a painstaking analysis of the many factors involved in attempting to plan the structure of jobs in the future and map out the training needed as a result. The factories of the future will certainly be very different from the factories of today due to the effects of decisions as to technologies, models of organisation and management procedures. The people who work in these new factories will not be expected to have the same expertise as today's workers, nor will work practices there be the same. Research conducted in workplaces in European

Community member states over the past few years gives a reasonably clear picture of trends in the future.

We do not have such a distinct picture of the nature of work itself and all it implies; pay, status, conditions of access and the social prospects it affords. The factories of the future and the training their workforce needs must still to a great extent be planned in the light of whatever is seen as the macro-social scenario.

Address for correspondence:

Centre National de la Recherche Scientifique, 15 Quai Anatole, 75700 Paris, France.

REFERENCES

Bullinger, J. *et al.* (1986) Towards the factory of the future. Paper read at the Symposium on 'New production systems: the implication for work and training in the factory of the future'. Turin, 2–4 July.

Cofinneau, A., and Sarraz, J. P. (1985) Impact social et organisationnel des automatismes et de la robotique—Peugeot Mulhouse. IECE Développement, Programme Mobilisateur Technologie Emploi Travail, Ministère de la Recherche et de l'Enseignement Supérieur, October.

Fix-Sterz, J. *et al.* (1986) The present state and development tendencies of FMS and FMC in the Federal Republic of Germany. Turin Symposium, 2–4 July.

Haywood, B. W. (1986) Organisational aspects of FMS in the United Kingdom. Turin Symposium, 2–4 July.

Hollard, M., and Margirier, G. (1986) Nouveaux procès de production et implications macro économiques: contribution au débat sur la flexibilité. *Revue Formation-Emploi*, **14** (April/June), 22–34.

d'Iribarne, A. (1985) La nécessité d'une éducation professionnelle. *Revue Formation-Professionnelle*, **11** (June), 15–19.

d'Iribarne, A. (1986) Innovations technologiques et compétitivité economique. *Revue d'Economie Industrielle*, **38**, 11.

Kristensen, P. (1986) Technological projects and organisational changes: the dissolution of strategies and structures in Danish firms working towards flexible specialisation. Turin Symposium, 2–4 July.

Maurice, M. *et al.* (1986) Des entreprises en mutation dans la crise. Apprentissage des technologies flexibles et émergence de nouveaux acteurs. LEST/CNRS, Aix-en-Provence, mimeographed copy, June.

Sorge, A. (1983) Polarisation of skills in the future? *CEDEFOP, Vocational Training*, **11** (June), 22–25.

Section 2

Conditions Which Make Flexible Production Work

6. Organisation and Integration of Production Systems

Bill Haywood and John Bessant

Department of Business Management, Brighton Polytechnic, Brighton

SUMMARY

The main focus of this chapter deals with research on how far the diffusion of automated manufacturing technologies has progressed in British firms. Flexible manufacturing systems (FMS) (and flexible manufacturing cells) were seen as the first major step towards full computer integrated manufacturing (CIM). The first part of this chapter is concerned with the metal removal industries (FMS is, of course, applicable to a wide range of other industries such as furniture, rubber and plastics, foundries, etc.) and gives a brief outline of the research and its findings. The latter sections deal with a number of policy issues.

INTRODUCTION: THE TREND TO COMPUTER INTEGRATED MANUFACTURING

As in all other countries, the introduction of computers in the UK has tended to be rather fragmented. There was little of it, it was expensive, physically energy and space consuming, few people knew how to run it effectively, and it was devoted to specific functions, such as salaries or tool stocks. All these factors are now rapidly changing (see Bessant and Haywood, 1985) and the integration of all aspects of manufacturing is growing from the receipt of orders through design, planning, production, assembly, despatch, etc. This state of affairs can be understood by reference to a model offered by Kaplinsky (1984). He suggests that manufacturing can be divided into three distinct spheres of activity: design, manufacturing, and coordination. Historically these activities tended to be discrete and the process has been one of technological and organisational change leading first to integration within spheres and later to integration between spheres. A good example of this process can be seen in the case of machine tools; in the early factories, each

New Technology and Manufacturing Management   Edited by M. Warner, W. Wobbe and P. Brödner
Published 1990 by John Wiley & Sons Ltd

operation was carried out by a single special purpose machine. Gradually there was an integration, first of the functions which a single machine tool could perform and later, with the advent of numerical control, of the skilled operator input. Later still came the principles of direct numerical control whereby a set of multi-function machine tools can be controlled within a production cell by a master computer.

Current interest is focused on FMS which permit handling and transport to be automated (via robots, automatic conveyors, automated guided vehicles, etc.), with production scheduling and overall operations control all under computer control. This is a clear example of integration between spheres, bringing together the coordination and production activities. Other examples include computer aided design and manufacturing (CAD/CAM), and CAD links into computer-based inventory control and purchasing systems. This integration is facilitated by the fact that electronics provides the common language necessary for inter-sphere communication. However, integration does not stop there, for increasingly companies are looking at links, with both their customers and their suppliers. In both cases they are examining their relations at the technical level where CAD/CAM can be so important, and the links that exist organisationally with other companies.

In the later Kaplinsky (1986) model we were offered a picture of integration within the firm. Here we anticipate growing links between firms as well. If this is the case then there will also be a growing need to establish an overall communications system which would allow common standards within Open Systems Interconnection networks, e.g. the General Motors initiative, Manufacturing Automated Protocol (MAP), or the Initial Graphics Exchange Specification (IGES).

THE BENEFITS OF FLEXIBLE MANUFACTURING SYSTEMS

Flexible manufacturing systems offer a number of solutions to both the internal and external competitive pressures being increasingly felt by companies. *Internally*, of particular importance are the wide range of problems associated with batch manufacture. Such problems include:

— Long production lead times.
— High inventory levels of raw materials, work in progress and finished goods.
— Low machine utilisation due to long set-up times and product changes.
— Low machine utilisation downstream of bottlenecks.
— Queuing problems at bottleneck operations.
— Problems in introducing new products.
— Poor delivery performance.
— Poor quality control.

— High scrap levels.
— Poor production control, leading to high overheads; for example, in progress chasing, etc.

One indication of the extent to which such manufacturing conditions represent a threat to efficiency is the fact that in many firms a product will spend up to 95% of its time in the factory moving around or queuing, with value adding operations often accounting for only 2% or so of the time spent in the factory.

The potential benefits of FMS style technologies are considerable. In our study we discovered quite dramatic changes in a whole series of important manufacturing criteria, such as:

— Lead times, reduced on average by 74%.
— Work in progress, reduced on average by 68%.
— Stock turnover, increased on average by 350%.
— Machine utilisation, increased on average by 63% (up from say 50% with CNC to more than 80% with FMS).

Given that an estimated £23 billion is currently held in materials and components in UK manufacturing engineering the benefits for the average company are obviously very considerable. Data on FMS is still fairly limited since such systems are in the early stages of diffusion and most have only recently been installed. However, one of the key points which is emerging from this early experience is a need for significant organisational change to obtain the full benefits from new technology. It appears that this factor is likely to be an important determinant of how well firms are able to appropriate the benefits of CIM; at present there is considerable lag between the adoption of new technology and organisational adaptation.

These moves towards highly integrated technology for the 'factory of the future' will require a major rethink about production organisation and management. Traditional 'best practice' in production engineering will have to be combined with new management techniques and organisational forms, including a re-examination of the relationships between the workforce and the technology, and the political and social objectives of management.

Externally firms are being forced to respond much more closely to customer demand. This means shorter lead times on delivery, better delivery performance, high and consistent quality, and particularly, the ability to meet an increasingly customised product specification. With many markets becoming much more fashion-like with shortening product life-cycles, this puts severe pressure on firms to develop more flexibility and responsiveness, characteristics which have been termed 'manufacturing agility'. It is significant to note that these pressures for agility are confronting even firms in the mass and flow line sectors, where traditional patterns of scale economy are being replaced

by growing demand for smaller quantities of more customer specific production and variety—what have been termed 'economies of scope'.

It is in response to these trends that the various elements of CIM have
begun to evolve and converge, and FMS are one of the major innovations in
this area.

CIM OR C/HIM?

Much of the current discussion of integration has centred on computer
integrated manufacturing (CIM). However, our research convinces us of the
need to think more in terms of computer/human integrated manufacturing.
Although many benefits can be obtained and give support to the claims for
the potential of advanced manufacturing technologies, getting the best performance from them involved considerably more than simply taking the
decision to adopt the technology. This confirms the findings of other research
(such as Fleck (1984) and Voss (1986)), who point out that getting up to best
practice performance, or achieving the kind of benefits which suppliers offer,
can take months or even years. In particular, as Voss (1986) suggests, what
is needed in successful implementation is simultaneous technological and
organisational change.

In terms of skill, theories based on the division of labour and economies of
scale are being supplanted by multi-skilling and economies of scope. These
are much more relevant to production requirements where in batch manufacturing, for example, around 70% of output in metal manufacturing lies in
batches of less than fifty. FMS and cells, which answer many of these
production problems, call for multiplicity of skills (e.g. setting, programming,
simple maintenance, diagnostic skills, etc.), rather than employing a wide
range of specifically skilled people. This can be seen in a study of the
German firm Messerschmitt–Bolkow–Blum (MBB) (one of the largest FMS
installations), which needed exceptionally high levels of highly skilled maintenance personnel in order to keep it running effectively (Handke, 1983).

Attempts to develop a fully automatic factory with no human intervention
whatsoever are unlikely to meet with much success because of the enormous
risks and costs associated with developing suitable software to control such
systems.

Research by Wall (1986), for example, has begun to demonstrate the
importance of rethinking operator roles within advanced manufacturing systems. In work on small flexible cells it was found that in addition to a
deskilling machine minding role, there as a need for a highly skilled 'operator
midwife' role which involved intervening when problems with the largely
automated control system emerged. It is important to note that the objective

in such systems moves from one in which labour is seen as a necessary evil and a cost item to be reduced or eliminated wherever possible, to one in which it is seen as being an important aid to keeping the utilisation of the system high, and thus to recovering its high capital costs.

There has also been some debate regarding the erosion of distinctions between 'direct' and 'indirect' labour, with increasing dependence on the traditionally defined indirect workers to keep such systems running. Perhaps of greatest importance is in the fields of maintenance where there is a need to examine the pattern of skill availability and its development. Technological integration is bringing a number of new demands in the skills required of an individual, particularly in the areas of more flexibility and breadth.

Arnold and Senker (1983) identify this need in a number of applications and industries; they show the major influence which provision of (or lack of) suitable skills and training can have on the speed with which firms are able to achieve best practice performance with CAD systems. Handke (1983) has also observed, in his study of MBB in Augsburg, the extent to which maintenance skills, especially the newer ones such as systems analysis and diagnostics, contribute to the utilisation of advanced manufacturing systems, and hence to the rapid repayment of their initial costs.

The 'indirect' element is harder to quantify, but most firms appear to have used increased levels. For example, in Japan, only six people were employed directly on running the now well-known Yamazaki installation. However, 10 times more were employed in support of it (e.g. for programming, for swarf removal or parts movement, button pushers, etc.). While direct labour saving might be quite high, overall levels of employment were much less dramatically affected.

As far as the UK is concerned it may still be appropriate to employ these distinctions of direct and indirect labour. We have found that while there may be less 'direct' skilled labour required as a result of the introduction of FMS, manpower demand in the UK has tended to be for a higher quality of labour.

Our study shows job loss amongst direct labour as a general trend, but that job growth and quality of life improvements have probably occurred in many of the cases studied. In the past, most emphasis has been put on this direct labour impact—with good reason given the social implications. However we define 'quality of life' (e.g. less division of labour, health and safety improvements, enlarged job opportunities or skills, etc.), it appears that at this stage of the diffusion process, the impact in the UK has tended to be positive. We should keep in mind though, that quality of life changes *within* a group might well vary considerably. It is also likely that the diffusion process will dramatically change these early findings and that as such systems proliferate, there will be greater job loss if we fail to redefine the relationships between the worker and the computer.

ORGANISATIONAL FACTORS

Much of the preceding discussion has been about technological problems and opportunities posed, but the importance of methodological routes to improved efficiency was also stressed. When accounting for overall improvements in efficiency, estimates of the importance of organisational change varied between 40% and 70% of the total improvement. Clearly around half of the improvement tended to come from these types of change. One company which had not introduced FMS/FMC had reduced the level of stocks held by 60% and increased output by 30% just by adopting 'good management and methodological practices'. This together with investment in stand-alone computer numerically controlled (CNC) machine tools led to a trebling of turnover, from £20 million to £60 million, in the period 1981–4 when most UK engineering companies were in deep recession. During the period employment was declining in our sample companies by an average of over 30%; yet employment grew in this non-FMS company by some 14%. In other words, what was important here was not so much the technology but the adoption of good management and production practices.

The move to FMS and other integrated automation technologies also poses questions about the traditional pattern of functional specialisation. For example, there is the need for the design and production departments to work together to develop products which are suitable for manufacture on an FMS. Such a 'design for manufacture' philosophy is of particular significance in the flexible assembly automation field where small modifications to the design of an item can eliminate the need for complex manipulation of operations within an automated system. In one case, redesign of the product led to a reduction in the number of operations (handling and machining) from 47 to 15 with significant implications for cost and lead time savings. As one manager put it 'FMS is going to drive the shop—but it's also going to drive the people who design the product, and production engineering.'

The essence of such functional integration is not to eliminate specialist skills but to bring them to bear in a coordinated fashion on the problems of designing, producing and selling products—creating a single system view of the process rather than one with many parochial boundaries and little interchange across them. A good example of this can be found in the area of financial appraisal of FMS. Given the high costs of such systems, often running into millions of pounds, conventional accounting methods are often inappropriate since they would reject projects which were unable to show a payback of within two years or so.

FMS is not, however, only a production technology but also a strategic one and the question of whether or not the firm has such flexibility in the future might determine whether and what share it has of future markets. In many of the cases we examined firms commented that the actual justification for their projects was little more than 'an act of faith', confirming the view that qualitative judgements were at least as important as quantitative appraisal techniques. Thus the question of whether or not to invest needs to be a mixture of quantitative techniques and qualitative judgements expressed by those with different perspectives, such as, marketing, production engineering and corporate planning, in addition to the cost accountants.

In the same way as integrating technologies require closer functional integration, so they imply shorter hierarchies and greater vertical integration in organisational structure. In order to exploit the full benefits of a rapidly responsive and flexible system it is necessary to create a managerial decision-making structure which is closely involved with the shop floor and which has a high degree of delegated autonomy. As yet our experiences of the UK sector display almost twice the depth of managerial hierarchies as that found in Sweden, and a lower likelihood of shop-floor autonomy developing in comparison with similar enterprises in Sweden.

At the level of the shop floor, considerable changes are implied for the pattern of work organisation. With greater reliance on a small group of workers and managers comes the need to look for models of production organisation which have less to do with task fragmentation, division of labour and control by external regulatory systems of sanctions and rewards, and to evolve alternatives based on small autonomous working groups, with high flexibility and internal control. There appears to be a growing awareness of the inappropriateness of Tayloristic approaches which are based on a fundamental dis-integration of work for activities surrounding a fundamentally integrating set of technologies.

The rethink required encompasses both the hardware and the software elements of production, right through to the organisationally efficient management of production. It is becoming increasingly clear that factors such as just-in-time production, total quality control, supplier and customer relationships, etc., are all extremely important in improving efficiency, and that it is not merely the technology that we should consider. Significantly, it is precisely in these areas of organisational and methodological techniques that the Japanese are strongest, and which are somewhat belatedly attracting the attention of the West. There has been growing interest in these areas in Australia, the US and the UK. No doubt there are many similar experiences that could be highlighted from other countries.

Such aspects of organisational change come with the adoption of different approaches to the layout and methods of production. Here the influence of Japanese manufacturing techniques can be clearly seen, with emphasis on simplification and planning to achieve smooth flow through manufacturing; making batch processing resemble flow production as closely as possible. The precise configuration of layout and the range of techniques adopted vary. However, in many of the firms we spoke to technological change involving

FMS was taking place in parallel with programmes for quality improvement, changing supplier and purchasing policies and moving towards implementing a just-in-time philosophy, both in purchasing and within the production process as a whole.

Many people have talked of the cultural reasons why such 'Japanese' style methodological developments are inappropriate for Western countries. However, it would be difficult to think of many 'Japanese' production methods which do not have their roots in Western ideas, taken and developed by the Japanese since the 1950s. Theorists such as Sloan, and particularly Deming and Juran, have been extraordinarily important to the Japanese.

THE POLICY IMPLICATIONS OF PRODUCTION PROCESS INTEGRATION

In very broad terms it can be argued that although there are fundamental differences in the nature of manufacturing processes, the demands placed upon enterprises in the manufacturing sector are becoming increasingly similar. Although high volume flow process production (e.g. petrochemicals or food processing) involves very different basic processes to batch engineering work, both sectors are now facing pressures from their environment such as:

— Increasing competition, especially on a world-wide basis, with emphasis not only on price factors but also on non-price variables like design, delivery times and quality of product.
— Increasing demands for smaller batches tailored to suit customer needs; even in petrochemicals, flexibility in meeting a wider spread of needs is a high priority.
— Increasing demands for high quality products.
— Increasing demand for better customer service, delivery performance, after-sales support, etc.
— Increasing demand for new products on a decreasing life-cycle basis.
— Increasing demand for improved linkages with suppliers to facilitate just-in-time deliveries, reduced component costs and improved quality of parts.

A direct consequence of this is that firms are being forced to examine their internal environment closely to try and reduce costs. Labour costs are, usually mistakenly, given the highest priority, followed by materials, energy, and other factor inputs. In addition, firms are also trying to improve quality, reduce lead times, reduce the overall uncertainty in the production process, and so on.

The tools with which firms choose to tackle these problems can be drawn from a large toolbox. Most commonly used are the new, largely computer based technologies with which we have become famliar. The trends associated with these are essentially integrative at the purely technical level, bringing together physical and control functions into systems and complex machines. In the longer term these are also converging towards what has been termed computer integrated manufacturing (CIM) and which represents a full exploitation of the possibilities opened up by convergence of physical and control functions enabled by information technology. Further, this process does not stop at the boundary of the firm but moves on outwards, integrating along both the supply and distribution chains, as we noted earlier.

The point about this is that it is the product of extrapolating one kind of integration at the technical/physical/control function level. Whilst it is easy to make projections of this kind, there is growing evidence that achieving such integration in practice is much more difficult. First, there are technical problems at this level, such as the urgent need for suitable standards and protocols to establish the rules for systems interconnection. Second, there is growing evidence that even when the technical systems can be integrated, the full benefits which might be expected from such systems do not materialise because of a lack of integration at other levels in the organisation. This experience varies across the industrial spectrum and with firm size.

This suggests that other tools must also be used to support, or in some cases to substitute for, the new technologies. Probably the most significant group are those new methods of production organisation and management which have been exploited by Japanese industry. Examples here include total quality control and just-in-time scheduling and inventory management, which have strong Japanese roots, and group technology and value analysis, which have been tried in a much wider context. The point about all these is that they represent proven production engineering practices which can contribute to solving the problems outlined at the beginning of this section. These can be achieved at relatively low cost, involving a much lower level of risk for the organisation. It also affords the opportunity of examining the role that the workforce can play in interacting with new technologies. Recent experience suggests in very many cases of pre-installation justification for, and post-installation experiences of FMS, that firms who had wished to eliminate labour from the production process found the use of skilled workers a profound contributory factor in its efficient use.

Evidence suggests that implementing changes in either methods or technology in organisations requires some adaptation on the part of the organisation if the benefits expected are to be realised. The importance of this adaptation can be gauged from a variety of estimates. The benefits of technologies like FMS come before the technology itself is implemented; in other words from the organisational changes which it forces the firm to make. The nature of these changes is beginning to be documented, though its detailed mapping remains an important research task for the future. They include:

— Changes in organisation structures, especially functional integration, e.g. closer coordination of the activities of the research, marketing, and manufacturing engineering departments.
— Hierarchical integration, e.g. in the structure of task and work organisation.
— Changes in the linkage between manufacturing and business strategy, e.g. what is to be made, for which markets, and how it is to be made.
— Changes in the basic culture of organisations.

Characteristic of these is the idea of organisational integration to match the pattern of technological integration in the move towards CIM. Thus progress towards the future factory could be represented on a simple matrix, which has as its axes increasing technological and organisational integration. The goal—in which the full benefits of integrated systems are to be realised— involves integrated technology in an integrated organisation. The starting point for many firms is a basically disintegrated pattern in both the use of discrete items of production equipment and in the extent of organisational integration. The question posed is how to get to the goal—and the suggestion is that, although pressure is strongly on firms to choose the 'technology first' route, their chances of successful implementation may be enhanced by following an organisations and technology route, or at least one in which organisations and technology are adopted in parallel with one another.

CONCLUDING REMARKS

Much of the research, whether into the design and implementation of advanced systems or the organisational consequences of such innovations, has focused very narrowly on the production area. At worst, systems are measured against purely technical and system specific performance criteria such as machine speeds and flexibility. For a few systems some form of performance appraisal pre and post installation takes into account some of the wider benefits to the manufacturing system (such as improvements in lead times, inventory levels or machine utilisation); although even here many benefits were unanticipated whilst other, expected benefits failed to materialise. But very few firms extend their appraisal to the strategic domain and look at the contribution of such new technologies to a manufacturing strategy which is also linked to an overall business strategy. As Voss (1986) points out, there is an urgent need to plan investments at this level, to appraise their financial implications with this length and breadth of a strategic overview rather than a narrowly short-term one, and to assess the effectiveness or otherwise of the investment post installation against these strategic criteria.

Address for correspondence:

Department of Business Management, Brighton Polytechnic, Moulsecoomb, Brighton BN2 4AT, UK.

REFERENCES

Arnold, P. E., and Senker, P. (1983) Designing the future: the skills implications of interactive CAD. Engineering Industry Training Board, Watford, UK, Occasional Paper No 9.

Bessant, J. R., and Haywood, B. W. (1985) FMS as an example of CIM. Innovation Research Group, Brighton Polytechnic, UK, Occasional Paper No. 1.

Fleck, J. (1984) The employment effects of robots. In T. Lupton (ed.), *Human Factors in Manufacturing*. Bedford: IFS Publications.

Handke, G. (1983) *Design and Use of FMS*. Bedford: IFS Publications.

Haywood, B. W. (1986) Organisational aspects of FMS in the UK: Paper prepared for EC Symposium 'New Systems of Production'. EC–FAST, Turin.

Kaplinsky, R. (1984) *Automation: The Technology and Society*. London: Longman.

Kaplinsky, R. (1986) *Economies of Scale and Economies of Scope*. Brighton: Institute of Development Studies, Sussex University.

Voss, C. (1986) *Implementing Advanced Manufacturing Technology: A Manufacturing Strategy Perspective*. Bedford: IFS Publications.

Wall, T. (1986) *New technology and skills*. Paper to Manpower Services Workshop, Aston University, Birmingham, March.

7. Process-related Skills: Future Factory Structures and Training

Rainer Schultz-Wild

Institut für Sozialwissenschaftliche Forschung eV (ISF), Munich

SUMMARY

In all likelihood, uniform factory structures will not exist in Europe in the near future. The differences are too great regarding basic conditions and developmental perspectives between regions, countries, economic branches and market conditions, as well as the differences concerning the problems and potential solutions in the area of production technology and also workforce and skill availability etc. Even if the production technology offered does tend to become more uniform due to market conditions and/or international standardisation efforts, it nevertheless remains highly doubtful whether questions of technology utilisation, work organisation and the division of labour within companies and between companies will in all regions be solved according to a uniform structural pattern.

INTRODUCTION

It is widely agreed among experts that the concept of the so-called 'unmanned factory' has only very limited chances within the near future and that this concept is, at best, suitable only for certain marginal areas of highly standardised manufacturing. There are also numerous voices stressing the limitations of the long prevailing Taylorist or Fordist model of manufacturing organisation and work structuring, strongly centralised and based on a strict division of labour; this particularly within the context of the utilisation of modern computer aided technologies and the necessity for adapting to rapidly changing market conditions (compare, for example, Brödner, 1985; Piore and Sabel, 1984; Warnecke, 1985).

In view of these factors, particularly with regard to European industry, factory structures are being advocated which make use of the existing wealth of skills and qualifications and which seek to secure the potential for innovation and the capability to adapt, particularly in the case of the often smaller

New Technology and Manufacturing Management   Edited by M. Warner, W. Wobbe and P. Brödner
Published 1990 by John Wiley & Sons Ltd

and medium-sized companies, by preserving the scope for taking action and decision-making in proximity to the basis of the manufacturing process, on the shop floor. Such concepts are oriented less towards maximum utilisation of computer-based automation technology up to the total exclusion of human labour, and more towards a combination of technology and labour, whereby the production knowledge and experience held by workers closely involved in the manufacturing process is systematically integrated.

The process-related utilisation of skills and qualifications offers companies a number of advantages, particularly when strategies of so-called 'hard' automation, with their standardisation requirements concerning the product and remaining human labour, meet with restrictions and strategies of flexible automation are pursued instead:

— Process-related utilisation of skills and qualifications can save planning costs and other investments for complex and extremely expensive automation technologies in the areas of hard- and software, when workers are able to bridge gaps in the process sequence.
— Process-related utilisation of skills and qualifications permits savings in implementation costs as well as a comparatively rapid introduction of technological and organisational innovations to the manufacturing process. When extensive basic skills already exist on the shop floor, the introduction of new technology components will lead to less qualification deficits, thereby resulting in a considerable reduction of training expenditures. In addition, the implementation work performed by the user company's workforce will shorten the running-in period of the new facilities so that they will operate productively at an earlier date.

In view of the continuously high costs for components of computer aided flexible automation, the fact that the process-related use of skilled labour can reduce the risks and duration of system failures is of particular significance. The use of qualified, skilled workers familiar with the specific manufacturing equipment increases the latter's availability and reliability. Such personnel can not only prevent disturbances by intervening and correcting the ongoing manufacturing process, but also shorten breakdown times by performing repairs themselves so that specialised maintenance personnel need not be called on nor waited for.

Moreover, the process-related use of skills can also permit a better utilisation of manufacturing equipment, not only with regard to the extent of operational flexibility for various products or product variants within the framework of the given technical corridor, but also in terms of coordinating machine schedules and/or production capacity with the requirements of the ongoing production flow.

Finally, the process-related use of skilled personnel in the production process can also result in lower labour costs. On the one hand, this refers to the savings in costs arising outside the immediate area of manufacturing for technical services like work planning, programming, manufacturing control, maintenance and quality assurance. On the other hand, the number of workers can be reduced compared to highly specialised forms of work organisation, or those aiming for a minimisation of the use of skills because broadly skilled workers are able to replace each other and fill vacancies caused by illness or other reasons.

All these reasons point to a company interest in making use of a skilled and qualified workforce which is familiar with the special requirements of flexible automation and in employing these workers in the immediate proximity of the manufacturing process and of the mostly complex manufacturing equipment. In terms of manufacturing organisation, widely differing solutions are conceivable with this strategy, starting with more traditional workshops specialising in certain manufacturing technologies, up to 'production islands' for the complete processing of products or components of a final product. The forms of work organisation and the division of labour can also vary, for example between the following two basic models:

1. In the first case, the traditional forms of job classification and hierarchical division of labour are dispensed with to a large extent and instead, a homogeneous group of equally qualified production workers are employed who share the various and changing work tasks within a given manufacturing area according to internal agreements and who also share the responsibility for the fulfilment of the assigned jobs. For example, employees such as the German skilled worker, having practical and theoretical production knowledge and experience and having had further training in the field of information systems and control technology, are suitable for this form of team-work.
2. The second model adheres more to the traditional forms of functional and hierarchical division of labour and the different specialised jobs thereby resulting. Accordingly, the workforce structure is differentiated depending on the areas and also the extent to which individual workers are qualified, and personnel may be arranged in groups containing differently specialised workers. In this case, a mixed staffing of a production team is conceivable, with semi-skilled and skilled workers, technicians and even engineers, and associated with a more hierarchical distribution of responsibility as well as—compared to the other model—a considerably restricted capacity for employees to replace one another if needs be.

Both models, between which various gradations and numerous design forms are imaginable, are in varying degrees suited to different forms of technology utilisation and requirements of manufacturing processes. The first model, for example, makes far greater use of the work organisation design within modern manufacturing technology when the binding of work tasks to the machine's operational cycle is largely reduced due to the automation of workpiece handling and transport. The second model seems to possess more advantages in those cases where automation gaps must be bridged by routine activities or where the deployment of specialists is imperative for one reason or the other. These latter forms of organisation, however, also hold higher risks of a polarisation of skills and the creation of permanent barriers between different employee groups.

PRECONDITIONS FOR A PROCESS-RELATED USE OF SKILLS AND QUALIFICATIONS

A common characteristic of the two models of work structuring previously described is the fact that they both increase 'shop-floor autonomy' by means of process-related use of qualified employees and reduce the significance of planning, control and supervising departments outside the manufacturing area, as opposed to the more centralised Taylorist/Fordist factory structures. Both models correspond to a development concept which is currently being discussed not only in Europe but also in the US under the heading of 'The factory within the factory' (Priore and Sabel, 1984), the intention of which is underlined by the demand 'CIM only with HIM' (Everitt, 1985). The realisation of such forms of manufacturing structures and work organisation depends, however, on a number of preconditions. We shall briefly mention the market developments with regard to the computer aided components of manufacturing presently offered, the implementation processes of new manufacturing technologies taking place within the companies, and the availability of different qualifications and skills for manufacturing work, as well as the question of reward systems, career patterns etc.

Market developments in computer aided components of manufacturing

In the past years, the spectrum of components for computer aided integration offered by the market has expanded considerably. This description holds true for production planning functions (CAD, CAP) as well as for production scheduling and control (PSC) and manufacturing–technological functions of machine control, tool management, workpiece handling and transport and also quality assurance (compare the individual CAM components: CNC, DNC, FMC, FMS, CAQ, etc.).

In many cases, the use of computer aided integration technology is characterised by a pioneer situation in which manufacturers adapt the systems' actual design to meet specific customer requirements to a considerable degree.

However, there is an increased development of marketable, more standard-ised offers requiring the system users themselves to adapt to a certain extent if considerable costs for 'tailor made' solutions are to be avoided. Moreover, in many areas in which computer aided integration technologies are applied one can safely state that the manufacturers control the market, this having to do with specific aspects of information–technological products, the expensive development of the generally very complex software solutions as well as the lack of competency in information technology on the part of the users. Thus, it is of particular importance which organisational concepts are passed on to the user companies in terms of manufacturing and work organisation:

— Complete offers of factories with fully integrated computer technology hardly exist to date. But the CIM components on the market can be classed as those which are more open in terms of manufacturing organisa-tion and work structuring, or those which contain strongly centralistic concepts which aim for a definite division between work executed on the shop floor and the functions of planning, control and supervision else-where.

— In many cases computer aided production scheduling and control systems (PSC) follow a strongly centralistic–deterministic design as far as their inner logic is concerned and they aim for the most exact short-term detailed planning of shop-floor activities possible. On the other hand, there are PSC concepts which dispense with detailed work guidelines and regulations from the start and instead provide only central framework planning which is then to be worked out in detail at the shop-floor level and carried out there subsequently. This second concept is more strongly based on process-related decisions in the shop-floor area and permits a greater scope for the design of work organisation—from the use of a central control post for the execution of planning processes up to the management of manufacturing control functions by workers employed in the actual area of manufacturing.

— The concepts behind DNC systems can be based on a strong division of labour and result in a concentration of informing and supervising data in the work planning department, or else concepts can be realised according to which the DNC computer acts more as a data-bank for NC controlling and programming systems, which also allows shop-floor programming to be carried out.

— Also in the case of CAD/CAP or CAD/CAM systems, one can differenti-ate between concepts which from the start are either office oriented and aim for more efficiency in the area of pre-planning, including office programming, and concepts which are more shop-floor oriented whereby construction data are transmitted to a workshop computer or individual CNC control system, in order to facilitate or accelerate the programming process there.

The results of our analysis point to a present market dominance of CIM components of a centralistic–deterministic nature which are exerting a strong influence towards a consolidation or an increase of the hierarchical–functional division of labour between the areas of planning and execution. Such solutions are usually developed and offered by large computer manufacturers who have a strong market position and are backed by many years of cooperation with the users of their systems. But it is doubtful if these solutions meet the special needs of smaller and medium-sized companies.

In contrast, the offers usually coming from smaller software or machine building companies are more open in terms of work organisation and do not restrict their users so strongly to pursuing certain solutions of technology integration as far as manufacturing and work organisation are concerned and are therefore more compatible with forms of process-related planning, control and supervision.

Although even in the cases of more strongly centralistic–deterministic solutions one cannot say that the user companies are being definitely bound to certain forms of manufacturing organisation and work organisation, it is nevertheless undeniable that the logic inherent in such solutions will influence the decisions concerning the implementation process within the company. A process-related use of skills and qualifications is easier to realise or maintain when hardware and software components are designed so as to grant access from the shop floor. In this context it is interesting to note that recently there are indications that systems which started out with different basic concepts are beginning to converge. However, this is likely to prove to be a very long-term developmental process. An example is the development of NC programming methods. It can be assumed that due to the further development of interactive–graphic programming methods a standardisation of operating methods will take place between systems originally based more on office programming and those oriented to workshop programming.

Generally the concepts of open system architecture seem to suit better the manifold technical and organisational conditions of different users and open up market opportunities specially for smaller supplier companies.

Implementation processes of new manufacturing technologies

In spite of the factors of influence built into the existing market offers of CIM components, there undoubtedly still remains considerable scope for the design of manufacturing organisation and work organisation by the user companies. The question remains, however, as to whether and in what way this scope for decision-making is actually made use of during the course of implementation processes. In spite of the fact that the discussion among managers and engineers concerning the importance of 'human factors' for the successful introduction of new technologies has been given more emphasis during recent years, it can, on the basis of present experience, hardly be assumed that work organisation and manpower use will enjoy the same careful pre-planning as is the case with the technical and economical factors on which decisions are based. Many implementation processes are characterised by a step by step introduction of new technology components, whereby the existing manufacturing structures and forms of organisation are retained to the greatest degree possible. For the most part, changes remain limited to what is absolutely imperative from a technological point of view. Such tendencies towards structural conservatism stand in opposition to the experience that technical innovations often initiate or are the medium for a reorganisation of work processes, which can be far-reaching. Changes of a slower and more subtle kind may possibly occur which lead to a gradual undermining of forms of work dominant so far, while radical structural changes may also be brought about. The probability of the latter arises

— with the size of the 'automation leap' of a given technological innovation, thereby necessitating a reorganisation and extensive redistribution of work between machinery and manpower;
— with the degree in which the previously dominant forms of modernisation by small steps is deviated from or must be abandoned, for example due to the more system-oriented character of the new integration technologies being installed;
— according to the extent to which the new technologies contain concepts of work organisation which contradict the principles having so far prevailed.

Process-related use of skills and qualifications can thus hardly be expected where control and production systems of more centralistic–deterministic type are integrated into centralistic company structures based on a sharp division of labour. A process of this kind strengthens the control and supervision departments outside the actual manufacturing area and leads to a further reduction of autonomy on the shop floor. The introduction of similar technologies in companies where qualified shop-floor workers still enjoy a considerable scope for decision-making can result in a gradual undermining of shop-floor autonomy and will thereby, in the long run at least, jeopardise the utilisation of skills.

On the other hand, however, it is also conceivable that, due to the functional deficiency of centralistic control systems, alternative concepts will be employed from the start and that the preconditions in terms of organisation and skills for successful operating will be systematically planned and subsequently realised during the implementation process. Therefore it is of decisive importance which in-plant groups plan and implement technological innovations and what the former's interests and specific aims are. The realisation of company structures according to the model of process-related use of qualifications is, for example, more likely to occur when the (shop-floor) managers directly responsible for the manufacturing process have more influence on the latter than members of central departments for work planning or manufacturing control, for example.

Qualification structure of the workforce

Apart from the structures of the technology offers and the specific interests which come into play in the course of the user's implementation process, the quantity and quality of available manpower is certainly of considerable significance for shaping and designing manufacturing organisation and work structures. The process-related use of qualifications is easier to realise or maintain in those companies which already have a workforce with broad and relevant skills at their disposal or where qualification deficits can be made up with relatively low training expenditures.

In cases of stagnating or sinking employee numbers, it is particularly the qualification structure of the manpower employed within the company which is decisive. This is because an extensive exchange of workers via the external labour market (dismissal of insufficiently skilled workers on the one hand, recruitment of adequately qualified manpower on the other) would certainly meet with resistance from representatives of workers' interests and would therefore be hard to achieve.

Those companies which have previously established their organisation on centralistic, Taylorist structures, and which have mainly employed specialised semi-skilled workers in their production departments, will most likely have more difficulties and higher expenditures in carrying through a reorganisation process to permit process-related use of qualifications and skills than companies whose manufacturing jobs have traditionally been largely in the hands of qualified, skilled workers. This holds true not only for homogeneous qualified team-work, but also for structures in the shop-floor area based on a certain degree of division of labour. Returning certain planning, control and monitoring functions to the vicinity of manufacturing jobs when computer aided integration technology is introduced results in new types of jobs and job requirements which cannot readily be fulfilled by personnel previously employed within more centralistic structures based on a high degree of division of labour.

Although the qualification structure of the workforce will certainly have an effect on the choice and introduction of new technologies and the resulting reorganisation of work processes, this factor can only be regarded as invariable from a short-term perspective. Changes can be brought about more or less rapidly by further training and retraining measures carried out by the companies themselves, for example; or also, over medium and longer periods of time, by alterations occurring in the company external labour market and within the education and vocational training system.

THE PART PLAYED BY EDUCATION AND TRAINING IN THE DEVELOPMENT OF FUTURE FACTORY STRUCTURES

At present, the tendencies in industry towards technological–organisational change are meeting with workforce structures with varying degrees of affinity for a process-related use of skills and qualifications. While there are certain deviations within the national framework, between different branches, companies with different manufacturing, organisational and personnel structures etc., these deviations are likely to be considerably greater on a European level. Because of their central role in determining the quantity and the qualification structure of the workforce available for industrial work, the education and training systems, which are strongly conditioned by specific national norms and traditions, are of considerable significance.

As a systematic, comparative analysis of the different European education and vocational training systems is not the intent of this chapter, we will confine ourselves to pointing out several problem constellations which are important for the question of future factory structures.

1. An initial point concerns the ability of the education and training system to secure adequate manpower supply, in terms of quantity and quality, for industrial employment and particularly for work in the area of manufacturing. At least in the long term a definite affirmative answer to this question can by no means be taken for granted. It has been particularly the expansion of educational opportunities and the opening of schools, universities and colleges for sections of the population previously following other courses of education which has encouraged many young people to remain as long as possible within the education system and to then strive for positions outside industry, particularly those outside the actual manufacturing area with all its adverse working conditions such as noise, dirt, shift work, etc. This problem can certainly not be simply reduced to the question of appropriate training offers and functioning control mechanisms in the area of schools and training, but points most clearly to the conditions of working life and career chances offered by industrial work itself. The chances for recruiting employees for industrial jobs must, in the long run, be viewed in comparison with the working conditions, earnings and career patterns etc., offered elsewhere.

2. The question as to the necessary reform of the trades and the content of vocational training must be regarded in terms of education and training policies. There are many indications that in the course of computer aided rationalisation processes the lines traditionally drawn between existing trades and occupations will become obsolete and that new qualifications and skills will become significant. It is particularly the work forms of process-related use of skills and qualifications which seem advantageous to companies from many points of view and which push strongly towards a

dissolution of traditional job classifications and demarcation lines between trades. While technical knowledge and skills related to specific products and manufacturing methods obviously remain important, a knowledge of electronic data processing (EDP), control technology and the technology required for monitoring, controlling and maintaining more complex manufacturing systems is becoming increasingly important. At present, no general solutions exist for grouping and combining such qualification requirements to form new jobs and trades. This is partly due to the very lengthy periods of time required for establishing reforms within the education and vocational training systems, but also to the fact that in many cases the application of modern control and manufacturing technologies has not yet advanced beyond the pioneer stage and therefore company experiments concentrate on the reorganisation of the remaining work tasks.

In the Federal Republic of Germany, for example, a bill concerning the reorganisation of the industrial metal working trades was passed at the end of 1984 whereby the number of recognised trades was cut back significantly (from 42 to six trades) while the commonly required basic technical knowledge of various fields was increased and knowledge of EDP, system control and general process engineering more strongly integrated.

3. A similar educational problem exists concerning the combination of more theoretically oriented knowledge and skills and those more concerned with practical aspects. Not all European countries have a tradition of a worker type similar to the German industrial skilled worker who combines theoretical and practical skills as well as a considerable potential for adapting and learning. This type of qualification profile certainly offers favourable conditions for the realisation of work structures based on team-work with homogeneous skills, specially if there is a wider range of common technical knowledge than in a more differentiated structure of jobs and trades. However, when theoretical and practical knowledge and skills are taught in different educational and training courses and in different institutions (such as school and company) then more differentiated forms of work structuring and use of qualifications are likely to occur.

4. The form in which higher and advanced technical knowledge is taught at institutions such as technical colleges and universities as well as the training patterns and subjects emphasised will certainly be significant for the development of future industrial structures. There are several reasons for this:

First, technicians and engineers have a considerable influence on the developmental process of new control, monitoring and manufacturing technology; the research tradition and forms of logic followed here will surely have an effect—perhaps indirectly in many cases—on certain hardware and software solutions.

Second, the presence or absence of technicians and engineers from different professional fields and with differing orientations within company management will be reflected in the definition of company problems and in the technical solutions developed; thus certain market impulses (increased demands made on product variations, for example) will call for different reactions, so that solutions will be sought in the area of production and control technology in one instance or in the field of work organisation in another.

Finally, the engineers and technicians themselves constitute an important part of the company's total workforce and their varying availability and involvement in certain work situations is not without effect on the development of the structures of in-plant division of labour.

A comparison of the utilisation of flexible manufacturing systems in France and in the Federal Republic of Germany, for example, indicates that certain variations in system concepts and layout (greater significance of the central computer and software programs in France; stronger concentration on processing machines, handling facilities and transport systems in Germany) definitely have something to do with the differences between the countries with regard to the supply situation and the professional orientation of engineers in the user companies, and that these factors also have an effect on division of labour and job design within these manufacturing systems (Schultz-Wild, 1986).

In this context, the problem is also how to distribute the relevant technological, organisational and managerial knowledge concerning the use of modern computer aided technologies, specially in smaller and medium-sized companies and in less industrially developed areas of Europe. In the past, vendors of CIM components have made some efforts to offer not only hard- and software but also the relevant so-called teachware. Also, at least in Germany, a great number of intermediate, more or less independent institutions for knowledge distribution and retraining in this field have emerged. But there still seems to be room for greater activity, especially on a European level in research, development, education and vocational training.

5. When the introduction of modern control and manufacturing technologies evolves from the pioneer phase and becomes considerably more widespread and particularly when forms of process-related use of skills and qualifications are realised in the process, then the problem of adapting the existing workforce in the companies in terms of qualifications must be dealt with. When the initial introduction of new technologies only affects a few workers directly, then qualification problems can be avoided and training expenditure reduced by creaming off the best suited workers for the new jobs. Such a policy of creaming off cannot, however, solve the problems arising when larger sectors are affected by technological–

organisational innovations. The capacity and efficiency of in-plant and public training institutions and/or vocational retraining is now decisive. In particular, those companies with a large number of unskilled and semi-skilled workers will be confronted with the necessity of considerable expenditure and training (in-plant and/or company external) in order to achieve adequate further training suited to adult and already experienced workers. The fact that further training measures can lead to considerable qualificatory achievements when certain preconditions are paid attention to has been proved in numerous cases (Schultz-Wild, 1986).

6. Finally, it must be pointed out that process-related use of skills and qualifications within complex manufacturing systems necessitates new forms of cooperation, particularly when a hierarchical distribution of responsibility is rejected and more open and less rigid forms of task distribution are practised. The capability and willingness to cooperate are specific requirements which to some extent run counter to traditional forms of individual learning and individual work performance. As far as this issue is concerned, it does not suffice merely to state that education and vocational training systems must place a stronger emphasis on collective learning processes; it must also be emphasised that new forms of cooperation require the support of adequate wage and reward systems within industrial companies. Particularly when team-work is preferred this also means that new career patterns must be developed or other ways and means must be found of ensuring that manufacturing jobs will also, in the long run, continue to offer sufficiently attractive chances of earning and reasonable working conditions.

CONCLUDING REMARKS

More differentiated observation and analysis is surely necessary in order to establish in detail how the problems mentioned here could be solved in the light of the different traditions and conditions in education and employment prevailing in the various European countries so that favourable conditions could be created for the development of future factory structures.

Address for corespondence:

Institut für Sozialwissenschaftliche Forschung eV (ISF), Jakob-Klar-Strasse 9, D-8000 Munich 40, FRG.

REFERENCES

Brödner, P. (1985) *Fabrik 2000—Alternative Entwicklungspfade in die Zukunft der Fabrik*, Berlin: Sigma.

Everitt, P. (1985) The manufacturing cell 'A plant within a plant'. SME Technical Paper MS 85–901, Dearborn, Illinois.
Piore, M. J. and Sabel, C. F. (1984) *The Second Industrial Divide. Possibilities for Prosperity.* New York: Basic Books.
Schultz-Wild, R. (1986) New production technologies and their implications for manpower and training policies. EC Symposium 'New Production Systems', 2–4 July, Turin.
Warnecke, H. (1985) Von Taylor zur Fertigungstechnik von morgen, *Zeitschrift für industrielle Fertigung*, **75**, 669–74.

8. Technocentric–Anthropocentric Approaches: Towards Skill-based Manufacturing

Peter Brödner
Institut Arbeit und Technik, Gelsenkirchen

SUMMARY

This chapter contrasts the 'technocentric' with the 'anthropocentric' approach to applying new technology. There are strong forces of inertia, which prevent the human-centred approach from disseminating widely. Such restraints result from a firm's hardware, software, social system and prevailing ideology. While hardware seems to have the weakest inertia and software already needs fundamental changes, the social system and ideology establish the highest barriers. Since the transition to group manufacturing deeply influences social positions and relations, it can only be arrived at on the basis of a bargained and agreed strategy. To establish such a strategy, it is first necessary to overcome the prevailing thinking that cannot imagine any other improvement of production than replacing human capabilities by machine artefacts. A 'real choice' now exists *vis-à-vis* the implementation of integrated manufacturing systems.

GLOBAL COMPETITION

During the last two decades, we have witnessed dramatic changes in world markets. The demand for industrial consumer goods and, consequently, that for capital goods too, has shifted from steady expansion to stagnation. For some capital goods, this tendency may even be reinforced, as the example of the machine-tool industry demonstrates, by the fact that the performance per unit of their products increases faster than their functional value.

Such a global trend will not be affected by the large potential of unsatisfied demand in the developing countries, since the terms of trade in general and their immense indebtedness in particular prevent them turning their needs into spending power for industrial goods for a long time to come. Thus, the world markets are and will remain confined to the highly industrialised areas

New Technology and Manufacturing Management   Edited by M. Warner, W. Wobbe and P. Brödner
Published 1990 by John Wiley & Sons Ltd

and so-called threshold countries comprising the areas of North America, Western Europe and South-East Asia (the Comecon countries being only marginally involved).

The overall low growth rates of these limited markets, indicating the change from expansion to stagnation, have the effect that competition also changes its character from supplying expanding market shares, where suppliers are able to set the conditions to a large extent, to displacing competitors, whereby customers gain the power for buying products adapted to their needs. Under these new market conditions of competition by displacement, price and quality of unified products are no longer the only assets needed to win the race. The abilities to adapt the products to customer requirements with increasing variety and yet to guarantee short delivery times are becoming rather more important competitive factors. This development has, in turn, an impact on the internal conditions of operation of the entire manufacturing process, as will be shown below.

In this respect, the European industrial core might potentially even be better off, or at least those parts of it that have long experience with 'flexible specialisation' (Piore and Sabel, 1984), an appropriate production system and a skilled workforce at their disposal. While the stagnation in world markets and, hence, competition by displacement prevail, Europe's comparatively favourable position will tend to improve even further, and the industrial system of the US will lose ground due to an ageing technology and wasted human resources.

However, the potential superiority can be transformed into real competitive power, if and only if the decision-makers at all levels become aware of this situation and realise that they have to develop future manufacturing technology, work organisation and skill profiles according to the specific requirements of 'flexible specialisation' or, looking at high volume production, to those of 'diversified quality production' (this being a hard lesson to learn for some countries and industries, of course). Instead of merely imitating Japan, it is necessary for survival to develop Europe's own manufacturing technology suited to its own needs. The factory of the future is thus at the crossroads (Brödner, 1985a; Piore and Sabel, 1984; Sorge and Streeck, 1986).

INTERNAL CONDITIONS OF OPERATION

The substantial shift in the world markets from expansion to stagnation has a strong impact on the internal conditions of operation in production processes. They now have to:

(a) become highly flexible with respect to alterations of products and process innovations,

(b) ensure at the same time high performance of machinery, increase productivity and cut down lead times and work in progress,
(c) enable improved quality and functionality of products.

However, the existing production structures as they have developed are in conflict with these new requirements in one way or another.

According to recent systematic analysis of the relationship between technical change, work organisation, skill profiles and the impact of product markets, these are loosely coupled only by some degree of affinity rather than being completely determined by each other. A given product and its market do not determine the technology to produce it, nor does technology determine work organisation or skill profiles. Hence, there always is room for *strategic choices* for products, technology and work organisation. Two main variables underlie alternative product strategies: the type of competition to which they are exposed and the volume in which they are produced. These factors divide production into standardised price-competitive and customised quality-competitive production on one side, and low and high volume production on the other (see Sorge and Streeck, 1986).

In this schema, traditional production concepts fall either into the category of low volume production of customised quality-competitive goods (order-bound production) or into that of high volume production of standardised price-competitive goods. With the advent of high performance electronic data processing (EDP), the range of options for product strategies has widened considerably. Its most important impact is that the new type of high volume production of customised quality-competitive goods (e.g. in the German or Swedish car industry), or in short 'diversified quality production', with the potential of economies of scope, has been made possible. The strategy of 'flexible specialization' enables a 'quantum-leap' towards improved profitability and competitiveness and traditional mass production can move towards smaller batches. Although these different types of production will most probably coexist for a long time to come, the main focus of this chapter is on small-batch production for the strategic reasons discussed above.

Past development of small-batch production can be briefly characterised by three stages. In the first stage, labour was horizontally divided according to the concepts of Smith and Babbage making it possible gradually to use machines. In the second stage, Taylor's principles enabled planning to be separated from execution. The third stage deepened this vertical division of labour by introducing NC machines and making programming an additional subtask of planning. Each of these has been caused by the 'political–economic' prospects of better control of production, higher productivity and lower costs rather than by technical necessities.

The result of this is the highly differentiated job-shop manufacturing process with very complex design, planning and control tasks that we now have. This way of organising batch production has serious drawbacks, however, such as long and variant throughput times, an unfavourable ratio of indirectly to directly productive workers, and low quality of work (being far better than in mass production, however).

In particular, there are three substantial economic difficulties the factory of today has to contend with. First, there is the continual increase in the capital-intensiveness of factory equipment which compels the management to make better use of it. Second, the very long and variant lead times caused by the functional principle of job-shop manufacturing give rise to high costs for work in progress. Third, the ratio of 144 indirect to 100 direct workers in the average machining firm in the Federal Republic of Germany causes excessive personnel costs, since well-organised plants with comparable products demonstrate that the ratio of 90 to 100 is generally sufficient.

THE TECHNOLOGY-CENTRED APPROACH—THE 'UNMANNED FACTORY'

This technology-centred approach leaves the basic job-shop structure of the production process unchanged and follows the same fundamental objectives as in the past: to reduce direct labour costs and to gain better control over the production process.

Applying this development to the shop floor, management attempts as far as possible to automate setting and operating functions for machine tools and handling systems. The activities focus on automatic part and tool change, measuring devices and monitoring systems. They are, of course, limited by the rapidly growing costs of this equipment. Although fully automatic operation might be temporarily possible, there still remain gaps to be filled by human operators.

The largest potential of rationalisation lies in the technical office, however, where many attempts have already been made to automate parts of the immense information-processing work (which can easily exceed half of the total amount of labour). Since the use of computers requires analytical models of the process in question, by means of which objects and sequences of work can be described as data structures and algorithms, their application started in areas that were the most accessible or promised the largest economic effects, for example drafting, process planning, inventory control and scheduling. All these systems helped a little to save time and costs, but did not improve the situation fundamentally, particularly as their separate development and application make it very costly, if not impossible, to integrate them (Sigismund, 1982).

Coinciding with the broad dissemination of CAD and CAM systems, a new polarisation of qualification occurs. In order to use them effectively, objects and sequences of work become extremely formalised and at the lower end the user's work loses important parts of its former skill, whilst at the upper end, only a few, well-qualified workers are required to plan and maintain the system. In addition, functional differentiation leads to further division of mental labour with similar effects.

The repeated and fault-intensive input of the same data in different functions demands integration of computer assistance. Owing to the high degree of formalised and concrete knowledge, more functions of mental work have become accessible for computers. This has led to the development of the computer integrated manufacturing (CIM) system, which comprises at least three basic devices:

— *a common database* with which all function programs may interact, since most data are used in several functional areas,
— *a data highway* to link subsystems, since a CIM system will be widely distributed,
— *a set of data-exchange interfaces*, since both users' and suppliers' demands need to be able to link subsystems of different origin.

Integration is not the only issue of the technology-centred strategy, however. Others are to create knowledge-based and expert-systems for use in all key areas of production in view of the arrival of fifth generation computers. There are two motives behind this: one is management's fear that, since most human labour has been reduced to low-grade functions except for a few high-grade experts, conventional programs might not be able to cope with complex and changing situations; the other one is its wish to have the expensive human experts' knowledge at its own disposal. Although this development is accompanied with great hopes stirred up by the 'artificial intelligence' community (Feigenbaum and McCorduck, 1983), it is rather questionable whether it will ever achieve its promises.

At the end of this far-reaching development, an integrated computer system on the one hand and a dismembered work structure on the other will be found. Most of the production knowledge will then be incorporated in the computer system, while the workers' qualifications will waste away, since they

The concept of the 'unmanned factory' runs into several difficulties, however, making its success appear rather questionable. First, the extremely high costs and risks, caused especially by the software needed, conflict with the weak financial power of the many small and medium-sized firms. Despite their growing economic importance, such firms would be bypassed by the development.

Second, firms following this strategy would suffer from relative inflexibility with respect to both alteration of batches and process innovation. This is because every change in a customer order or a piece of production equipment has first to be modelled in the computer system. In the long run, the firm might even lose its innovative capability, since production knowledge and creativity on the human side have been wasting away over time; all this is in contrast to market requirements.

Third, existing skills (a very important resource especially in Germany) would be rejected, while skills which do not exist would be required. In order to avoid these difficulties, it seems necessary to look for an alternative approach.

THE HUMAN-CENTRED APPROACH—SKILL-BASED MANUFACTURING

The human-centred approach is based on completely different principles of organising small batch production. By splitting orders instead of dividing labour, job-shop manufacturing with its fundamental drawbacks can be changed into group manufacturing where part-families are manufactured in their entirety.

Group technology principles can be implemented in four major stages (see Mitrofanow, 1980). In many cases, management feels content with structuring the firm's entire part-spectrum into part-families (first stage) only, in order to gain more transparency and better classification for the geometric and manufacturing data pools (such as drawings, part-lists, process plans and so on). However, the idea of group technology obviously denotes a general organisational concept rather than a single technique.

If the organisational changes are restricted to this first stage alone, the economic effects that can be achieved are limited. Experience with actual cases has shown that major advantages can only be achieved by advancing to the higher stages of group technology. As compared to job-shop manufacturing, these advantages are as follows (Spinas and Kuhn, 1980):

— short throughput times (time reduction by 60 to 88% and benefits of 44 to 60% for in-process inventory have been reported),
— enriched job-content and wide margins of action (reducing stress and challenging the worker's skills),
— easy production planning and control (since each production island can be regarded as a single uncoupled unit).

The main disadvantage is the unbalanced utilisation of machining capacity. However, this can be mitigated in its economic effects if capacity requirements are oriented at the full load of the most expensive piece of equipment and if limited cross-utilisation of idle capacity between production islands is allowed. The extra costs for higher qualification of the whole working team as compared to specialised workers is easily compensated by the other benefits of group manufacturing. Besides these main advantages, considerable reductions of set-up times and improvements in overall engineering and productivity give rise to further benefits.

In a similar way, as has been demonstrated for the manufacturing process on the shop floor (where the knowledge exists how to make machines), these organising principles can also be applied to the design office (where the knowledge exists how to invent machines). The design process being split up according to families of products, or their modules, the designers (single or in team work) perform the whole design process comprising tasks such as finding the functional structures and the dimensions, calculating, single part design or geometric modelling. Thus, two skill-centred production subsystems equipped with local computer assistance and connected by electronic data exchange will be formed: production and design islands.

In order to work efficiently, these largely autonomous subsystems still need some data exchange and so they have to be interlinked by the basic components of the CIM architecture, that is, a common database, a data-highway and data-exchange interfaces. However, the way in which computer assistance is implemented differs completely from the technocentric approach. Instead of incorporating almost all knowledge and the sequences of work as far as possible in the computer system, in this case the computer serves as a general, and consistent information system also performing routine operations, but leaves the planning of working actions to the workers' and designers' skill.

A substantial increase of productivity can be expected from both production concepts. Many indications suggest that productivity grows even faster when following the human-centred development path. Paradoxically, production requires less labour, the more it uses its quality. This has important implications for employment in general and the structure of labour markets in particular, especially since the required high level of skill profiles tends to further segmentation trends. Therefore, combined counteractions at both firm and society level have to be developed (appropriate skill formation for all, reduction of working hours, etc.) in order to avoid a segmented workforce and unemployment.

KNOWLEDGE OF PRODUCTION

By conceptual analysis of 'acting', the worker is able to construct an abstract model of generalised actions comprising the objects and the rules to change them. Hence, machines are nothing else than implemented theory.

However, the prerequisite for being able to do so is that workers recognise the recurring factors in the changing situations. Unless they realise the general in the specific, the experience gained is private. Because of this 'tacit knowledge' (Polanyi, 1966), there exists a barrier to objectifying production knowledge, that is, production processes cannot in principle be completely modelled.

On the other hand, the 'acting' subject knows how to act in a goal-oriented way even in uncertain or unstructured situations. His concretised experience or 'tacit knowledge' is much more comprehensive than the rule-based or objectified knowledge which is all that can be implemented in machines. It forms the basis for the unique human strength to be able to conceive and evaluate complex situations, to make adequate decisions and to take appropriate actions.

While humans, thus, can act creatively in an unknown surrounding, proceeding unsystematically and inconsistently, however, because of a not very impressive information-processing capability, machines are bound to programs made by humans to change their state and to operate on data structures, and work in rule-based and consistent fashion. In order to join these opposing attributes of humans and machines productively, some basic principles have to be regarded corresponding to a hierarchical system of design criteria (Hacker, 1978).

Work design, that is the determination of the division of labour, of the partition of functions between man and machine and of the modes of man–machine interaction, has to be done in such a way, that in the working situation a wide margin of action is preserved leaving initiative, evaluation and decisions up to the worker and ensuring that his work comprehends planning and executing tasks. For the computer to be used as a tool here, its functions and its behaviour have to be completely transparent. In particular, its reactions have to be self-explanatory and adapted to the actual working situation. In interaction it is extremely important that the worker can perceive the connection between his own intention or action and the effects it produces.

Accordingly, technical equipment needs to have an appropriate user surface. The man–machine interaction therefore has to be designed in such a way that it is:

— transparent and self-explanatory (by use of direct object manipulation),
— adjustable to different degrees of user experience (presenting flexible dialogue procedures),
— reliable (following the principle 'what you see is what you have got').

In addition, the terminals and screen masks need to have correct ergonomic shape. Looking at existing CAD/CAM systems, most of these conditions are not fulfilled or to an insufficient extent only.

POLITICS OF PRODUCTION

The history of industrial production is, from one perspective, a history of the manifold attempts of the management to get control over production processes. At the beginning of the first industrial revolution, when craftsmen were hired to work under the unified command of a capitalist owner, they still worked in exactly the same manner they were used to. Since all knowledge of production was at their disposal alone, the owner depended on their goodwill to produce something with the required quality.

Seen with the owner's eyes, this was a very unsatisfactory situation establishing a substantial problem in capitalist production. It is true that, by force of the working contract, he owned the working capacity, but that did not determine the material form, in which the work was actually being done or the working capacity was productively used. Since the productive forces, the abilities to produce or create something, are not separable from the worker, whose abilities are not 'alienable', the owner is compelled to cooperate with the worker. This is the basic issue underlying the politics of production.

The owner's situation could only be improved by modifying the modes of manufacturing. The first major attempt to get more control over production was the horizontal division of labour proposed by Adam Smith. Besides the economic benefits of more output with less costs which he had in mind as the basis for the 'wealth of nations', the workers' specialisation on specific tasks within the working process had the effect that they lost, as time went by, most of their production knowledge in favour of the entrepreneur, who was now able to set the basic manufacturing structure (Marglin, 1977).

In general, the horizontal division was also the basis for introducing machines in manufacturing. The repetitive operations the workers had to perform could be easily analysed and conceptually modelled and, thus, be objectified in machines. Besides the increased work performance caused by the use of machines, they also enabled owners to gain better control over production.

In spite of the horizontal division of labour and the limited use of machinery, control over production still remained full of gaps, since within the frame of divided labour the workers could act autonomously. This was the point where Taylor stepped in and established his 'principles of scientific management'. By empirical analysis of workers' operations and of cutting metals, he was able to objectify essential parts of the production knowledge and, thus to separate planning from executing tasks. Managers were now able to plan working processes independently from the workers and to prescribe how and in what time they had to perform their operating tasks. Later on, the introduction of partly automated machinery and of computer systems in manufacturing (Fordism in mass production, NC technology in small-batch production, CAD/CAM systems) further increased the potential for management control over production.

This kind of development has its price, however. Manufacturing processes are becoming more and more inflexible to the extent that workers' autonomy and production experience are declining. This state of affairs appears in mass production that has been explicitly designed for single products with few variants. But it also holds for small-batch production, where Taylor's principles could be applied only halfway and produced its unfavourable structures (job-shop manufacturing with a skilled workforce despite central planning), considered earlier. Both types of manufacturing processes, the inflexible mass production and the hybrid small-batch production being partly Taylorised, partly based on skilled work, are coming into conflict with the new requirements of global competition. Substantial flexibility of manufacturing is incompatible with deskilling and constraining the autonomy of workers. Hence, new production concepts with altered politics of production and alternative forms of controlling production are needed.

The principles of group technology and autonomous working groups provide such a production concept. Yet, the autonomy of production and design islands can only be developed within limits which leave the management without fear of losing control over production as a whole. Control changes its form, of course. According to the technology-centred production concept it used to be exercised by objectifying knowledge, by the detailed working instructions derived from it, and by the machine system. In contrast, it is now exerted through computer assisted central planning and supervising of production in its entirety, but leaving much wider margins of action to local planning and execution, and through a performance policy challenging the workers' competence, autonomy and responsibility as well (Kern and Schumann, 1984). Controlling autonomy instead of defeating independence is the issue.

CONCLUDING REMARKS: THE SUPERIOR CHOICE

Taking all these considerations together, it becomes obvious that we are in a situation of choice. Different strategic options for computer integrated manufacturing are at hand, delivering different economic benefits.

Taking into account the problems that the technology-centred approach is going to run into, the human-centred one clearly shows its superiority in both economic and human respects, especially under disturbed market conditions. It reduces throughput times dramatically (with a huge potential for saving costs and gaining market strength) and it is less capital intensive, above all on the software side, since existing qualifications are essentially preserved and not replaced by programs causing high expenses. For the same reason production becomes very flexible, particularly since changes in the order of processes can be considered without being modelled first. Working conditions allow for wide margins of action and enhancement of skills, thus preserving the innovative capability. It can be implemented stepwise and so can also be followed by smaller firms.

Address for correspondence:

Institut Arbeit und Technik, Florastrasse 9, D-4650, Gelsenkirchen 1, FRG.

REFERENCES

Brödner, P. (1985a) *Fabrik 2000, Alternative Entwicklungspfade in die Zukunft der Fabrik*. Berlin: Sigma.
Brödner, P. (Ed.) (1985b) Skill based automated manufacturing. Preprints of the IFAC Workshop held in Karlsruhe, Sept 3–5, VDI/VDE-GMA, Düsseldorf.
Feigenbaum, E. A., and McCorduck, P. (1983) *The Fifth Generation*. Reading, Mass.: Addison-Wesley.
Hacker, W. (1978). *Allgemeine Arbeits- und Ingenieurpsychologie*. Bern: Hans Huber Verlag.
Kern, H., and Schumann, M. (1984) *Das Ende der Arbeitsteilung? Rationalisierung in der industriellen Produktion*. München: C. H. Beck Verlag.
Marglin, S. A. (1977) *Was tun die Vorgesetzten? Ursprünge und Funktionen der Hierarchie in der kapitalistischen Produktion, Technologie und Politik*, Bd 8. Reinbeck: Rowohlt.
Mitrofanow, S. P. (1980) *Wissenschaftliche Grundlagen der Gruppentechnologie*. Berlin: VEB Verlag Technik.
Piore, M. J. and Sabel, C. F. (1984) *The Second Industrial Divide. Possibilities for Prosperity*. New York: Basic Books.
Polanyi, M. (1966) *The Tacit Dimension*. Garden City: Doubleday.
Sigismund, C. (1982) The structure and strategy of factory automation. Research Report 661, Business Intelligence Program, Menlo Park, SRI International.
Sorge, A. and Streeck, W. (1986) Industrial relations and technical change: The case for an extended perspective. Workshop on 'Coping with New Technology in Japan and the Federal Republic of Germany', Berlin, August 29–30.
Spinas, P. and Kuhn, R. (1980) Gruppentechnologie. Ein alternatives Fertigungskonzept. Report, Lehrstuhl für Arbeits- und Betriebspsychologie der ETH, Zürich.

9. Design for Human–Machine Interfaces

J. Martin Corbett

School of Industrial and Business Studies, University of
Warwick, Coventry

SUMMARY

A desirable alternative approach to design for human–machine interface rejects the notion of comparability and focuses on how people and technology can complement each other. New skills will, however, be needed emphasising the social interaction between the operator and the designer. Proactive research and development are called for.

STATE OF THE ART AND FUTURE TRENDS IN PRODUCTION SYSTEMS

Within the engineering community in Europe (and elsewhere) there persists a vision of 'people-less' production systems of the future. In this view, the explicit incorporation of human factors in the design of production technology is a temporary and rather short-term problem which is becoming increasingly redundant.

Such a claim for the future of production systems should be taken seriously, although it is hard to answer since it is probably the case that the evolution of such systems will be somewhat haphazard and unpredictable. In part, this is due to the uncertain nature of technical innovation during rapid periods of change. But it is also due to the inevitable uncertainties concerning the diffusion of such technical changes. Nevertheless, one can make some reasonable predictions about the nature of change and speculate on whether or not, in the foreseeable future, the design of human–machine interfaces will remain relevant.

A number of trends can be discerned from the current pattern of change. First, all commentators agree that the introduction of stand-alone CNC machine tools, CAD work stations and industrial robots will continue to accelerate. But at the same time, more and more companies will experiment

New Technology and Manufacturing Management   Edited by M. Warner, W. Wobbe and P. Brödner
Published 1990 by John Wiley & Sons Ltd

with, and introduce, integrated systems such as flexible manufacturing systems and CAD/CAM. Considerable effort will also go into developing computer integrated manufacturing systems but, except in research and development cases and in some instances of highly predictable production environments, these will not extend to fully automated 'people-less' factories on any widespread basis. In large part this is because reliable enabling technologies are not yet in place, and furthermore, most companies are simply unable to address the complexities involved, to say nothing of the expense, particularly in the field of systems integration. Overall, such systems as do evolve will get larger and, so far as both the designer and the user are concerned, more complex.

These opportunities will probably be greatest in small and medium batch production firms, which account for around 70% of British engineering output. Such innovations as are implemented will be operated in the midst of relatively old technologies such that there will be 'islands of production' amongst traditional technologies.

Human aspects of systems technology will thus remain important for the foreseeable future. In particular, as production systems get larger, more sophisticated and complex, they will need well-trained personnel to run them. They will also need to be designed so that they are comprehensible to the operators if performance levels are to be satisfactory. We are now hearing talk of the 'multi-skilled craftsman' in relation to new production technologies—a craftsman capable of operating and maintaining complex electro-mechanical systems.

State-of-the-art production systems are flexible manufacturing systems (FMS) which combine the benefits of a highly productive, but inflexible transfer line and a flexible, but relatively inefficient, job shop. An FMS is a system dealing with high level distributed data processing and automated material flow using computer-controlled machines, assembly cells, industrial robots, inspection machines and so forth, together with computer integrated materials handling and storage systems. Such systems are typically centrally programmed with little or no part programming facilities available on the shop floor.

The next generation of production system is the computer integrated manufacturing (CIM) system. These systems extend integrated computer control to the ordering and re-supply of parts and materials and work scheduling.

MAJOR PROBLEM AREAS

There are three, interrelated problem areas associated with the human–machine relationship which stem from the technical trends discussed above.

These are:

1. The reliability of new production technologies.
2. The effect of these technologies on the design of jobs.
3. The design of appropriate human–machine interfaces.

Reliability and new production technologies

The historical trend in the design of shop-floor production work has been towards the incorporation of human skills into automatic machinery. The development of the digital computer and the microprocessor offers the potential to extend this skill incorporation to both physical and mental capabilities. The operators of state-of-the-art FMS technology are typically required to carry out those functions which are not yet automated. The current lack of technical sophistication in sensing devices and error recovery software has led to a concentration of human operators in monitoring and error recovery tasks. As such, individual vigilance and responsiveness is critical to overall system performance and the wealth of craft skills available in Europe remains under-utilised.

It is one of the great ironies of technological design that the human element is regarded as the major source of uncertainty in system performance (and therefore one to be eliminated whenever possible), whilst at the same time it is generally accepted that the operator's ability to cope with uncertainties and unforeseen disturbances during system functioning is the factor governing system reliability. A further irony stems from the fact that, when software is developed to replace certain operator functions, this software itself tends to create uncertainties which are more difficult to control because they are less 'visible'.

The historical development of manual to automatic control of shop-floor machines therefore has an important consequence for the overall efficiency of production systems. In all realisable systems, there will be some undesirable disturbance or noise which may enter the system at one or more points during the production process (e.g. poor castings, worn tooling). These disturbances can be eliminated in one of three ways.

1. Remove all disturbances at source (e.g. reject all sub-standard materials before they go on the shop floor).
2. Predict all possible disturbances and develop software and hardware mechanisms to control them.
3. Utilise a skilled operator who, with an almost completely open-ended repertoire of skills and behaviour, will drive the production system to its goal despite unforeseen disturbances.

The predominant trend in engineering design, fuelled by the dream of the 'people-less' factory, is to take the second option. This trend stems from a technology-centred or 'technocentric' approach to technological design.

The development of solid modelling in CAD systems, which permits simulated metal-cutting and the direct generation of part programs from geometric data, is widely heralded as an important key to the success of this strategy. However, the failure to design and develop a 'people-less' factory at the present time bears witness to the complexities (and expense) involved in pursuing the totally predictable (reliable) production system. Indeed, many commentators are now fostering the belief that, as the complexities of production technology increase, the role of the human operator will become more, rather than less, important for efficient system functioning. In this view the design of operator jobs becomes a critical factor for system reliability.

A 'technocentric' approach to design, therefore, overlooks two factors. firstly, that designer errors can be a major source of operating problems, and secondly, the designer who tries to eliminate the operator still leaves the operator to do the tasks which the designer cannot think how to automate.

The legacy of 'technocentric' design can be stated as follows: Having fragmented the job of the new production system operator and removed a large part of his/her skilled control of the system, the designer then relies on him or her to deal with all unforeseen (unprogrammed) disturbances. However, a technical system that does not provide the experience out of which operating skills can develop will be vulnerable in those circumstances where human intervention becomes necessary.

Take, for example, the direct numerically controlled (DNC) machine tool, which is a basic building block of second and third generation 'technocentric' systems. Here, almost all uncertainty and discriminatory choice is removed from the operator because the program that controls all the machine functions is written away from the machine by an office programmer. The high cost of such machines and the subsequent high value of the finished product are such that it is important to keep the machine running and to avoid scrappage. As virtually all disturbance occurs at the machine (Corbett, 1985) the operator sometimes has to override the program. But a DNC lathe is designed primarily as a machine–workpiece system rather than a human–machine system and it is more difficult to avoid making control errors because shop-floor intervention was not explicitly designed for.

New production technology and the design of jobs

Whereas traditional manual and semi-automatic production technologies enabled manual skills to be incorporated into the design of machines, the development of the digital computer and the microprocessor enables human cognitive and decision-making skills to be complemented or replaced by machines. It is the historical trend towards this incorporation of human manual and cognitive skills into machines which is equated, by many writers (e.g. Braverman, 1974), with the historical tendency towards the simplification and fragmentation of manufacturing shop-floor jobs.

Empirical research on the impact of new production technology on the design of jobs has not lent support to this deskilling theory, but it is important to note that studies which offer counter evidence are predominantly case studies of jobs with stand-alone CNC machine tools. Although CNC machines are the basic building blocks of new production systems, they are not integrated together by computer control systems or automatic materials handling machines as are the next generation FMS and CAD/CAM systems. Hence the CNC case studies 'are all sampling organisations/firms at a particular historical point, one in which the form of the technology has not been closed off by a series of decisions and technical developments which, in combination, constitute sunk costs such that unwinding them, making a series of different choices, becomes an impossible cost burden' (Littler, 1983; p. 144).

There is growing awareness that the designers of the second and third generation technical systems are the job designers of the future and there is therefore an urgent need for occupational psychologists and other personnel experts to become involved in the design of such systems at the earliest possible stage.

There are two distinct options open to systems designers at this point in time. One which is currently dominating design thinking can be termed the 'technocentric' approach to design. In this perspective, the aim of automation is to displace human skill and place it within the technology. Typically, the allocation of functions between human and machine is based on the idea of comparability—functional requirements being realised with respect to the technological state of the art, where the human takes over those functions that are not yet solved. But, as Rasmussen (1979; p. 2) has argued:

> The fact that all control functions which can be formally described also can be automated by means of computers, leads to the danger that the role of the system operator will be to plug the gaps in the thoroughness of the designer's work. On the one hand, as a convenient, movable manipulator, he will have a category of trivial, infrequent actions for which automation is unfeasible; on the other hand, as an intelligent data processor he will be expected to respond to ill-structured and unforeseen tasks.

The impact of 'technocentric' production technology on the design of jobs is one in which human operators are increasingly becoming subordinate to machines: humans become passive as machinery takes a more active controlling role in the production process. The development of 'fifth generation' intelligent knowledge based systems (IKBS) enables this impact to be all the more pervasive.

In the occupational psychology literature, there is now mounting evidence that this automation of discretionary skills traditionally exercised by manufacturing shop-floor personnel has a detrimental effect on both the physical and mental health of these personnel (Karasek, 1979). Furthermore, research in cognitive and developmental psychology suggests that the loss of control that is experienced by many operators of second and third generation production systems may well spill over into their home and social lives to create a state akin to 'learned helplessness'.

The alternative, 'anthropocentric' approach to systems design rejects the idea of human–machine comparability and focuses instead on how they may complement each other. The computer and the human mind have different but complementary abilities. The computer excels in analysis and 'number crunching' computation, whilst the human mind excels in pattern recognition, synthesis and intuitive reasoning. By combining these different abilities in technological design it is possible for humans and machines to help each other achieve an effect of which each is separately incapable. It is to this endeavour that the human sciences need to contribute through involvement in technological design. Present and future strategies for this endeavour are discussed later in the chapter.

The design of appropriate human–machine interfaces

One of the problems associated with 'technology-centred' systems is that their operation often requires skills that are unrelated to existing skills, with the resultant problems of poor transfer of training and the under-utilisation of the rich seam of machining skills to be found in Europe.

The development of CNC technology has produced a shift in decision competence from human to machine, whereby the operator of a machine tool, for example, is not alone in the control of the machine but, owing to the decisions and choices taken by the designer and stored in the computer, is now forced to cooperate intimately with the designer.

The number of design decisions and choices open to the designer is almost infinite, but research in the field of ergonomics points to three key choice points in design which have the most impact on operator skill and control. These are:

1. The allocation of function between human and machine.
2. The control characteristics of the human–machine interface.
3. The informational characteristics of the human–machine interface.

With regard to the first of these choice points—the allocation of functions—

ergonomists stress that there are choices over what humans do and over what machines do in any automated system. The conventional 'technocentric' approach to this choice is to leave the operators only those tasks which cannot be automated. The irony of this approach has been discussed in the previous section.

This approach to the allocation of functions typically leads to the concentration of operator tasks in monitoring and error recovery functions. Where an automatic control system has been put in because it can do the job better than an operator, the operator is also asked to monitor that it is working effectively. In complex modes of operation, the operator will need to know what the correct behaviour of the production system should be. Such knowledge requires either special training or special information displays. The alternative 'anthropocentric' approach to function allocation needs to be based on the idea of human–machine complementarity as discussed above.

A second key choice point in technological design concerns the control characteristics of the human–machine interface. Design decisions here concern how the control of the production system is to be shared between human and machine. For example, CNC machine tool control software can be designed to enable operators to interrogate databases in order for them to take important controlling decisions (such as determining tool path geometry, work scheduling and pacing). On the other hand, the software may contain complex algorithms which enable the computer to take all the controlling decisions, thereby restricting the operator's role to that of machine minding.

Rosenbrock (1983) sees two paths open to designers in respect of the control characteristics of new production systems technology, corresponding to the 'anthropocentric' and 'technocentric' distinction made above. Using the example of computer aided design (CAD) technology, he describes one approach (the 'anthropocentric') as involving the acceptance of the skill and knowledge of the designer and attempting to give the designer improved techniques and facilities for expressing that skill and knowledge. Such a system would amount to a truly interactive use of computer technology that allows the very different capabilities of the computer and the human mind to interact to the full. The alternative, 'technocentric' approach to this is to break up design processes so that they are reduced to a set of simple choices (Rosenbrock, 1983). The 'anthropocentric' approach therefore places the human in control of the system, whereas the 'technocentric' approach reverses this and leaves the human subordinate to the system (see Chapter 8).

The third key choice point in systems design concerns the informational characteristics of the human–machine interface. The invisibility of many software functions in complex production systems means that the operators must rely heavily on information and data that are transmitted or generated by computer in order to structure their work behaviour. Software which only presents machine-specific information to an operator in the event of system malfunction, for instance, will not enable the operator to see the overall consequences of his or her actions for overall system performance. Restricting information in this matter inevitably restricts operator control as one can never fully control a system without understanding it.

The interaction between human and computer may thus be viewed as a social interaction between operator and designer, in which the designer predefines the situation through the type and scope of the information given to the operator. Because of this, the designer has a further means to restrict or enhance operators' control of a production system. One has only to recall Milgram's (1974) dictum: 'Control the manner in which a man interprets the world, and you have gone a long way toward controlling his behaviour.'

An operator will only be able to generate successful new strategies to control disturbances if he or she has an adequate knowledge of the production system functioning during the production process. Bainbridge (1983) points out two problems that this creates for 'machine-minding' operators. One is that effective retrieval of knowledge from long-term memory depends on frequency of use. The other is that this type of knowledge develops only through use and feedback about its effectiveness.

STRATEGIC OPTIONS FOR RESEARCH AND DEVELOPMENT (R & D)

Given the technical and social advantages of 'anthropocentric' new production systems technology, there are now two main areas of R & D that need to be addressed. First, there is a growing need for these advantages to be communicated to engineering designers, production engineers and organisational decision-makers. Although the intransigent conservatism of many of these job holders is, undoubtedly, one factor which has contributed to the present failure of such a communication, organisational and occupational scientists themselves must shoulder some of the blame.

At present in the UK and other European countries, there is little social science research taking place into the human and social aspects of new production systems technology. This situation is probably due to three interrelated factors, namely a shortage of funding for social science research generally, the lack of recognition amongst social scientists of its importance, and a shortage of skills in this area.

Within individual companies, the picture is scarcely any better. Many engineers are loath to adopt more organisational and psychological views in their work, especially when these extend to areas which are difficult to quantify. At the same time, other professional groups, such as line managers, general managers and personnel/industrial relations specialists, are reluctant to adopt a more proactive role in the design, development and implementation of technology, preferring to leave these issues to the technical specialists.

Similarly, eventual users and their representatives rarely put these items high on their agendas, perhaps because their interest in new technology is dominated by whether or not it affects their job security and job prospects.

The second area of R & D that needs to be addressed is the need for the 'anthropocentric' perspective to shift from its theoretical and philosophical critique of current practice, towards a more practical and proactive role in technological progress. One of the most productive ways of making this shift may be through the design, development and implementation of alternative 'anthropocentric' technology in the 'real' world of manufacturing. Through the implementation of exemplary 'anthropocentric' systems, the benefits of such technology can be demonstrated to all. Such a shift will not be made without difficulties, and there is therefore an urgent need for research and development into the process of designing these alternative systems. Rhetoric needs to be backed up by constructive example.

PROACTIVE RESEARCH AND DEVELOPMENT WORK

This method of working involves the explicit consideration of the human aspects of new production technology from the beginning of design. Whilst work scientists have had very little involvement in work of this kind, some notable efforts have been made in some areas and virtually none in others. Some examples are offered below.

Collaborative design methods

Overall research into designing 'anthropocentric' new production systems is on a minute scale compared to the amount of research being carried out on their 'technocentric' counterparts. There are, however, notable attempts to develop collaborative design methods, which need to be developed and extended.

A pioneering example is the UTOPIA project based at the Swedish Centre for the Quality of Working Life in Stockholm (Ehn *et al.*, 1982). UTOPIA is an acronym in the Scandinavian languages for Training, Technology and Products from the Quality of Work Perspective. This project involved the design of powerful computer-based tools for skilled graphic workers in the newspaper industry, and utilised a radical new approach to the design process. This approach was essentially experimental and involved experienced end-users, i.e. skilled graphic workers, in the design process. The emphasis was on 'designing by doing' using mock-ups and rapid prototyping.

In the UK, the best known example of this kind of proactive R & D work is that based at the University of Manchester Institute of Science and Technology (UMIST) under the leadership of Rosenbrock (1983). This project involved the development of a flexible manufacturing system in which operators are not subordinate to machines, although in practice much of the work focused on developing human-centred software for a CNC lathe. This work is now being extended by funding from the European Commission to incorporate the wider field of computer integrated manufacturing systems. As in the UTOPIA project, the research team undertaking this work comprised work and social scientists collaborating with computer scientists, skilled workers and engineers.

Experiences within these projects suggest that social scientists should not concentrate solely on the drawing up of human-centred work design criteria in the hope that engineers can and will use them in the way that is desired. Design is not merely the application and trading-off of design criteria: intuition and aesthetic considerations play an important role in the design process. Accordingly, the use of scenarios, rapid prototyping and design mock-ups may prove particularly useful in counteracting the dominant technology-centred approach to engineering design.

Control system design

The field of human factors engineering (ergonomics) potentially has a major input to make to 'anthropocentric' control system design, but, at the present time, the predominant emphasis in ergonomics research has been at the informational level of systems design (the third key design choice point identified in the previous section). The output from such work is 'user friendly' software and it is rare that the more fundamental control aspects of the human–machine interface are studied. It is also unlikely that such research will be funded from the normal human factors funding bodies. Hence R & D work on the control aspects of human–machine interaction, such as the direct manipulation of new production system machinery, has progressed little since the pioneering work on record–playback machine tools control systems and analogic part programming techniques at the Massachusetts Institute of Technology.

R & D work on the design of control system technology is important because, although CNC machine tools generally have some provision for shop-floor part programming and editing, the development of DNC is liable to push these functions back to the office (as they were with NC). This push will receive further impetus as CAD solid modelling techniques are refined and developed.

Information system design

The highly integrated systems architectures associated with FMS and CIM technologies necessitate research effort in the area of distributive information networks as well as decentralised control systems (see Chapter 10). We have already stressed the impact of system complexity on the design of shop-floor work, and it seems likely that a decentralisation of information and control will be a crucial element in the usability and flexibility of new production systems.

The UMIST project illustrates how information that has traditionally been kept in the hands of the production department may be presented to shop-floor personnel via terminals located at the machines in a way that is compatible with traditional machining skills and decision-making. In this example, the emphasis was on information concerning the determination of cutting parameters and sequences, but there seems to be no reason why this principle should not be extended to include information on overall system performance, targets, scheduling priorities, tool path geometry and so forth.

The development of expert systems and artificial intelligence techniques is another crucial element in the design of future production systems. The announcement from Japan of the 'fifth generation' initiative created a response in Europe based on the perceived need to compete, rather than a critical evaluation of whether such technology was suitable for European needs. Certainly, in the manufacturing arena, much of Japan's new production systems technology is designed to incorporate human machining skills because of the chronic shortage of skilled craftsmen. Europe, on the other hand, has a wealth of craft experience and expertise. It makes sound economic sense for technology to be developed in Europe which allows this important human resource to be expressed and not displaced.

CONCLUDING REMARKS

The continuing trend in 'technocentric' design towards the centralisation of programming activities means that very little research and development effort has been concentrated on the design of human–machine dialogue structures for shop-floor programming and decision-making. Many such designs impose a fixed sequence of actions and strategies on the user which may be inappropriate for actual, rather than normative, production demands.

Work on direct object manipulation and on user-definable macros offers encouraging signs that flexible and reliable dialogue structures can be designed which allow skilled machinists to follow their own preferred methods and sequence of working.

Address for correspondence:

School of Industrial and Business Studies, University of Warwick, Coventry CV4 7AL, UK.

REFERENCES

Bainbridge, L. (1983) Ironies of automation. *Automatica*, **19**, 775–9.

Braverman, H. (1974) *Labor and Monopoly Capital*. New York: Monthly Review Press.

Corbett, J. M. (1985) Prospective work design of a human-centred CNC lathe. *Behaviour and Information Technology*, **4**, 201–14.

Ehn, P., Kyng, M., and Sundblad, Y. (1982) The UTOPIA Project. In U. Briefs, E. Ciborra and J. Schneider (eds.), *System Design with, for, and by the Users*. Amsterdam: North-Holland.

Karasek, R. A. (1979) Job demands, job decision latitude and mental strain: Implications for job design. *Administrative Science Quarterly*, **24**, 285–308.

Kusterer, K. (1978) *Know-how on the Job: The Important Working Knowledge of Unskilled Workers*. London: Macmillan.

Littler, C. (1983) A history of new technology. In G. Winch (ed.), *Information Technology in Manufacturing Processes*. London: Rossendale.

Milgram, S. (1974) *Obedience to Authority*. London: Tavistock.

Rasmussen, J. (1979) Notes on System Design criteria. RISO: Danish Atomic Energy Commission.

Rosenbrock, H. H. (1983) Social and engineering design of an FMS. In E. A. Warman (ed.), *CAPE '83*, Part One. Amsterdam: North-Holland.

10. Strategic Options for CIM Integration

Gunter Lay

*Fraunhofer Institut für Systemtechnik und
Innovationsforschung (ISI), Karlsruhe*

SUMMARY

The progress which the CIM concept and its components have made in practice is
described in this chapter in terms of its individual parts and the relevant integrations
between them. The individual courses of technical and organisational developments
are presented, and the role which computer integrated manufacturing plays in these
developments is examined. Strategic options for the integration process are described,
with an emphasis on human-centred systems.

INTRODUCTION

Computer applications in production planning and production departments
have increased continuously during the last few years. Using the key word
'computer aided manufacturing', firms installed computer numerically controlled (CNC) machine tools and flexible manufacturing systems on their shop
floors. Production planning and control systems were introduced to assist
material requirements planning and capacity planning. Furthermore, in the
planning departments the work planning, especially the programming of CNC
machine tools, is nowadays equipped with computer aided systems. In product design and development processes the firms increasingly use computer
aided design (CAD) systems.

All these developments in production engineering are characterised by an
increased use of computers in all areas of the manufacturing process. Abbre-
viations, such as CIM (computer integrated manufacturing) or CAI (computer aided industry) are concepts of the factory of the future which are being
talked about everywhere. The new developments in production engineering
are technical developments, on the one hand, and organisational concepts
which are discussed as supplements or alternatives to the technical measures,
on the other.

New Technology and Manufacturing Management   Edited by M. Warner, W. Wobbe and P. Brödner
Published 1990 by John Wiley & Sons Ltd

TECHNICAL DEVELOPMENTS

Computer aided design (CAD)

The term CAD means the assistance computers can give in the design and drawing process. It includes not only the direct grapho-interactive generation of two- or three-dimensional data models with subsequent graphic output, but also supporting activities, such as calculations (e.g. the finite-element method) or simulations (see Maier, 1985).

A CAD system consists of the following component parts: CAD computer, computer peripherals, operation software, and user software. The initial CAD systems were installed on large-size computers. Now, CAD systems are available for all computers irrespective of price and size, from large-size computers over work stations down to personal computers (PCs). Today, it is apparent that the tendency of the now wider diffusion of CAD is towards work stations and PCs. A distinction is thereby made between computer-bound and computer-flexible, portable systems. Whereas in the initial phase of the diffusion there were mostly computer-bound systems which were offered as 'turn-key' systems, there is now apparently a trend towards an increased application of computer-flexible, portable systems.

The number of CAD systems installed in the Federal Republic of Germany has grown rapidly over the 1980s. The number of CAD working places, however, is even more extensive since several working places are connected to one system. Among other things, the number is dependent on the efficiency of the computer applied. About 52% of the CAD systems are applied in mechanical design, about 40% in electronic engineering, mainly to design circuits and to delink printed boards, and 8% in other sectors, such as architecture, layout planning, cartography, etc.

It is expected that in future the number of CAD installations will rise considerably since the lower the hardware costs (tendency towards work stations), the lower the financial risk involved in venturing into the CAD technology. (However, CAD application also requires certain technical and qualifying preconditions which involve considerable costs and have a retarding effect on the speed of diffusion.) This prognosis is backed up by data which has been gathered out of the evaluation of the public subsidies for the introduction of CAD/CAM systems in Germany (term of the programme: 1984 to 1987). Accordingly, approximately 950 mostly small- and medium-sized firms are presently engaged in extending and/or introducing CAD applications funded by this programme.

Computer aided planning (CAP)

CAP means the application of computers in production planning, for the purpose of elaborating operations schedules, calculating time standards, selecting machines and operating material, and above all programming numerically controlled (NC/CNC) machines, manufacturing cells, manufacturing systems, etc. Owing to the wide spectrum covered by this term the diffusion of CAP has to be assessed quite differently. Computer aided NC programming systems are widespread, since they have definite advantages as to time as compared with manual programming.

In the case of programming systems, the development tends to be away from language-oriented systems towards graphic programming including simulation of the contours of workpieces and the tool path on the terminal. By now, the programming systems are also fully developed as regards operating and programming comfort and facilitations, such as geometric macros, parameterisable subprograms, automatic generation of all cuts necessary to come from the rough workpiece to a finished size. Systems for the computer aided generation of operations scheduling, however, are not very common. There do exist some developments, mostly by university institutes, which, however, have hardly been adopted by the industry. Automatic generation of operations scheduling must not be mistaken for the computer aided management of operations scheduling which forms part of production planning and control systems.

Production planning and control (PPC)

PPC refers to the application of computer aided systems in the planning and control of contract filling and manufacture as regards disposal and organisation, including determination and management of material needs, dates and capacities; that is, the administration of bills of materials, operations scheduling, materials, and time as well as the recording of operating data, the planning of production and/or the management of customer orders.

Electronic data processing has been introduced in the PPC sector rather early. Diffusion is, therefore, very much advanced. In many cases, the initial PPC systems were batch oriented and integrated into the commercial electronic data processing. Therefore, the IBM hardware is dominant in PPC systems. In some cases, this causes serious problems today since PPC will increasingly be integrated into the technical data processing, a market which is controlled by other hardware producers.

Today's PPC systems are mostly dialogue oriented and one can point to differences between two types of development.

The initial PPC systems, which were mainly applied in industrial scale manufacture, were based on the concept of a centralised total planning, in which every process step was exactly planned as to time and sequence. This concept is functioning in large series manufacturing where the production can easily be surveyed due to a technically realised, prescribed manufacturing process—even here the state of planning is often already undermined due to unforeseen events—but it can hardly be applied to small and medium batch-size production. Because of customer orders, rush orders, etc., the manufacturing conditions of this sector are not transparent enough to enable effective planning.

Recently, there have, therefore, been a rising number of PPC systems where only a rough frame-planning is centrally preset; detailed planning will then have to be made by the personnel in the workshop. These systems of a frame planning with decentralised use of competences are much more flexible and can, therefore, be better adjusted to manufacturing conditions, particularly in small and medium batch-size production.

Computerised numerical control (CNC)

The development of numerical controls had already started in the 1950s. The initial controls still consisted of link-programmed, discrete or integrated circuits. The diffusion of machine tools with NC control was very hesitant. This changed fundamentally in the early 1970s when computers began to be integrated into the control units and CNC control was developed. By integrating computer and storage capacities into the control units, the operating and programming comfort of machine tools has considerably improved.

The market in Germany is not yet saturated; on the contrary, there is a trend towards an even further diffusion of CNC machines. NC machines are hardly produced any more, but due to their long life the number of machines in use has not yet declined.

Today, CNC controls are mostly applied for turning machines, boring and milling machines, horizontal boring machines, and machining centres (approx. 40%). Other machining work holds a share of over 20% in NC/CNC machines, the principal share being held by grinding and erosion machines; but CNC controls exist for almost all types of machining.

If this distribution of CNC machines on machining processes is compared with the distribution almost 10 years ago (1977–78), clear structural changes are noticeable. At that time, the share of turning machines was higher than 60%, boring and milling machines held a share of just under 20%, and the other machines came to less than 10%. So, it becomes apparent that a disproportionate diffusion of CNC machines took place in the boring and milling sector, in particular for machining centres and other machines. There is an obvious tendency towards applying CNC machines for all manufacturing processes.

Almost half of all NC/CNC machines (46%) are used in mechanical engineering and predominantly in the small and medium batch-size production. Because of their higher productivity and mostly more intense utilisation (two shifts) NC/CNC machines can be regarded as basic modules of computer aided manufacturing, although today they hold a share of less than 10% of the total machine tools in Germany.

Various forms of work organisation are possible with CNC machine tools, in particular in the organisation of programming. They range from programming by the operator directly at the control unit to computer aided programming in the planning department or even external programming. In recent years, programming methods have been the subject of much debate. Nevertheless, no one alternative has become predominant, and all possible forms of organisation are to be found in parallel, even though the individual alternatives hold different shares. This makes it evident that the work organisation is not determined by the new technologies but can be laid out individually, the layout process in the end being a 'matter of arrangement' depending on a mixture of objective, subjective, and interest-bound criteria.

Industrial robots (IR)

In the past, discussion about the application of new technologies, guided by the example of the industrial robot, has often been very vehement. On the one hand, there was the view that they were 'indispensable for maintaining competitiveness' and on the other, that they were 'job killers'.

In Germany, in contrast to Japan where the definition is much broader, industrial robots are defined as: universally applicable handling systems to be used in industry, with at least three axes the movements of which can be freely programmed, capable of being equipped with manufacturing means, such as gripping devices and tools. On the basis of this definition, about 6600 industrial robots were installed in Germany in the mid-1980s. This proves that in reality the controversy over the IR is out of proportion to its quantitive importance, if one compares the number of IRs in use with, for example, the use of over 50 000 NC/CNC machines.

In the German case, the IR is mostly used for handling tools and in particular for spot-welding, which makes up about 60% of the cases in which IRs are used. In about 38% of cases, IRs are used to handle workpieces, of which a minority are used for loading and unloading of machine tools.

It is expected that in future the application of IRs will continue to increase but this development should also be accompanied by structural changes. As far as IRs for spot-welding and coating are concerned the saturation limit should be reached soon, whereas handling tasks, such as storage and transport, charging of machines, and in particular assembly, seem to be the potentials of the future. At present, the diffusion of IRs is impeded by the fact that so far there does not exist a fully developed sensor technology. The 'grasp into the box' is strived for everywhere, but has not yet been realised. Among the flexible manufacturing systems portal robots, in line and area construction, are a particularly important means of automatising the exchange of tools and workpieces.

Automation of the material flow

Automation of the material flow is crucial in computer aided manufacturing processes. In this context, automation includes storage, transport, and handling components.

There are numerous technical solutions for each of these components and concentrated efforts are being made to develop them further and to improve them, e.g. as regards exactness.

— Storage automation is mostly effected by means of (elevated) shelf storages which are operated by automatic high-lift trucks.
— Transport automation is in most cases undertaken by driverless transport systems, such as automated guided vehicles (AGVs) or rail-guided vehicles, but also by suspended conveyors and roller conveyors or conveyor belts.
— Flexible linkage of several machines is increasingly done by robots.
— The handling functions are mostly carried out by handling devices which have been specially matched to the particular task, for instance pallet exchangers, tool exchangers, etc. Part of the handling work is also done by universally applicable industrial robots.

Flexible manufacturing systems (FMS)

The term 'flexible manufacturing system' was first introduced in 1967. It refers to a series of manufacturing installations which are interlinked by means of a common control and transport system, thereby enabling automatic manufacturing, but also allowing varying machining operations at different workpieces to be performed within a given area. An analysis of the companies using flexible manufacturing systems according to numbers of employees shows a significant concentration of use in larger companies with more than 1000 employees (approximately 60% of all installations) and a general increase in frequency of use associated with rising employee numbers. Thus FMS and FMC technologies are presently of little relevance to the large number of small and medium-sized companies.

The classification of the flexible manufacturing systems and manufacturing cells installed according to system size shows the following distribution: The majority of installations are flexible cells (70%), whereby the groups of two-machine and three to five machine systems are nearly equal in size (approximately 11% each), while only 7% of the installations consist of large systems with six and more machines. This distribution is in marked contrast to the system sizes recorded in the early phase of FMS/FMC diffusion during which 70% of the systems installed were large ones. In the meantime a definite trend towards flexible manufacturing cells and smaller systems, from five machines downward is apparent.

Initial installations of FMS/FMC in German companies took place around 1972, which is in accordance with first installations in other countries. Until 1980 the development was hesitant. In 1980 only 14 systems were in use; a total of 25 systems were operative by 1983. From 1980 onwards, an increased diffusion was noticeable and by the mid to late 1980s, there had been a further expansion.

A more detailed analysis of the installation count according to system size and periods of application yields the following picture. The initial development is characterised by flexible cells on the one hand and by large flexible manufacturing systems on the other (six and more machines). In the early 1980s, notable numbers of smaller flexible manufacturing systems (between two and five machines) were beginning to be installed, while all the size groups continue to run approximately parallel to each other during this period. In recent years, a different course of development has taken place which is characterised by a marked increase of flexible cells and small flexible manufacturing systems (two to five machines)—the latter to a somewhat lesser extent—while the installation of large flexible manufacturing systems (six and more machines) is not only stagnating, but actually decreasing. While flexible cells and small flexible manufacturing systems will apparently play an increasingly significant role in the future, one can safely state now that it was the employment of these smaller, less complex systems involving less risks that paved the way for the wider diffusion of FMS/FMC. Thus, the initial philosophy of large systems has failed to find wide scale acceptance.

The typical area of application of FMS/FMC lies between the opposite poles of highly productive, but inflexible large series manufacturing of single parts on transfer lines on the one hand, and the highly flexible, while less productive manufacturing of a variety of parts in small and medium-sized series using all-round machines on the other.

Thus, two completely different basic structures can be given when flexible manufacturing systems are installed. Analysis of the types of manufacturing replaced by FMS/FMC revealed that in only 11% of the cases examined were transfer lines replaced because of decreasing batch sizes and a demand for more variety, that is for a higher degree of flexibility. In the majority of cases, flexible manufacturing systems are replacing unlinked conventional machines or NC/CNC machines which have so far been employed in the extremely flexible, while less productive manufacturing of small and medium-sized series. In these cases FMS/FMC installation serves to increase productivity by raising the degree of automation of small and medium-sized series manufacturing for which the means of rigid automation previously offered were not suitable.

This context, however, is dependent on the size of the systems installed. While large flexible manufacturing systems (six or more machines) are replacing transfer lines in a third of the instances, their share decreases steadily with decreasing system size. Because of the increasing use being made of flexible cells and small flexible manufacturing systems, the aspect of productivity increase will become more important than that of flexibility in future.

Flexible manufacturing islands

The concept of the flexible manufacturing island follows the organisational principles of group technology. The characteristic features of a flexible manufacturing island are as follows.

— In the manufacturing island, a limited spectrum of parts consisting of part families which have been selected according to group technological aspects is manufactured.
— Apart from special working processes, the manufacturing island has to do the machining of the entire spectrum of workpieces. The operating material (machine tools, fixtures) required for this task is included in the manufacturing island.
— Apart from NC/CNC machines, conventional machine tools and manual working places can also be integrated in the manufacturing island. To assist the automatic control and to program the NC/CNC machines the island can make use of a microcomputer.
— To a large extent the island controls itself, that is, almost all planning and organising work concerning the part spectrum is assigned to the staff within the manufacturing island.

The autonomous manufacturing island is particularly suitable for small and medium batch-size manufacturing of parts which are not very complex and the demand for which is fluctuating considerably.

The concept of the flexible manufacturing island represents, primarily, an organisational approach, but it does not refrain from using new technologies, such as NC/CNC machines, PPC systems with decentralised competence, and systems to program the NC machines; these are integrated in this special form of organisation.

It is difficult to judge how far the flexible manufacturing island has been adopted in practice. As far as we know, there do not exist any special studies about the diffusion of this concept. There are few user-reports in the literature, perhaps because switching production over to the principle of the flexible island does not represent a spectacular change which involves great investment and can be used for PR purposes.

Just-in-time manufacture (JIT)

Originally, the organisational principle of the JIT manufacture was developed in Japan and became known under the keyword 'KANBAN'. With the aid of KANBAN or JIT it is possible to reduce throughput times and stocks considerably.

KANBAN can be used not only within the firm, but also between several firms (for instance between the automobile industry and its suppliers). The characteristic features of the method are as follows (Wildemann, 1984).

— Setting-up of multi-loop, automatic control systems between manufacturing and consuming areas.
— Implementation of the principle of 'go and get' for the respective subsequent consumer stage.
— Flexible use of personnel and operating material.
— Assigning of short-term control to the operating staff.

However, certain preconditions have to be met before this method can be applied effectively. First, by standardising the parts and by forming part families, a steady manufacturing process has to be achieved. Furthermore, a workshop organisation orienting itself on the material flow is required. The responsibility for quality lies with those who hand the parts over; they must only hand over perfect parts, which fulfil the quality requirements. As the method requires a steady manufacturing process it is particularly suited for firms producing larger series. However, if identical products are less frequently manufactured and the composition of the orders fluctuates, the method can only be applied in a restricted way.

In Germany, the KANBAN method was the subject of intense discussion, quite a number of firms experimented with the process, and many factories introduced at least some elements of KANBAN. In only a minority of cases, however, is it possible to adopt the method without any modification.

The original KANBAN method functions without any assistance by electronic data processing (EDP) and uses the KANBAN card as an instrument to control the manufacturing. However, it is possible to introduce EDP assistance for KANBAN and/or to integrate KANBAN principles into existing PPC systems. In this way, the economic applications of the method can be extended still further, especially if flexible transport systems are also used.

Concept of a departure from Taylorism—alternative forms of employing labour force

At present, two different concepts of employing labour can be noticed in German industry. The first one which Kern and Schumann (1984) called 'technocratically borne' and Brödner (1985) 'technocentric', tries—in the traditional way of a division of labour according to Taylorism—to automate production, to replace the human being as far as possible, and to centralise planning and control at the remaining workplaces in order to make the work flow transparent.

The second concept, which Kern and Schumann called 'empirically un-ideologic' and Brödner 'anthropocentric', tries to develop the creative powers of the human being. Instead of building machines which imitate the human being, reduce him to the functioning method of a machine, or push him completely out of the production process, it is intended to combine the opposing characteristics of man and machine in a productive way (see Brödner, 1985, p. 118). In practice, this means that the structures of Taylor's division of labour are revised by transferring 'indirect' activities, such as quality control, maintenance, production control, NC programming, etc., back into production again, that is, by assigning this work to the trained worker in production.

This also means that many small and medium-sized firms, which still have structures with only a limited division of labour, do no longer necessarily want to introduce the 'rationalisation ideal' of Taylor's division of labour.

Opinions on the importance of this concept for industry vary considerably. Kern and Schumann state that the rationalisation strategy of firms has undergone a real change of paradigm. Brödner sees it as the response of firms to the changed production situation, although the aims of the rationalisation did not change.

Brumlop (1986), too, deals critically with this empirical concept. On the basis of a study she made in the car industry, she does not see any change in the rationalisation as regards paradigm, but a trend towards a concentration of the remaining activities and individual functions. These, however, remain within the framework of traditional concepts of work structures and do not include a revaluation of production work. The principal aim is to make more effective use of working power through flexible forms of employment, which may lead to a changed division of labour, and hence changed qualifications. As she says, this manifests itself above all in cases where the extension of functions combined with higher demands on flexibility, attentiveness, and concentration leads to an aggravation of the overall stress situation, which runs counter to the possibly positive effects of less narrow work schemes (see Brumlop, 1986, pp. 182ff).

Thus, the new production concepts will not automatically lead to a total departure from Taylorism and the hitherto prevailing principles of rationalisation. On the one hand, they are obstructed by the resistance of established structures and controversies within the managements as regards competence; on the other hand, they bear the above-mentioned risks.

Moreover, there is the risk of segmentation, that is, new production concepts are only introduced in the central sectors of production; the marginal sectors (being rather important from the quantitative viewpoint), however, are organised even more according to the principles of division of labour and provided with 'everyman's' workplaces, a development which finally leads to a greater separation of staff qualifications.

COMPUTER INTEGRATED MANUFACTURING AS TECHNICAL–ORGANISATIONAL LINKAGES

Development trends

Under the key word 'computer integrated manufacture' (CIM), information linkage beyond company departments by integrating computer systems became the target of more efficient production. In the last few years, the technical possibilities of linkage have become more promising. Nevertheless, it is difficult to find comprehensive CIM concepts on the market. Up to now, partial integrations which link CAD with NC programming, CAD with the generation of bills of material, and CAD with calculations according to the finite-element method can be obtained. In these sectors, the degree of development as well as the options of linkage have increased. At present, the integration of CAD and PPC is on the threshold to more comprehensive supplies.

The kinds of computer aided systems mentioned above have until now been more or less limited to within firm departments. The exchange of information between departments and their computer systems was organised in a conventional way: drawings, bills of material, work plans, etc., were produced with computer assistance and then passed on to the places where they were to be used.

The idea of CIM is to bridge these gaps between departments working with computer aid by linking hardware and software. The aim is to link islands of computer application in the firms. It is noticeable that CIM is not one software system but a variety of single elements designed in a specific way to link already installed systems. Such elements are, for example:

— interfaces between CAD systems and systems for the programming of CNC machine tools for geometric data exchange;
— exchange interfaces for geometric data between design systems and calculation systems;

— transfer links from CAD systems to material requirements planning systems for bills of material or for using parts from a computer aided inventory control in the design process;
— interfaces between shop-floor data-collection systems and capacity-planning systems;
— direct numerically controlled systems to interlink computer numerically controlled machine tools with programming and program managing systems.

All these interlinks follow two principal ideas:

— creating an uninterrupted digital information flow between all computer assisted technical and administrative departments of a plant;
— avoiding multi-programming and multi-keeping of the same data in the memories of the computer systems in different departments.

CAD/CAP integration

In Germany the integration of CAD with NC programming is provided for in about 20% of all CAD systems installed. With about 40% of these installations, the mechanical engineering industry is the main user.

Large-size firms employing more than 1000 people are the main users, they put two-thirds of these integrated systems into practice. There are three technical alternatives in integrating CAD and NC programming:

— geometric interface to the NC programming system,
— integration via interface: out of CAD–NC module 'source program and/or CL-data transfer',
— integration via NC module in the CAD system: output of the control program.

The differences between these alternatives are as follows. In the case of an 'interface for geometry transfer', the CAD system generates an output file containing the complete data set required for NC programming. A conversion module re-formats these data in such a way that they can be read into the NC programming system to be integrated.

The concepts of interfaces for 'source program transfer' or 'CL-data transfer' require a NC part to be integrated into the CAD system, allowing generation of the tool path for the NC process in the dialogue mode of the CAD system. When generating the NC source program at the graphic terminal of the CAD system, it is possible to define the geometry of the tools to be used, to determine the technological data of the manufacturing process, and to optimise the tool path. Depending on whether or not the NC module of the CAD system includes a NC processor, the NC source program (processor not running) or the CL-data file (after run of processor) is transferred to the subsequently arranged NC programming system.

In the case of complete integration of NC programming into the CAD system, the latter contains a NC module including NC processor and a library of NC postprocessors. The CAD system supplies the finished NC tapes for the different NC machine tools to be programmed.

All these methods of integrating CAD with NC have one thing in common—the NC programs can be generated without requiring a new definition of the geometry. The data relevant for the NC have to be taken out of the CAD file instead. This is done by separating the data which are not required for NC programming, such as dimensioning, texts, hachures, etc., of the NC contours.

As far as the organisation is concerned, each of the above alternatives allows the distribution of labour in different functional groups within the firm, as described below.

With an integration via geometry interface, the organisational concept may be such that the designer working with the CAD system is charged with the duty to generate the information relevant for NC programming out of the database and to transfer this information within the computer to the system of the NC programmer. As an alternative, the duties may also be assigned in such a way that the programmer has to search for the relevant information in the database, to separate it, and to transfer it to his NC programming place for further handling.

Where the integration is realised via the 'source program transfer' and/or the 'CL-data transfer' interfaces, depending on the particular organisation, either the CAD designer or the NC programmer programs the geometry instructions for the tool path and the technology data by using the NC part in the CAD system.

If the NC programming is completely integrated in the CAD system, it will be a question of whether the entire organisation of NC programming is assigned to the design department or whether arrangements are made for the CAD system to be used by both the design department and the planning department. In the latter case, it would be necessary to provide the planning department with CAD workplaces as well.

What has been said above makes evident that with all technical integration options, the organisational concept has either to provide for a way to transfer the work from the design department to the planning department or to give the planning department the right of access to the CAD system of the design department. The organisational layout of the CAD/NC integration is still completely open, whereas the technological development is proceeding very rapidly.

CAD/PPC integration

CAD and PPC are integrated via the bill of material. As a matter of tradition, the administration of bills of materials is one of the central duties of the PPC system. The generation of the bill of material, however, is done either manually in the design department or automatically by means of the CAD data. In Germany, this is realised in about 30% of CAD systems. The real problem of CAD/PPC integration, however, is the conversion of the bill of material produced by the CAD system into a format which can be reasonably handled by the PPC system.

Conversely, the CAD/PPC integration is capable of supplying additional data for the design work. Information from production planning and control, such as calculation rates, bills of materials, operation schedules, stock inventories, is increasingly regarded as essential for design work, to ensure that it meets the requirements of manufacture and assembly.

Such a mutual exchange of information between CAD and PPC can be achieved in the following ways (see Förster, 1985):

— development and transfer of intermediate files,
— redundant data filing with identical data administration systems,
— common database,
— integrated user software.

These alternatives imply the following different approaches to integration. According to the first concept, which provides for the generation of intermediate files, CAD and PPC systems are linked by the fact that data can be transferred from one area to another via an interface file. CAD and PPC systems have to be specifically adapted to one another to enable the data to be exchanged in such a way that they can be handled by the receiving system. In systems which are integrated in this way, it is possible to transfer a bill of material which has been generated by the bill of material processor of the CAD system to the PPS system. However, it is impossible for the users of the CAD and PPC systems to change over at will from one system to the other by using inquiry languages.

A closer integration of CAD and PPC is provided for by the concept of a 'redundant data file with identical administration systems', and the concept of a 'common data base' respectively. Here, CAD and PPC systems whose hard- and softwares are still separated have access to one common database and/or both systems operate with the same data administration system. In this case, it is essential to have a uniform composition of the data.

The most developed form of linking CAD and PPC is represented by the concept of the 'integrated user software'. Here, the CAD and PPC softwares are linked to one another in such a way that the user of such integrated solutions does not notice that he is working with two separate systems. At his respective terminal he can use all programs and data. This means, for instance, that a part of the program of the PPC sector is automatically called in the course of CAD dialogue, and vice versa.

In quantitive respects, CAD/PPC integration is not yet very successful. Approximately 1% of CAD systems applied can be linked with a PPC system. These systems usually operate according to the concept of a 'development and transfer of intermediate data files', that is, on the lowest integration level. However, great efforts are being made to improve the technical side of CAD/PPC linkage, so that in a few years an increase in diffusion may be expected.

Organisational alternatives are of particular relevance with the concept of an 'integrated user software', that is, on the highest integration level. Since the technical side of this concept allows the CAD designer to have full access to the PPC functions, it will be necessary to organise the assignment of competences. Therefore, it will be some years before the organisational problems of a CAD/PPC integration become important.

Direct numerical control (CAP/CNC integration)

The integration of CAP, in particular the partial sector of NC programming, and CAM (computer aided manufacturing), that is, the control of machines and systems which as far as time and location are concerned is directly allocated to manufacturing, is also called DNC operation (direct numerical control). DNC systems may be subdivided into two groups. On the one hand, there are programming systems containing the basic DNC functions for the administration and distribution of control data, the management of tools, and the recording of operating data; on the other hand, there are process control systems for the administration and distribution of control data, the recording of operating and machine data, and for the control of storage, transport, and handling systems.

The latter group is especially important for the application of flexible manufacturing systems. Analyses of the extent of DNC systems in Germany are not yet available, but it may be assumed—at least as far as process control systems are concerned—that their diffusion will increase in parallel to the growing diffusion of flexible manufacturing systems.

Different CIM strategies and alternatives to CIM

The realisation of computer integration between the different computer systems installed in all departments of a firm brings economic benefits for the enterprise by achieving the aims characterised above. For example, the interlink between computer aided design and computer aided programming of numerically controlled machine tools shortens the programming times, reduces the possibilities of making mistakes in the programming process and accelerates the throughput times by using the geometric definitions out of the CAD systems. An additional programming of the same geometric data of the workpiece in the NC system can be avoided.

In view of the economic potential of integrated computer systems, and the enormous subsidies that individual countries and the European Commission are investing in this technical development, as well as the state of diffusion reached so far, it is unrealistic to believe that current discussion on the desirability of CIM in society would have any effects on industrial practice. Even if such a discussion process did lead to a broad agreement in social science that CIM concepts should be rejected, the decentralised decisions on CIM investment and the different definitions of CIM would prevent any moves to restrain the further diffusion of CIM.

But CIM does not look like a technical trend that is necessarily connected in every case with bad effects on human work. Like most of the new technical developments, computer integration in manufacturing can result in completely different effects. On the one hand, the technical concepts and the organisational implementation of CIM in firms can be formed in such a way that computer integration over the borderlines of firm departments is another step towards centralisation, increasing division of labour, deskilling, etc. But this scenario is not the only one possible.

On the other hand, CIM may also be used in a way that combines economic benefits for the firms with technical and organisational structures that favour qualification processes, holistic job structures, the ability to make decisions in the different workplaces, etc. In the following section, some principles are described for designing CIM concepts along these lines.

One point here should be stressed. The discussion about old and new concepts of production, to which many people contribute with different terms for the different concepts, is not a discussion about the 'yes' or 'no' of computer integration. CIM is not the same as the 'technocentric production concept'. Conversely, the 'anthropocentric method' of organising production does not necessarily mean a production without computer integration. The 'anthropocentric production concept' has to use computer integration in supporting its aims by technical means, ensuring that CIM is developed and implemented in a way that is compatible with its requirements.

Demands on human-oriented CIM concepts

In the following section, several elements that should be part of such CIM concepts which are not only economically centred but which also favour human aspects will be described. Some of these aspects can at last be put into practice because the possibilities of CIM enable organisational structures which the traditional forms of computer application prevent. The elements listed are not grouped systematically, but are the results of a 'brainstorming' process and should be used as input for further discussions.

— The architecture of the computer system in CIM should not be a main-frame concept. Decentralised computers linked in a local area network bring a lot of advantages for the people working with the system. Some of these are the possibility of tailoring the decentralised computers exactly to the needs of the different users, the shorter times of computer reaction, the independence from central computer maintenance staff, and so on.
— The database in CIM concepts that is created, administered, distributed and used by different departments in the firms should have only one format. If this is not the case, it will be necessary to process the data structures so that the data created in one department can be used in another. Such processing hinders communication in CIM. By processing of data structures the technical concept often creates one-way connections between the CIM components. This means the people working with the CIM components in the individual departments have less scope for decision-making.
— The different components of CIM, i.e. the software modules for different tasks in CIM, should have a common 'human interface'. The structure of commands, the dialogues, the reactions of the system and so on should be standardised. Holistic job structures often require employees to use more than one CIM component. Thus differences in the software dialogues hinder such structures of job design.
— The software architecture in CIM should be formed so that decentralised decision-making is supported. Decisions aided by CIM should be made in the workplace, where their effects can be judged best. It is thus possible to adjust competence and responsibility.
— The work organisation in CIM and therefore the CIM architecture, too, should be formed in such a way that individual qualifications of the employees can be further used in the same departments. Task-shifting by CIM architecture from one department with people qualified to do these tasks to another department should be avoided, as this leads to deskilling.
— In structuring the CIM database, no attempt should be made to collect and centralise all plant information in one big memory. On the contrary, only that part of the information which is actually needed by others to do their work should be passed on from the individual CIM work station to the higher level in CIM architecture. The benefit of such a tree-like concept is dual: the amount of data that is to be kept in central memories remains in a form that can be handled, and the individual employee on his CIM work station is not kept under permanent control.

— The possibilities of CIM should be used to create holistic job structures. Within the framework of integrated systems adequate competence structures are best established by regrouping the departments vertically. For each product or group of products in a firm the people working in design, planning and production should be linked closer together.
— More than in the past CIM offers the possibility of supporting the so-called concept of design, planning and production islands.
— Training programmes are necessary to give employees knowledge of information processing in CIM. Only this understanding enables the workforce to use fully the scope they have in decision-making.
— CIM concepts should have a form in which decision-making by humans is supported, not automated. This means, for example, that CIM systems offer simulations of the consequences of different decision alternatives to aid the decision-maker.

Technical bottlenecks for establishing human CIM concepts

The realisation of the demands listed above on human CIM concepts requires several preconditions:

— The CIM components which are offered on the hard- and software market need to have certain options. The technical standard of these products must reach a level that makes it possible to realise in industrial practice what is possible in principle.
— Human CIM concepts, which can be established in principle and after specific technical developments for industrial practice, are also an object of bargaining processes in firms. In these bargaining processes power balance, good will, thinking in the short or long term, and other factors play a role.

Regarding the technical preconditions, the following of the above listed demands can be realised in industrial practice because of the 'state of the art' of the market supply.

— It is possible to decentralise computers. There is a tendency towards work stations or even towards the increasingly powerful personal computers. Mainframe computers are used more and more for data keeping and network managing.
— There is a 'supply side' on the software market that offers software modules for CIM concepts by which the process of aggregate planning is aided on a central level and the process of shop scheduling is assisted on a decentralised level.

— The market offers not only software that tries to automate decision processes by mathematical algorithms but also software products which simulate the consequences of decision-making alternatives for the user.

With this background on the market situation, the 'state of the art' suffers in the following areas. In these fields the present software supply of CIM components hinders the realisation of human CIM structures.

— Common data structures, especially between CAD systems and, for example, material requirements planning systems, are not available.
— Common 'human interfaces', i.e. 'man–machine dialogue', etc., have not yet been developed for the CIM components. Even within one CIM component, there is a broad variety of dialogues offered by different vendors.
— Certain interfaces for data exchange which would enable alternative forms of CIM are not available. The vendors offer partial software solutions for CIM concepts which are interconnected with specific organisational solutions.

CONCLUDING REMARKS

In the last few years, 'shop-floor programming' of CNC machine tools has established itself in Germany to a reasonable degree beside the central computer aided programming. As a means of keeping a high level of qualification on the shop floor, and for economic reasons, too, shop-floor programming is regarded in some cases as superior.

For the future, it is doubtful whether the economic advantage of shop-floor programming will remain. By an integration of CAD and computer aided programming of CNC machine tools in CIM concepts, the programming times will become shorter. Until now, integration interfaces were available for CAD systems and central NC programming systems only. Therefore, there will probably be a marked trend to central NC programming. The limited importance which shop-floor programming has achieved will diminish.

This trend is, however, not inevitable. Two alternative concepts are possible which enable the exchange of geometric data of workpieces between CAD systems and the shop floor. To achieve these interfaces additional development work is required. The task is to transfer geometric data out of CAD systems into shop-floor terminals or the CNC units of machine tools.

If we are successful in the technical realisation of such concepts and in proving their economic advantages in industrial practice, shop-floor programming even in CIM could have a chance in the future. The requirement is to make up the lead which central NC programming systems have gained, as quickly as possible.

Address for correspondence:

Fraunhofer Institut für Systemtechnik und Innovationsforschung (ISI), Breslauer Strasse 48, D-7500 Karlsruhe 1, FRG.

REFERENCES

Brödner, P. (1985) *Fabrik 2000—Alternative Entwicklungspfade in die Zukunft der Fabrik*. Berlin: Sigma.

Brumlop, E. (1986) *Arbeitsbewertung bei flexiblem Personaleinsatz*. Schriftenreihe HdA Band 71, Frankfurt/New York: Campus Verlag.

Förster, H. U. (1985) CAD/PPS-Kopplung—ein Meilenstein auf dem Weg zur rechnerintegrierten Produktion. CAD/CAM-Report 1/2, pp. 54–9.

Kern, H. and Schumann, M. (1984) *Das Ende der Arbeitsteilung? Rationalisierung in der industriellen Produktion*. München: Beck-Verlag.

Maier, H. (1985). CIM-Expertise im Auftrag des ISI und des ISF (Unpublished), Leopoldshafen.

Wildemann, H. (1984) Anforderungen an PPS aus der Sicht der Zeit- und Mengenminimierung—Einbindung der KANBAN-Philosophie. In *Mit Technologie die Zunkunft bewältigen, Band 3, PPS für den mittelständischen Maschinen- und Anlagenbau*. Frankfurt: Maschinenbauverlag.

Section 3

Selected European Perspectives

11. A European Overview of Work and Vocational Training

Arndt Sorge

Department of Business Administration, University of Limburg, Maastricht

SUMMARY

This chapter argues that education and training are not to be thought of as directly influenced by technical change. The tendency towards flexible automation attests to the importance of a strong, institutionalised, practically relevant and academically demanding system. A sensible way to influence technical change may be indirect, through promotion of better and more widespread vocational education and training. The author draws on examples in British, French, German, and Italian firms based on empirical research carried out under the sponsorship of CEDEFOP and the FAST Programme of the European Commission.

INTRODUCTION

— To what extent will new technological developments lead to full automation and computer integration?
— Do computer-based highly integrated production systems lead to more flexibility, or will this aspect mainly be ensured by human qualifications and work organisation?
— Which new man/machine relationships will arise?
— Which measures have to be taken to meet future requirements?

Such questions may be fruitfully discussed with the help of research results from a comprehensive investigation under the FAST programme for which FAST and CEDEFOP had carried joint responsibility. The study focused on various aspects of flexible automation of manufacturing in Denmark, the Federal Republic of Germany, France and Italy (some examples of which are

New Technology and Manufacturing Management   Edited by M. Warner, W. Wobbe and P. Brödner
Published 1990 by John Wiley & Sons Ltd

discussed in several chapters later in this section). These aspects included:

— technical developments and their applications,
— organisational aspects of enterprises and work,
— vocational training and education on staff and manpower policies,
— the situation of smaller sized firms.

THE RESEARCH RESULTS: AN OVERVIEW

Technical choice

A conventional approach is to predict or describe technical developments and then find out the economic, social, training or other consequences which they entail. It may certainly be that a particular technical trend appears to be indisputable, such as increasing control, monitoring, transport and feeding link-ups between previously independent or stand-alone machines. However, the economic and social consequences of such developments vary much more depending on which kind of technical solution is found or designed, rather than being specific to the more global trend. There is thus a need for an increasing awareness about the fact of technical choice. Questions should be asked about the purposes for which flexible manufacturing systems or cells are used, how they compare with alternatives, how they ought to be designed and used. Such considerations are particularly pressing with flexible manufacturing systems, firstly, because these are not produced and sold in standard versions, and secondly, because it is not clear whether, in an individual case, flexible manufacturing systems or cells are preferable to their alternatives, for example, stand-alone CNC machines without automatic workpiece handling. Every user, therefore, has to make careful specifications of the kind of system he wants. An important point about technical choice is that it must be based on a clear definition of work organisation, manning, training, skills required and other factors necessary. Otherwise it is not possible to arrive at reliable estimates of rates of utilisation of machinery, operating costs, revenue and, finally, economic justification of the investment. Choices with regard to organisation of work, education and training are therefore not merely consequences of technical choice but must also be made before a technical alternative can be selected (see Campbell *et al.*, 1989).

The economic justification of flexible manufacturing systems may often appear dubious when alternatives are compared. They ought therefore to be mainly considered as indicative of a possible long-running trend to increase the continuity of operations by automation in areas outside mass or large batch production. But one should guard against speculating about economic and social effects on the basis of presently visible technical configurations.

Organisational choice

Just as a user or designer may choose between technical alternatives, so he also has a choice of work organisation. This possibility was discussed at two levels. At the level of company strategy, development and selection of technology should be integrated into a wider strategic choice which the organisation has to make. At the level of work organisation in the factory, a choice has to be made about the allocation of work functions to workplaces and individuals, and to human beings or machines. Greater prevalence of allocating functions to humans and of linking machine operation with setting, programming and planning functions was seen to be linked with organisational choice geared to more differentiated product markets. This strategy ('flexible specialisation') was considered to be of increasing importance, and makes appropriate vocational education and training even more important than in the past (Warner, 1985).

To some extent, technical choice entails organisational consequences. But it is equally true that different forms of work organisation may be chosen for the same technology. The design of the French flexible manufacturing systems (FMS) studied seems to have followed a philosophy of making the mechanical engineering part of them appear more like an appendix to a central control computer. This was less so in Germany, and this ties in with a difference in work organisation approach, in that the use of skilled craft workers was stressed more in Germany. Although organisational differences existed between France and Germany, research was interpreted as showing that national differences between organisational strategies were not as important as differences between individual company strategies in each country (see Maurice *et al.*, 1982).

Education and training challenges

Organisation differences are linked with education and training differences. For instance, in the case of an FMS, greater involvement of operators in machine-setting and programming requires more frequent and more extensive training of skilled workers. Also, the more widespread and extensive the training of skilled workers, the less dramatic are problems of retraining and conversion of workers. FMS and FMC, as well as other forms of flexible automation, do not directly suggest that it is preferable to have manning and skilling arrangements which stress broad-based skills at the operator level and lesser hierarchical differentiation of manpower by separated skill levels. However, it can be shown that the interests of companies are slowly, gradually and in an increasing number of cases moving in this direction. One main reason for this is the increasing differentiation of product markets. This fact suggests reductions in batch sizes; it gives rise to interruptions (conversion, retooling, reprogramming) in the workflow, which require more skilled, experienced and quickly-reacting kinds of workers than increasingly came on the scene during the past growth of mass markets. It may thus be said that both the technical and the organisational choices are becoming loaded in favour of education and training concepts that emphasise broad-based training for multiskilling or polyvalence, that link school and work as well as education and training and are less likely to be socially divisive by opening a gap between highly trained engineers and unskilled workers (see Wagner, 1983).

The factory of the future

Factories will, as in the past, be subject to a long-running drive to increase continuity of operations, thus speeding up throughput and reducing work-in-progress. The development of electronic control and monitoring devices, of transport, storage and feeding facilities serves this purpose. On the other hand, there also appears to be a break with a previous trend. The increasing flexibility required of companies with regard to product innovation and variation cannot only be assured by matching technology. Greater frequency of conversion in design and production raises barriers to automation. Thus, increasing continuity of operations makes for automaticity whereas greater frequency of conversion makes for barriers to automation. In view of such countervailing tendencies, what we are witnessing is a trend towards partial rather than full automation. Such a factory will feature greater proportions of more highly trained engineers and technicians, but it will also have to upgrade the training of workers and make sure that the training, education and experience of workers, engineers and technicians do not drift too far apart.

It is not clear how many people will work in factories or in manufacturing in the future. But the job potential of manufacturing will also depend on the extent to which education and training systems create the right calibre of worker, technician and engineer for manufacturing in more differentiated markets with more customised products.

Supportive network and environment

In view of their less bureaucratic organisation structures, smaller companies are likely to become increasingly successful in a context that puts a premium not only on the flexibility of technology but also on that of work organisation and manpower. Indeed, the employment statistics of many countries bear out a more recent trend of increasing employment shares in such firms. On the other hand, smaller companies suffer from a number of drawbacks. They are less likely to attract highly trained engineers, cannot provide the range of specialised internal services that large companies have, cannot afford a very large marketing, sales and service organisation, find it more difficult to finance capital-intensive ventures and cannot afford the training and retraining facilities of the quality and quantity that larger companies may have. Smaller companies are, however, not only competitors of larger ones but often connected with them through intricate networks of sub-contracting, supply and service. The notion of networks seems to provide the key for a concept to explain the situation of smaller firms. This matter is less a question of whether these have more or less FMC and FMS or other forms of flexible automation. It can of course be demonstrated that, in many countries, the exponential growth in the use of CNC machines occurred in smaller companies more than in larger ones. But again, this is not the heart of the matter. Instead, one should first think about how smaller companies may possibly turn their valuable potential for organisational and manpower flexibility to better use by obtaining access to qualified manpower, specialised services and consultancy to the same extent as that enjoyed by larger companies.

THE RESEARCH RESULTS IN DETAIL

The technical scenario

By and large, the development of technology for enterprises in batch production (notably in mechanical and electrical engineering, the automobile industry, aircraft manufacturing and similar industries) will be likely to follow a trend which is already visible. CAD/CAM is being developed to establish more and more technical linkages between machines, previously separate computers, files and programs. In parallel, mechanical linkages are being developed between machines and with buffer stocks and stores. Robots extend their application beyond welding and handling into quite a number of functions including assembly. However, it is not easy to predict the speed and pervasiveness of this tendency. It can also be seen how technical development has come and will go on to be orientated towards ease of conversion of machines, tools, computers and programs. This trend is visible in CNC, programmable controllers, CAD, robots, FMS/FMC, electronic production control, CAE and other developments. All this is best thought of not as aiding full automation of the factory but rather as facilitating human intervention despite increasing technical continuity of operations. There are, of course, always opposed technical concepts of development. But the scenario of the fully automated factory has probably had greater publicity than it deserved, over and above certain far-flung plans and individual showpiece plants. Although the number of fully automatic factories may increase, these do rely on substantial engineering, maintenance, planning, programming, tooling and setting effort, and they are linked with more labour-intensive suppliers of parts and services.

Countervailing tendencies between replacing and facilitating human intervention are inherent to the process of technical innovation throughout. What is significant with regard to a particular innovation cannot be determined on the basis of its momentary technical properties. It will only become clear when the context of technical change is taken into account. This connection, however, is likely to encourage greater compatibility between human intervention and automaticity than in the past.

The organisational scenario

The technical emphasis on the continuity of operations is linked with changing organisation concepts. At various levels in the workforce, employees are being encouraged to see their own work in the perspective of its wider implications in the factory at large. There is thus greater use of work teams across functional or occupational specialisms.

The organisation of workflow becomes more geared to a sharing or overlap of functions between places of work, departments, work groups and occupations. All this is to enable the organisation to be less rigid and set to exercise well-known and standardised tasks. Rather, organisational concepts appear to be evolving which facilitate the pragmatic solution of problems that are hard to standardise, by bringing together different sources of skills and knowledge. At the level of operators, for instance, this change is shown in the increasing willingness of FMS and FMC users to unite loading/operating and setting/programming functions. It also shows in the reduced importance of the traditional separation between the different metal-cutting techniques (turning, milling, drilling, grinding, etc.). Another example is the growing link between mechanical and electronic specialisms in maintenance. In the same spirit, one can notice that design of parts is increasingly done with a view to improving practicability and economy of production. Such developments are linked with the assimilation of 'blue' and 'white-collar' workers, and with the continuing trend towards greater quantitative importance of indirect production functions and workers. This upgrading of skills and qualifications may, of course, imply that the discrepancy between technically advanced manufacturers and their suppliers, between independent and dependent firms is increasing. To redress such a threat of polarisation is the task of education and training, and the supportive networks, discussed below.

As the organisation structure becomes more differentiated and new occupational specialisms emerge, it becomes less rigid. There seems to be a premium on a division of labour which is mostly not less than before but is more fluid or 'organic' rather than mechanistic. Naturally, this is not to detract from the importance of organisational choice. There are enough reasons for moving more, or less, in the direction indicated, and companies may have different ways of doing this. But on the whole, this seems to be the trend which will continue as long as we witness a relative decline in the importance of mass markets. It is also important to realise that companies cannot adapt organisational recipes with infinite smoothness, to suit the strategic choice which they happen to make. Instead, this adaptation requires certain conditions to be fulfilled in the system of education and training.

The education and training scenario

It is essential to separate the consideration of vocational training somewhat from that of technical change. Well-known orientations, such as in the direction of a broader skills basis, better links and alternation between school and work, recurrent education, and links between manual and intellectual work, retain their significance. A more organic or fluid division of labour, suited to a regime of technology in which continuity of operations through automation and human intervention are combined, presupposes an education and training arrangement which provides workers that fit into this sort of organisation and are able to make sensible use of such technology. It may be suggested that in a country such as Japan, where the appropriate manpower is expected to remain in the larger company until they are about 55 years of age, the appropriate system of training, if not of parts of the education system, can be provided by an individual company. But in labour markets with mobility during working life, a sound national or at least regional system of vocational education and training must be one of the most important prerequisites for successful technical change. Some countries have grave problems equipping themselves with a system of vocational education and training to start with, let alone one which is well adapted to the most recent technical innovation. In such countries, vocational training often disappears in importance behind general and higher education.

New technology increases the importance of further training and education, particularly if the rate of technical change is rapid. But this should not disguise the fact that many further training problems are due less to technical change than to deficits in basic education and training. The educational and economic returns of further training measures may be much greater when these do not hit unsuspecting targets who are ill-prepared both through lack of sufficient grounding in a relevant occupation and by not having acquired the capacity to learn in a more structured way. Another problem is that, often, further training is too short and too specific with regard to particular equipment or techniques. It is thus important to give a broader and more institutional basis to further training.

In a European context, most of what has been said so far raises the issue of regulating and institutionalising training and education between a multiplicity of agents: national or other governments, federations of employers or groups or clusters of companies, representatives of employees including trade unions, specific training or education institutions outside companies. Probably more than the technical and the organisational scenarios, that with regard to education and training needs to achieve concerted action between many agents. This process may involve informal accords, formal consultation, written agreements and statute law. It is also no accident that in this context, there was frequent reference to the right of employees and their representatives to have an influence on company, government or other policies. Such demands also appeared under the technical and organisational scenarios, that is, a case was made in favour of specifying technical, organisational and training choices with the involvement of employees and their representatives.

There may be many different ways of orientating education and training in the directions mentioned above. Sometimes the German 'dual system' of vocational training is held up as the model for a pervasive diffusion of enriched skills as well as of technical change (see Sorge and Warner, 1986). Leaving the answer to the question about the 'best' system aside for the moment, it is certain that every institutionalised system will and must assure its continuity. In France, upgrading of basic vocational training more or less automatically involves training for the CAP (certificat d'aptitude professionnelle) while in Germany this occurs within the 'dual system'. In both cases, there are proposals for making increasing use of such qualifications as well as improving them. The countries may be moving in the same direction, parallel with each other, but on separate tracks. The direction is the same because, under different systems, there is a necessity to intertwine training on the job and in the classroom more frequently and systematically.

The supportive network and environment scenario

It has been suggested that smaller companies can make an even more substantial contribution to the economy and employment because of their organisational flexibility, if the problems of training facilities, access to highly qualified manpower and specialised services can be overcome. One solution is the creation of supportive networks to provide these. Such networks can be of different kinds: they may consist of companies alone, or of companies and education, training, consultancy or other supportive organisations. They may be informal or formalised, possibly in the form of public or quasi-public bodies, such as chambers of industry and commerce.

Part of the problem is, of course, the provision of training. Here, one may envisage, for instance, the proliferation of regional training centres which are geographically and in their practical orientation close to the potential of such firms. There are also examples well worth heeding, of one company using the training facilities of another one which is possibly larger. In a similar way, on some sort of contractual basis, firms may share consultancy, development, marketing or other service functions which they would not feel able to provide individually. The region of Emilia-Romana in Italy has become well known for developing such a cooperative-style network. In many cases, such functions are also offered by independent suppliers on a commercial basis. Noteworthy examples are those of software houses or designers and producers of semi-customised microelectronic circuits. These are examples of small firms with technically qualified specialists that provide an input of competence for other companies.

Often, however, small companies will simply be unprepared to deal with highly qualified specialists either in their own organisation or in suppliers. Such a gap may be reduced through quite substantial further training for existing personnel or by alleviating the risk a small company may incur when hiring a calibre of manpower to which it is not used. Conceptually, this approach is very similar to that under the organisational scenario. The trick is to remove or narrow down gaps which had previously been created. In the case of the organisational scenario, it is gaps between functionally and hierarchically differentiated specialisms within a company. In the case of the networks and environment scenario, the problem consists of closing gaps between different kinds of companies to which different, more or less demanding and encompassing, ranges of functions have become allocated. Once again, the concept does not imply that different types of companies will become less distinguished by their main kinds of activity. It does imply, however, that the more refined division of labour between companies ought to become more fluid, being tempered by overlapping functions. It is not sufficient to characterise this relationship between smaller and larger companies by competition alone; cooperation between smaller and larger companies as well as between smaller companies is of increasing importance. Such cooperation includes commercial transactions and more institutional affiliations, including public or quasi-public corporations. This scenario blurs the institutional boundary between training, consultancy, financial support, informal mutual support through sharing of equipment or other resources, and purely commercial services offered on an open market. Nevertheless, it is firmly connected with the training theme since the aim is to make particular kinds of human effort and its output available to those who have profited less from it in the past.

It is important to conceive of technical change as occurring through a series of successive steps, like flexible automation and, specifically, flexible manufacturing systems and cells. Each step does not merely entail organisational or skilling consequences but defines new options or choices with regard to the organisation of work and the generation of skills. In principle, basic choices thus go on to exist under new technology, and in concrete details, they acquire new forms and definitions. It may even be that the range of choice becomes larger with new technology. The crucial problem is, therefore, not to elaborate new consequences of technical change but to redefine, discuss and implement organisation and skilling options which are not radically new in principle.

In the field of *research and development* (R & D) this means that in flexible and integrated manufacturing, organisation is a key issue for the future. This has to be taken into account when formulating industrial innovation policies and developing production technology and manufacturing facilities. R & D policies must not only rely on 'technocentric' concepts, which are guided by a development logic of technology. In this way, the demands of prospective production might not be met. What is required now is a new R & D approach, which is based on organisation and skills for the elaboration of adapted technologies.

In the field of *education and training*, this leads to the following considerations:

— Mastering technical change implies, to a large extent, mastering the generation of skills and knowledge, i.e. vocational education and training.
— The key role of vocational education and training is closely connected with the organisation of work. We should be more concerned with the organisational requirements for generating and utilising skills than with their technical causes.
— Mastering technical change through skilling raises the problem not only of individual but also of collective skills. Differentiated specialist skills have to be integrated. This requires an organisation and a strategy of the type described above.
— Supportive networks ought to be developed to make training, specialist human resources, consultancy, development, marketing and other services more available to smaller firms, so that they can turn their asset of organisational flexibility to more effective use, in the prevailing context of technical change. Relations between companies or other units and their environment are increasingly characterised by greater interdependence.
— Further training appears as a new, strategically important element in companies. It poses acute problems to small and medium-sized companies, which can only be solved through supportive networks.

In the form presented here, such concepts are far-ranging but general. In order to be more instructive and concrete, more research and development on technical, organisational, training and network concepts specific to different cases, is needed. To specify such cases requires identifying in particular those which are less currently discussed but probably important. Cases of technical change are often seen as applications of new technology in process technology rather than product technology. Against this, it may be said that there is a need for considering, in addition to 'new production systems', new products, that is, changes in the product spectrum, product technology, and what these require, entail and are conditioned by.

CONCLUDING REMARKS

The central conclusions reinforce the approach adopted by CEDEFOP, through its work on or in connection with international comparisons, for about a decade, before discussion of new technology became trendy. Such work has focused on the importance of 'alternant' education and training, the links between organisation of work and vocational training and education, which have been shown by comparisons between France, the Federal Republic of Germany, the Netherlands, and the UK, and the persistence of choice and flexible automation concepts in the case of CNC machines. A discussion of new technology should not amount to reinventing the wheel.

Address for correspondence:

Department of Business Administration, University of Limburg, F EW-BE, PO Box 616, NL-6200 Maastricht, The Netherlands.

REFERENCES

Campbell, A., Sorge, A., and Warner, M. (1989) *Microelectronic Product Applications in Great Britain and West Germany: Strategies, Competence and Training.* Aldershot: Gower.
Maurice, M., Sellier, F., and Silvestre, J. J. (1982) *Politique d'éducation et organisation industrielle en France et Allemagne.* Paris: Presses Universitaires de France.
Sorge, A., and Warner, M. (1986) *Comparative Factory Organisation.* Aldershot: Gower.
Wagner, K. (1983) *Relation between Education, Employment and Productivity and their Impact on Education and Labour Market Policies. A British-German Comparison.* Berlin, European Centre for the Development of Vocational Training.
Warner, M. (1985) Microelectronics, technical change and industrial economies. *Industrial Relations Journal,* **16**(3), 9–18.

12. Technical Projects and Organisational Changes: Flexible Specialisation in Denmark

Peer Hull Kristensen

Institute of Economic Planning, Roskilde University Centre, Roskilde

SUMMARY

The first part of this chapter describes the difference between two industrial strategies: neo-Fordism and flexible specialisation; it is this difference which forms the conceptual framework for the Danish case studies. The second part of the chapter presents some of the results of the case studies of the processes of reconstruction and the application of the new technology in production in Danish industry. These case studies show that flexible specialisation is playing an increasing role in Danish industry, and that the reorientation toward flexibility and the application of CNC technology is very evident. The prerequisites for and the trends in this process of reconstruction are analysed in relation to career and education patterns in the Danish iron industry.

INTRODUCTION

Firms that move in the direction of flexible specialisation try to create new markets rather than to defend or recapture existing ones. Their strategy is to develop new products that correspond to, and even help define, the needs their eventual customers were only beginning to realise they had, and for whose satisfaction they are willing to pay a premium over the price of the most suitable alternative standard goods. Because of this intimacy between client and producer, flexible specialisation creates its own demand, but in a way that limits competition.

This relation to the market implies a profound break with the Fordist model of organisation and a reversal of the postulates, first described by Adam Smith, on which it rests. In Fordism, the continual subdivision of tasks, by itself, increases the productivity of labour, and makes possible the gradual substitution of special-purpose or task-specific machines for workers

---

New Technology and Manufacturing Management   Edited by M. Warner, W. Wobbe and P. Brödner
Published 1990 by John Wiley & Sons Ltd

performing increasingly routine and simplified jobs. Increasingly specialised use of resources makes possible ever cheaper production of generally useful goods. The increasing specialisation of the entire system undermines the integrity of each stage of the manufacturing process. In mass production, whether geographically concentrated or dispersed, the parts are completely subordinated to the whole.

Flexible specialisation excludes this use of resources by definition. It is pointless to invest in product-specific machines and workers capable of doing only one thing if markets are in constant flux. Where the goal is to minimise the total costs of manufacturing a range of different goods rather than the price of any one product, technology must be general purpose. Accordingly, workers must possess craft skills, defined simply as the comprehensive knowledge required to perform many different, unforeseeable operations with one piece of equipment. All this means that each stage of the manufacturing process retains some autonomy with respect to the whole. Because each combination of craftsmen and general-purpose machine can be turned to different uses, the manufacturing system is defined at any one moment by the way its parts are combined, and its flexibility is determined by the ease with which they can be rearranged.

How a system of flexible specialisation is organised varies from industry to industry, according to the properties and capital requirements of the relevant technologies. Put the other way around, there is no single form of industrial organisation that follows from the strategy of flexible specialisation. Within each industry there will be a flexible variant of the dominant pattern, sometime superficially similar to, but often conspicuously different from the Fordist model.

At one extreme are the continuous-process industries such as petrochemicals. Here, efficiency requires a direct connection between manufacturing operations, each one of which, moreover, employs large amounts of fixed capital. A move in the direction of flexible specialisation means internal decentralisation within the existing or renovated plant. As the number of products and the frequency with which a plant switches from one to another increases, the range of capacities of the equipment in each department becomes greater, and the skill level and the level of responsibility of the workforce must rise accordingly. There is simply no time to get help in the solution of minor problems, and production workers must understand enough of the technology to be able to collaborate with maintenance personnel to solve major ones. This development is one central pattern in the chemical and steel industries in the Federal Republic of Germany. These factories look much as they did before; and it is necessary to examine their organisation and, above all, the higher skill levels of their workforce and the greater sophistication of their products, to determine the extent of the changes.

At the opposite extreme are industries where capital requirements for many, if not all, operations are low, and there are no economies of scale to be achieved by directly linking successive machines in a sequence. Three different machines are at least as efficient in three separate locations as under one roof, provided each is the optimal size for its type. Under these conditions, a move to flexible specialisation is likely to take a decentralised form: an explosion of the factory into its separate pieces. In the limiting case, one worker owns one machine, and goods are produced by federations of one-man shops, each specialised in one phase of production (see Sabel, 1982; Piore and Sabel 1981, 1984). Most cases of flexible specialisation consist neither of networks of one-man shops nor of large, self-contained factories operating as a collection of technologically linked artisans' shops under one roof. Most are networks of small and medium-sized firms operating as a loose and shifting federation, often but not always, led by a larger company that assembles or simply markets the final product.

Complications in the study of choice of strategy

It is difficult to make a direct, accurate assessment of the extent to which firms are moving in the direction of flexible specialisation rather than neo-Fordism. Earlier, we suggested that the shift from Fordism to internally decentralised factories is hard to detect from the outside; so is, at certain stages of development at least, the difference between a small sweatshop subcontracting to a large neo-Fordist firm and a unit of a modern flexible-specialisation system. Nor are there good aggregate statistics on changes in the composition of output, as government publications and trade journals that treat questions similar to the ones raised here repeatedly point out. Products defined in the statistics as specialities, such as stainless steel, for example, are frequently mass produced, whereas many shapes of carbon steel which ought to count as specialities are registered as standard products.

Nonetheless, there is a good deal of circumstantial evidence in favour of the view that in many countries and industries, flexible specialisation is becoming increasingly significant. Studies of the automobile industries in France, Germany, Italy, and Japan, for example, unanimously report speed-up in the model cycle and a growing diversification of products. The international trade press reports that companies specialising in alloy steels and fine chemicals regularly show higher profits than standard commodity producers. Studies of the use of numerical control equipment invariably report its growing use in small shops and, more important, its role in meeting demand for more variable products.

Beyond these suggestive, though hardly comprehensive bits of evidence, a number of systematic considerations give weight to the thesis that firms are being driven toward flexible specialisation and away from neo-Fordist strategies. The fundamental reason is that the risks of holding tight to the traditional model are in many ways greater than the risks of innovation; and under these circumstances, cautious realists can act like revolutionaries.

It is not the new technological developments alone which determine the choice of a manufacturing strategy. It is an open question which can be put to the factories: is the acquisition of new technology primarily aimed at reducing costs or at achieving flexibility?

The answer to this very important question was surprisingly unanimous from the Danish case studies. While FMS technology was considered to be of lesser importance, CNC machines were regarded as being of the utmost importance. A report of the findings is given in the following sections of this chapter.

FLEXIBILITY AS A KEY WORD

During the past 10 years flexibility has become a key word in nearly all firms covered in this analysis (15 small firms and 13 medium-sized enterprises in Danish industry constituted the basis of the sample studied). Flexibility within production became necessary for some firms during the crisis of the 1970s and the 1980s due to radical changes in market conditions. One, a shipyard (company C), went from regular, stable production of supertankers to producing ships which differed substantially with each order. Another, a diecasting plant (company F), had to alter its pattern of production of large, homogeneous series to smaller, more heterogeneous series with subsequently higher quality standards. These firms have now begun to invest significantly in modern technology. Company C for example, purchased CAD/CAM equipment—a computerised laser cutting-machine to shape immense patterns in iron, and a computerised tubing mill. Another company, company F, invested in casting cells consisting of casting machines equipped with automatic blank handling, automatic form sprayers and modern systems for supervision and surveillance in addition to NC machines for tooling and finishing. But the question of whether flexibility also requires changes in the organisation of labour remains to be answered.

Other firms have been so successful in realising these kinds of market changes that they have reached a second or third phase in organising, selling and producing in accordance with a philosophy of flexibility. A fittings factory (company B) was forced to close down its production of standard taps in the early 1970s. They are now producing new models in special enamelled colours. Design changes have become important for this firm, which now considers itself a 'fashion industry', rather than a supplier of standard parts. Completely new types of modular taps that can be combined by the customer are being marketed. The firm has restructured its organisation so that it now produces in groups which can be reorganised and changed, and it is gradually replacing its production machinery with flexible technology in order to keep up with the market.

Some firms have invested in flexible technology—often by accident—and suddenly discover that they have a certain flexibility in their production which can be utilised in marketing and product development (companies G1, G2 and F).

But a surprisingly large number of firms (in this relatively small sample) have always survived by being flexible and have for a long time managed the large number and variety of products resulting from this flexiblity (companies A, D, E, H, I, K, L). A few believe that this can be resolved by investing in integrated flexible manufacturing systems (A, K and E), but have not gone further than the planning stage.

One firm (company D) built a new factory whose production was controlled—from the stamping of sheet metal on CNC punches—through a computerised transportation system which fed components into a single large assembly line. The system had problems right from the start. The CNC punches were flexible enough, but the integrating link between processing and assembly (automatic transport) and the integrated assembly line had to be abandoned. Company D is now attempting to integrate phases of production through organisational solutions which can help to regain flexibility and productivity, and this has proven to be successful.

Some firms (B, D, E, H, I) have attempted to solve the problems of flexibility through organisational means and tend to view technology as merely a supportive factor.

Hidden assumptions of flexibility

These changes in the lives of the firms in the analysis challenge the dimensions of Fordism, which form a *logical* unity. Some firms have so far only challenged one or two aspects, whereas others have assailed the whole spectrum of Fordism. But the analysis shows that as of yet none of the firms have discovered a new, consistent structure which one could call an assertive, conscious form of flexible specialisation. Most of the firms exhibit an ambivalent and contradictory pattern which can best be described as a schizophrenic mixture of Fordism and flexible specialisation. Some firms which have always survived through flexibility have planned their organisation, utilisation of resources and labour according to the tenets of Fordist efficiency: high operational efficiency, high utilisation of capacity, wage systems which promote productivity, stockpiling, etc. They are only now beginning to realise that their philosophy of management was unsuitable for the purpose. Upper management is now rejecting the constraints of Fordist principles of management, and discovering numerous alternative ways of organising labour, economising, and systemising production and sales.

In situations like this, organisms struggle with themselves in order to experiment with new forms, to seek new possibilities of structure and identity.

But in doing so, they also run the risk of subsequent injury due to the application of Fordist management principles in some areas and flexible specialisation in others. The process of transition, documented in our studies, can be seen in the light of psychological, biological and organisational theory as extremely painful.

In the light of such theories, most of the firms we have visited seem extremely vigorous. By using trial and error they have carried out a number of projects and have undergone radical processes which ought to have been impossible. These medium-sized Danish firms have not become stuck in a fixed pattern. On the contrary, they appear to have a 'hidden' resource for flexibility that allows them to experiment with differing degrees of flexible specialisation without sacrificing their economic survival on the market. This 'flexible flexibility' is most prominent in firms like B, C, G1 and G2, who, in the course of the 1960s, progressed from different forms of flexible specialisation to mass production. During the crisis of the 1970s, they reverted to new forms of flexible specialisation. How was this possible?

In terms of their formal structure, Danish firms resemble most other firms in the world. They see themselves in an organisational diagram that reflects specialisation of functions, divisionalisation, and differentiation and hier-archy among the employees, just as firms in other countries do. They see themselves in a classic Fordist mirror. The crucial question is whether or not this depiction conceals something which is not inherent in a Fordist firm.

In spite of great differences between the three cases we studied in depth, there is one common trait. After an intensive participatory transition, com-pany I was able to change a number of Fordist forms of management and supervision, after which their organisation of labour functioned, in spite of radical change, without complication. Firm D, on the other hand, reinforced a number of supervision and management forms without consulting their employees, the result of which was a decline in efficiency in a new factory with improved technology, to 62% of that of the old plant, which, by any standard, was impractical. They were unable to improve productivity until they began to listen to the employees' problems and suggestions. In a third case, company F faced a number of problems concerning morale, piecework systems and organisation of labour, which made it difficult to involve the employees in the decision-making process and to take steps toward more independence in production.

What is common in these cases is a relative ease in altering production when two conditions are met: first, those firms which had least difficulty in changing direction also have a higher percentage of skilled workers, and it is a fair guess that there exists a craft ethic concerning responsibility and efficiency in production that provides the individual worker with a certain degree of autonomy as well as the ability to cooperate across the lines of traditionally defined areas. Throughout the 1960s, in spite of the fact that managers assumed that they were operating under a Fordist system, it was still possible for workers and foremen collectively to maintain both a relatively flexible form of production as well as a high professional standard of craftsmanship as a 'concealed' fact.

Second, this 'concealed' organisation of craftsman-like production must be respected when new systems of supervision and management are instituted. This is difficult to achieve without giving the employees participatory influence because the organisation is, as mentioned, a concealed organisation within the organisation.

Company I met both conditions from the start. Company D had a production based on skilled workmanship, but during their restructuring neither this craftsmanship nor participation was respected, and problems ensued. Whether the drop in productivity occurred because the workers sabotaged production, or because the organisation of labour—technically speaking— did not respect the prerequisites for a craft organisation of production is irrelevant. The conclusion is the same: when there is a high percentage of skilled workers with a relatively autonomous craft organisation, it is easy to change the organisation of production as long as the basic organisation of labour is respected.

Company F is apparently lacking in both prerequisites in so far as production is concerned. Individual responsibility and autonomy are slowly being squeezed out of this foundry, which today relies on unskilled casters, who receive a rudimentary training and among whom there is a high rate of turnover. This fact has necessitated a supervisory apparatus to monitor quality and efficiency, thereby creating a vicious circle that makes it impossible for company F to hold on to casters who are responsible and independent enough to plan their own work. Company F's flexibility today is therefore limited to possibilities connected with technology and the organisation surrounding production itself (construction, tooling and finishing of castings). Progression toward greater flexibility is a tedious process in a firm like this, compared with company I and company D, whose only problem was to discover their own 'concealed' organisation of professional workmanship.

None of our cases indicate a problem in reorganising production, initiating new technology, changing wage systems, etc., when the two conditions already mentioned are met. On the contrary, there seems to be a readiness among production workers to improve organisation or to make work more expedient, to introduce new technology, e.g. obtain better equipment, and to meet new challenges. Some post-war Danish firms have certainly followed a Fordist ideology. Some have adopted hierarchical organisations, introduced wage systems that promote productivity, and specialised labour to increase operational effectiveness and utilisation of output. However, our studies confirm that production to a large extent involves general purpose machinery and a considerable degree of skilled labour, organisation in smaller workshops under the supervision of a foreman, and so on.

Is there—under the Fordist 'superstructure' in these firms—a shop floor 'base organisation' of craft production which, instead of opposing change, new production jobs, new technology and new ways of organising labour, has been able to effect these changes—so long as the conditions mentioned above have been met? If so, then the Fordist superstructure is almost a 'false consciousness', which has been reinterpreted by the skilled workers. There is considerable evidence that wage systems have not lived up to a Taylorisation of labour, if anything, piece rates have proved to be a system for designating status among various individuals and groups involved in production. Indeed, there are strong indications that a decisive separation of the planning and execution of labour has not taken place. In many of the cases, for instance, the products were so poorly documented that they depended on the 'man on the floor' knowing how a job, a product, or a variant was to be produced—or else knowing how to find out.

According to our hypothesis, it has been easy to combine this concealed organisation of craft workers with the new managerial ideologies that have spread like wildfire throughout Denmark during this decade. Production managers and technical and administrative executives in many of the firms we visited have been replaced by new people, all of whom are strongly influenced by the 'just-in-time' concept, that is, rebels against the old Fordist goals of efficiency. This new group has demonstrated a surprising compatibility with the 'concealed' organisation of work and has thus been able to reorient production, organisation, economising, etc., without difficulty.

Is this phenomenon peculiar to Denmark, or do other countries have similar conditions? The same ideologies of production and concepts of rationality have spread throughout other countries. Perhaps there is considerably more receptiveness within Danish culture. Perhaps the new ideologies, which in Denmark have established a harmonic relationship between ideology and the concealed organisation of labour, become, in other countries, ideological superstructures of a basically Fordist reality in organisation.

THE 'DANISH ROAD' TO FLEXIBLE SPECIALISATION

Flexibility without FMS?

If our case studies are at all representative of Danish firms, they show that FMS does not play a very important part in the efforts of medium-sized firms to achieve flexibility *at the present moment*. The case studies were selected on the basis of information that these firms were in the process of a significant renewal of their production technology. Nevertheless, none of them had invested in FMS; only two were planning to introduce an FMS (company A and company K); and two others (company B and company H) were planning to implement similar projects in the coming year. It is characteristic of all these firms (with the exception of company B) that they are using FMS to replace existing CNC machines, which are extremely flexible, in the machine shop. Only company B was considering the possibilities of replacing existing specialised machines with FMS. There is a possibility that several large Danish mass producers have introduced FMS as replacement for transfer lines (Asea, Danfoss, Grundfoss) but it must be kept in mind that these firms do not give a picture of the development in normal Danish firms, and that it was difficult—for various reasons—to obtain detailed information from these firms.

The major problem, at least for those who had gone furthest along in planning the acquisition of an FMS, was that the introduction of an FMS meant reduced flexibility and variablity. The intention was to diminish transition time in production. The firms were in doubt as to whether a sufficiently large group of components could be identified, together with a relatively limited number of fixtures, such that the system could exploit the production capacity of the machine. None—not even the firms with the most advanced plans—had an intimate knowledge of the production economy of FMS. It is apparently easier to assess when going from rigid, old-fashioned transfer lines to an FMS, in which case it is only necessary to calculate alternative costs. The increased costs incurred in 'flexibilisation' are thereby more easily estimated. In firms with CNC general purpose machinery it is the transition time, rather than flexibility, that is improved by FMS. But company K, which had proceeded the furthest in planning, found that foreign firms with FMS had a higher transition time than they were able to achieve in their own workshops as a result of investing in CNC machines. Another likely reason for the prolonged implementation of FMS in Denmark is—in addition to the insecurity concerning production economy—that few professional engineers influence the process of technological change in the firms we studied. The professional ideology that can make FMS an ambition was only evident in company A. Engineers in other firms were educated at technical schools. If FMS is to be implemented at the present time, a new department, staffed by professional engineers, whose function is to systemise components, production methods, etc., is necessary. Firms which already have such functional staff—who previously designed transfer lines—are better equipped to plan for FMS.

Danish firms invest in new machinery in small incremental steps; they usually do not plan toward a long-term technically integrated system. They purchase machinery the way a craftsman buys tools: when they hear about exciting new machines that are more precise, more efficient or more expedient, they buy them without paying much mind to economics or the 'final system solution' as such. Initially, the machines are used to rectify problems which were insolvable with the old equipment, and then they discover new possibilities which no one could imagine before the machinery was introduced.

The initiative for investing in new technology comes from many departments and hierarchical levels in the firm: skilled workers, foremen, production technicians and managers, as well as technical and administrative executives can all take the initiative to 'get some better tools'. Before the new machines are purchased, the employees concerned, as well as other interested parties, are often invited to visit exhibitions and suppliers; shop stewards, operators, and machine setters collaborating with production technicians and managers. Finished solutions are seldom presented for the workers on the floor to accept; when they are, they are usually unsuccessful.

This pattern of investment and the participatory decision-making process would easily be disrupted if Danish firms introduced FMS; and workers and shop stewards clearly had no say in the planning process in the two firms that were drawing up such plans.

Does this mean that Denmark has a tendency to lag behind in innovating production technology? There is no reason for such an assumption. But compared to other countries, the introduction of NC and CNC machines in Denmark indicates that the conditions for implementing new technology and the motivation behind and the methods involved, differ radically from many Western countries. Originally, American aircraft companies first introduced NC technology in order to control the machining of complicated mathematical curves. Noble (1979) has shown that the ensuing diffusion of CNC technology in the US was motivated by the desire to increase control over quality and efficiency of the work process, which previously were relegated to the skilled metal worker's (irritating) autonomy. NC became a method of Taylorising skilled metal workers. The possibility that Danish firms shared this desire cannot be ruled out. But the hierarchy of engineers, production planners and programmers that are necessary for the fulfilment of such a desire were not present. In the 1960s and early 1970s this aroused a degree of concern that Danish firms apparently were very slow in implementing new NC technology. But in 1979 the picture changed. The Danish Institute of Technology had been following the trend of developments and was able to confirm at that time that the number of CNC machines per employee in the iron industry was among the highest in the world.

Meanwhile, considerable changes took place in CNC technology. Machine coding was being superseded by more sophisticated high level programming. This in itself meant that programming became easier and quicker, and it became the crux of the matter for relatively small Danish firms. CNC machines could now be programmed on the shop floor, and it did not become necessary to hire a new class of technicians to replace the skilled worker and his machine tool. According to our survey, machine setters have in most cases become 'programmers', and work with the machines as autonomously as before.

In most firms, there was a specific 'ideology' that the machines should be programmed on the shop floor. The dominant picture in the three cases we studied in depth was that the machine setter did the programming. But there were also occurrences of a foreman programming and in several cases one skilled worker functioned as programmer, machine setter, operator, repair-man, toolmaker, etc. But apart from the fact that programming takes place in close proximity to the shop in most of the firms, work on the new NC machines takes many forms, selected in accordance with an ordinary sense of what is expedient and natural. Only company K has established an independent programming department (with three employees). Company K is also one of the two firms furthest along in the planning of FMS in our study.

While Denmark has kept up with the diffusion of CNC machines to a surprising degree, the country lags far behind in the use of robots, which are environmentally hazardous and relatively repetitive. Furthermore, robots have not yet been coupled with other programmed machines in a single computerised system. Such systems depend upon a certain amount of engineering and systems work at the present stage and therefore cannot 'automatically' gain admission to factories from the shop floor. When robots become cheaper, equipped with better sensors and more flexible gripping mechanisms, and above all, when robots can be programmed by means of a 'black box' to collaborate with a large range of machines from different producers, and when the programming of this 'black box' can take place on the shop floor, then it is likely that the use of robots in these areas will spread quickly and lead to a wide dissemination of FMS cells in Denmark.

Organising flexibility

The vogue of Fordism among small and medium-sized firms in the Danish iron and steel industry during the 1950s and 1960s finds expression in the 'functionally divided workshop'. Different types of jobs were gathered together here in different shops under separate managements: cutting and bending in one shop, tooling and lathing in another, welding in a third, and grinding and polishing in a fourth. Then a myriad of different products and variants were finally gathered together in one assembly department. The advantage of this arrangement was that each operator could be supplied with a stock of blanks to be prepared or assembled and in this way a high capacity utilisation could be guaranteed. This fact makes it possible to keep the operators occupied on contracts that have had time and method studies run on them. The intention was, of course, to produce stock according to fairly certain sales prognoses, which made it possible to run the same series as long as possible, so as not to disrupt the well planned work by rearrangements and machine resetting.

The crisis of the past two decades has made this type of organisation inappropriate, but at the same time managers realised that the system did not function in the 1950s and 1960s either. The prognoses never came true; plans had to be constantly changed; orders always had to be rushed through many different departments, zig-zagging back and forth, causing the interruption of many series with higher priority on short notice. The result was that blanks and products that were in preparation and assembly for five effective hours could take three to four weeks to run through all the departments on the way to the stocks.

The aura of rationality surrounding this 'system' was maintained in the 1950s and 1960s because sales prognoses tended to be artificially low, or else salesmen were able to sell everything that was produced. In the 1970s and 1980s markets became more difficult. Products and variants on stock could not be sold, and long production times made it difficult to make the kind of products and product variants that could be sold within a given time limit.

This problem was already latent in the 1960s as Danish firms survived even then by operating with a wide range and variety of products. After the crisis this range and variety have been extended. Company E illustrates the problem that arose. On the one hand, they continued to stockpile; large intermediate stores created full utilisation of capacity and production was organised according to sales prognoses. On the other hand, rush orders were constantly zig-zagged through all the departments, with the result that other series were interrupted and conversion time skyrocketed. Eventually production based on sales prognoses ended up half a year behind schedule. It was no wonder that company E felt that their capacity was too small.

'Just-in-time' (JIT) philosophy (and the Danish version) has made it possible for a large number of firms to view the problem in other ways. The problem of capacity arose by keeping the machines and personnel continually occupied with the aid of intermediate stores and sales prognoses. If it were possible to produce what was being sold instead and get it through the factory in a short time, it would be easier to utilise the existing capacity, decrease warehousing costs, avoid stocking obsolete components, blanks and products. Research and development would consequently gain flexibility in that the stock would not act as a heavy, conservative force. But this sounds like a general attack on Fordism's principles of management and work.

One way of changing production has been to gather various machines, welding equipment, assembly apparatus, etc., together in one group that produces all the stages in one or more products, often in many different varieties. Factories become, in principle, a number of small, relatively independent factories, each producing its own blanks and assembling its own product groups. This situation occurred in companies R, G and I, and was being implemented in company E. Company I's plant comprised four small factories: a pump factory, a valve factory, a pipe-fitting factory and a component factory. The component factory is broken down into a number of smaller groups, each in charge of every stage in the production of special components. One of these groups would typically consist of four men, a CNC lathe, a traditional milling machine and a polishing machine.

The process at company H was a bit different. They moved different kinds of machines together in the various departments so that the individual worker—when handed a blank—could take the piece to different machines and process it completely before handing it on again.

This reorganisation implies that a relatively small group of skilled and semi-skilled workers under the leadership of a foreman can handle the whole manufacturing schedule of a product that previously had to go through a long line of foremen and departments, with a lot of intermediary transport and subsequent delays. They can distribute the work between themselves, move men around from one place to another if a bottleneck should arise, and plan their work according to a comprehensive estimate. But big problems naturally arise in the wake of such changes. Piece rates become inexpedient because the important thing is to increase cohesion within the group, rather than to have the individual worker on maximal operative capacity. Producing on order, as opposed to stockpiling, entails new arrangement, new programs, etc., within the individual production group or mini-factory. Conversion and resetting time thus become more critical than machining time, and it is no wonder that CNC machines and machining centres have become the ideal tool for such production groups.

Company I exemplifies how such machines can be used in an extremely flexible way. As the sales of a particular product or variant increases, there is either too much or too little capacity in the various mini-factories. By moving the machines around—inserting two CNC machines here, three there, and a single machine somewhere else—and connecting them to fixed installations which can be dropped down from the ceiling (ventilation, electricity, compressed air), company I has been able to adapt capacity to sales in the respective areas. In this environment, a large integrated FMS complex surrounded by all this versatility would seem like a boulder among vines.

The factory has been transformed into a production laboratory which is constantly being recombined in new ways, disassembled and moved around to be regrouped in another location. In a factory like this, the basis for the organisation of labour is constantly changing, and the premises for the expedient arrangement of labour vary from group to group.

The image of a 'production laboratory' is also enhanced by the fact that product development and improvement, and the development of new production methods and arrangements, take place within the factory itself. Consequently, production and development do not become separate and final. Production workers naturally participate in making new things, changing old products, revising and arranging production. Perhaps this factor is not irrelevant when estimating the validity of the general assumption that Denmark's R & D expenses are low compared with its GNP. It is much easier to calculate the R & D expenses when it takes place in special departments.

The organisation of labour concerning CNC machines does not follow a fixed and predictable pattern either. Two CNC machines were placed together with a skilled worker responsible for everything from production planning to machine setting, operation, insertion and extrusion of blanks, tool purchase and repair, machine maintenance, etc. A similar processing unit in another place in the factory consisted of three CNC machines, where the work was divided between an operator and a machine setter/programmer. Finally, a former metal worker acted as a consultant for all the skilled machine setters, who, with his help and supervision, programmed their own respective machines.

A student of industrial relations could easily identify all types of work organisation in company I. In one place he could find fulfilling work, and in another an almost Taylorist monotony for an operator who, due to the division of labour, is not allowed to do the programming. In one area the workers are rotated, whereas in another they remain in fixed positions. If anything, company I reveals that work—in order to be expediently organised—must be arranged differently, according to the conditions at hand. From the employees' point of view, company I often undergoes changes, and whoever wants to change from a monotonous job to a more challenging one can easily do this, and, in fact, is encouraged to do so. But our analysis of the firm also revealed that the employees are made up of different groups with different desires. One-third wanted to learn something new and find new challenges, whereas the rest wanted a job that was fairly routine and easy to learn.

Due to changes in the firm's work organisation, it is now easier to make the work more challenging and unified. Whereas a skilled worker wanting varying and challenging jobs previously felt himself forced into a monotonous and disruptive position, an unskilled worker might now feel pressure to undergo new training, job rotation, and new adjustment. But there is still room for both workers who desire challenge and those who prefer routine.

This tendency applies not only within processing. Company I's assemblers, who are responsible for assembling total pumps and valves, have to be able to tell whether different parts can be joined and to test them, as well as to plan the day's work in an expedient manner, so that reasonable sizes of series are run together, and rush orders get through on time.

The same phenomenon can be observed in the changes in company D, who established for the first time a proper assembly line in their new factory. The problem was that the workers at the different stations were to put 'the same gadget' into different products, so that every time a new 'box' came to the station it was a new and different job. Only two years after this assembly line was established, it was split up into three separate lines, each with its own product group. In the future they plan for each man to assemble 'his own product', and they have developed a 'one-man factory', equipped with a hydraulic lifting table, assembly tools and parts. These 'one-man factories' are mounted on wheels, so that they can be combined in groups of varying sizes, depending on the need for capacity within the different products. Once again the goal is twofold: first the individual worker ought, in principle, to be able to work independently of the rest of the organisation; second, the factory should be able to be constructed, disassembled and readjusted in a new form in a short period of time, so that capacity can be used where it is needed.

Company F has plans to install a casting cell, consisting of casting machinery, filling automats for moulding material, measuring equipment to control the machines, in addition to handling automats for removing casting blanks, and finally, an automat for lubricating forms between castings. This modernisation will relieve the founder of the tasks of removing cast blanks, lubricating forms, and adjusting cycle time for processing. On the other hand, it will reintegrate a number of functions which at present are divided among several employees. The founder will be responsible for quality control, and, to a certain extent when changing series, mounting and dismounting of casting forms. His job will thus become to a large extent a matter of building up casting cells and controlling the quality of what is produced by the automatic machines.

These examples have several attributes in common: production must be frequently converted to form new combinations, and the individual worker has to be able to grasp and control a synthesis of naturally and expediently defined job assignments in such a way that he can plan his work as efficiently as possible. This step has meant a break with Taylorism and monotony in all cases, and has resulted in economising on conversion times instead of on operation time.

Danish firms' approaches to flexibility during the 'Sturm und Drang' period of the 1970s and 1980s seem then to have been threefold: to make the individual shop as independent of the rest of the organisation as possible; to make the individual employee responsible for the quality and organisation of his own work; and to ensure that the individual components can be converted as quickly as possible. But this approach has not been consciously arrived at, nor in universal collusion. The road to this approach was different for each firm. In company I it was accomplished as a 'fairy-tale' of participation and cooperation between bottom and the top; in company D as a 'drama', where a new Fordist factory had to become shipwrecked before the firm realised the extent of its dependency on flexibility and on its employees' cooperativeness; company F is still at the 'crossroads' of management's ambitions in one direction, and the employees' low expectations and morale—stemming from a systematic Taylorisation of work during the 1960s—in the other.

Technological renewal in the transition toward the flexible organisation of production

Technology plays an important role in this change, in that CNC technology makes it considerably easier to reorganise shop production and give individuals more autonomy in their work, thus facilitating cooperation.

Traditional tooling machines were certainly also universal machines, but they often had a much more narrow field of activity than modern CNC machines. These can set up in one jig what formerly required many different machines. Modification of programs facilitates frequent changing of small series. It would have been difficult for firms to separate the old special purpose workshops and merge the various types of machines into the present product/production groups without CNC machines. It would quite simply have required too many different machines and given a poor utilisation of capacity. CNC technology also permits a relatively low utilisation of capacity, the objective here being that production should run smoothly without bottlenecks, and that the necessary tools are present.

Many of the firms we visited stressed the difference between Danish and foreign machine shops. In Denmark entire factories are modernised with CNC (welding and tube-processing machines, lathes, cutters, drills and punches), whereas many foreign firms modernise one department with the latest FMS equipment, letting the rest continue with obsolete machines and equipment.

Taking company I as an example, it is difficult to see how, in the period in question, FMS could have been chosen as a viable solution. Machines have been moved around and regrouped. Some sectors of production were closed down, some were transferred to sub-contractors, and new products were introduced. Where capacity requirements rose, production groups could be complemented with a CNC machine or two. If an FMS installation had been able to meet these requirements, it would have required the planning and programming efforts of a whole group of engineers, and the firm should have been able to calculate a market that no one was able to predict. Isolated CNC machines, on the other hand, do permit this flexibility. A foundry (company F) introduced CNC machines in order to cast in larger series and then make variants by finishing in the processing shop. Further steps toward FMS would also in this case be contrary to their interests.

The principle in CNC investment is, then, that smaller machine groups have become relatively independent of the other areas of production and, in addition, can produce and be adjusted relatively autonomously. This necessitates a degree of independence from the other areas, which is in contrast to the close integration of machines that is characteristic of FMS.

A similar phenomenon is seen in the way computers are used in administration. Almost all the firms in the study have introduced a computer system which, in principle, can keep track of raw materials and component parts, items under production, production capacity, sold goods, delivery dates and stock. Some of the firms have not been very successful in implementing and using such systems. Firms which, on the other hand, have been successful are able to survey their various products and variants with ease. For these firms, the computer has proven to be a precondition for the introduction of JIT as opposed to stockpiling, as with a manual system it would be impossible to control and enter such complex and extensive amounts of data within the critical delivery dates.

In those firms where such systems are functioning, either the foreman (company F) or the individual production worker (company I) uses the computer system as a reference for organising his department or his own jobs. By using the computer system, it is possible to determine if there are enough stores to start a given production program, or if a planned production program has taken into consideration the relevant delivery dates, or if it is possible and expedient to gather production in large or small series. The computer system thus becomes the single factor that makes it possible for the increasingly autonomous worker to plan his own work according to expediency and his time priorities. Whether or not such a relationship is achieved, however, depends upon a number of other factors. Is the computer system, for example, relevant to the individual employee's work? Are there appropriate data procedures? Is there any risk of computer sabotage? Can the system be integrated with wage systems? Several of the firms have apparently had difficulties in achieving the proper relationship, but it was a common opinion that the system should be used as a reference, rather than to give the individual foreman or operator direct orders. The system ought to make it possible to organise the work in an expedient manner but not to directly determine the job sequence. The computer, therefore, becomes a tool that permits the individual employee to attune his increasingly independent job to the work flow. In a fully integrated FMS installation, this relationship has to be reversed: the individual's job must be determined by the 'system', so that no incalculable consequences arise. Company C attempted to establish precisely this kind of regimentation. Our findings show that a specific computer system or production layout cannot be set up against people's inclination.

Product development, the organisation of work and the future of FMS

JIT production makes sales and product development less dependent on what one already has in stock; it allows continuous product adaptations, introduction of new products and variants, etc. This new-found freedom is countered, however, by another tendency. Seven of the 13 firms we visited had systematically begun to 'modularise' their products, so that more types of products and variants could be constructed from a set of common building blocks. In connection with this 'modularisation' it had proved possible to introduce automatic flexible technology in a special sector of production in a few of the firms.

A shipbuilder had formerly placed pipe layout in the side of the ship, but had gone over to laying them in channels under the corridors. This permits 70% of the ship's piping to be standardised. A large CNC machine had been installed in the pipe shop that cut, threaded, bent and ground these standard pipes, which varied in length, diameter and curvature. The CNC machine ran these pipes with the aid of interactive CAD/CAM programs.

A few other firms developed products that were built according to the building block principle, i.e. products which the *customer* could construct and reconstruct with the help of standard modules. These standard modules could be produced on relatively automatic machines. Company L developed a new modular system for building wiring (installation) cabinets with eight possible door sizes. The shelves and construction rods could be combined in different ways, so that any number of different cabinets could be constructed with these elements. To produce the doors for these cabinets, an immense CNC machine had been installed that could handle all the steps in the production (shearing, bending, and punching the sheets of metal). Merely by reprogramming and replacing a relatively small number of tools, the machine could shift from one door size to another.

The effects of this kind of CNC automatisation of standard components is interesting. The rest of the workshop (the tube shop in the shipyard mentioned above, for instance) subsequently gets only varying jobs, and always in small series. In these cases, CNC has been the *sine qua non* for the automatisation of standard production, as it is only by being able to range within a product family that enough jobs can be gathered together for this kind of production line. In addition, the CNC production flow mentioned above was custom built for the respective factories.

Among our sample there were two firms that were in the process of reviewing their productions with the intention of regrouping them in families in order to improve production on an FMS installation consisting of four machine centres connected to automatically programmed transport equipment. This case occurred in one of the firms after a systematic change in production to CNC technology and production groups. Consequently, they have already obtained a substantial number of the economic advantages of converting to FMS. Only if they were able to force production far beneath levels experienced in foreign firms with similar production would conversion be a rational solution. It seems, therefore, that the reorganisation of production, the splitting up of older workshops and the combining of production groups for special products constitute an alternative to FMS strategy, in that much of the taxonomy, the ability to adjust quickly and the fast production flow—which are the greatest advantages of FMS—can also be achieved by a combination of organisational renewal, use of CNC machines, and administrative computer systems.

This relatively organic and gradual strategy makes it possible to go further in automatisation, but the possibilities here are almost self-evident. Firm I illustrates this. Several areas had achieved such a high output that three CNC machines had to be frozen in one group, where they were used to produce a relatively fixed product family. In these machine groups a machine setter did set-ups, programming and run in, whereas an operator took care of feeding and removal of the pieces on all three machines. On many of these groups of CNC machines it would be expedient for company I to replace the operator with a robot and thus create an FMS cell. There were plans for this in a few areas, but not all. Such FMS cells would tie up the flexible CNC machines, which were already needed to run new products in other areas of the factory.

It was under consideration, therefore to replace groups of CNC machines with special machines—partly because they would be able to replace and release three CNC machines, and partly because special machines could be constructed for the same price as one CNC machine and run with a much higher production speed. They would thus pay for themselves within three to four years, so it would not matter if they were scrapped after a few years in action. The example is illustrative. In a few years, when robots become cheaper, are equipped with sensors and more flexible gripping mechanisms, and can be programmed to work with a large number of CNC systems and programs it will be natural for firm I to have a few robots standing by. Thereby, an FMS cell can be constructed when production in a certain area becomes sufficiently stable. If this stabilisation exceeds a certain level and appears to be persistent, it would be profitable to invest in a special machine to release CNC machines, robots and men for more varied and challenging work.

If company I constitutes a model factory, it shows that all forms of production organisation can coexist in a complex and changing combination within one and the same factory, at the same time. FMS will be represented— as robots and CNC machines organised in smaller cells—but will not necessarily constitute a dominant strain. On the other hand, the shipyard pipe shop and company L's production of wiring cabinets show that CNC machines can be custom built for a particular product area and can make it possible to automatise production with specific variants in a completely automatic system without actually comprising FMS.

UNSOLVED PROBLEMS AND THE NEED FOR TRAINING

Careers and training

The conclusion on development in the firms in our analysis can take two directions. One is to stress the absence of FMS installations and indicate the preconditions for a reversal of this tendency. The second is to attempt to explain what actually has occurred and to try to reinforce the forces and institutions that have supported this development, as well as to solve the consequent problems that seem to arise.

The paucity of FMS is undoubtedly attributable to the relatively weak position that civil engineers, programmers and production planners have within the hierarchies of Danish businesses. Compared with other countries, little professionalisation has occurred in this field, so it is the experience of existing workshop organisation that influences continuing development projects rather than professional ideas on FMS, CIM, etc. If this is to be changed, it would require increased training of engineers and programmers at high level technical institutions and, furthermore, education of operators to train them to intervene, reprogram, and maintain established FMS installations, whose operation they must ensure with a minimum of interference.

The other standpoint is to view the developments (extensive use of CNC technology, reorganisation of production, changes in sales strategy, product development efforts) as the expression of a flexibility that is based on the individual employee's, the individual firm's, and the individual region's ability to adapt and to gain new knowledge as well as their desire and ability to try new possibilities. In other words, the second viewpoint is to see the actual development toward flexible specialisation as an expression of a capacity to adapt, which is supported—not by a limited class of professionals—but by a large body of employees. Taking the latter point of view, the question becomes: What has produced this capacity for flexibility and adaptation and made possible the assimilation of new technology along a wide front, with so few problems? These merits must be confronted with the problems that have arisen and will continue to arise due to the environmentally turbulent 'Sturm und Drang' period that Danish businesses are undergoing today.

We have already connected this capacity for flexibility and adaptation with the hypothesis that under the Fordist superstructure or surface of many firms an organisation of craft production has survived as a 'hidden' organisation within the organisation. This craft organisation has provided foremen and skilled and unskilled workers with a relatively high level of autonomy in planning work and creating natural patterns of cooperation, and given the individual a broad and comprehensive grasp of production which has made it possible to change production in step with changing needs. Naturally, such an assertion cannot be statistically documented. But recent studies indicate that the conditions of work in Denmark have certain characteristics that substantiate this hypothesis.

Hofstede's (1984) comparative analysis of 'work-related values' characterises Danish work culture and production culture by (1) an extremely low 'power distance'; (2) a large capacity to accept insecurity in one's job (activities and the job are not rigidly determined in writing, varying interaction on new assignments, high level of ambitions); (3) a relatively high degree of individualism (the individual employee desires challenge and the opportunity to show initiative and therefore is allocated a relatively high degree of responsibility for the area of his own work); (4) a radical shift toward 'feminine' values (emphasis on pleasant atmosphere, security in one's position and cooperation as compared to 'masculine' values, such as advancement, high income, education and the need to keep up to date). In a culture like this, 'success' would necessarily pertain to a collective, to human relations and to the environment and there is a preference to work together in a loosely structured organisation that changes its image organically in accordance with whatever one is occupied with at the moment ('the village market' organisation). The hierarchic supervision and coordination of Fordism and the rigid division of labour of Taylorism are, in all respects, in contrast to the cultural pattern that, according to Hofstede's analysis, is characteristic of Denmark.

Why this production culture arose and is retained seems to depend on two factors: first, the general level of education in Denmark, including the level of industrial training, is distinctly higher than in most other countries; second, career patterns in industry are tremendously open. The findings of Maurice et al. (1982) in their comparison of French and German patterns of interplay between educational systems and business organisations cannot, of course, be directly applied here, but our case studies indicate that Denmark resembles more the German model than the French.

A spiralling relationship between the access to and level of education on the one hand and career patterns on the other is substantiated in our case studies. When an apprentice becomes a journeyman his education does not necessarily end; a multitude of possibilities is open to him. In addition to courses at vocational schools, the choice of evening school courses is extensive and diverse. In many regions it is possible to take courses at business and technical schools in the evening. If he wants to aim for a formal technical degree this opportunity is also open. The engineering college is an example of the kind of programme that many skilled workers choose after a few years' experience as journeyman, foreman, production technician, master craftsman.

There are many reasons why craft workers continue their education. Career interests are one, but often the need for new challenges or the desire to live up to new assignments motivates this move. Cases of skilled workers gaining interest in computer technology and studying in their free time—either in private study or at night school—to become self-taught experts, are representative in our study. But interestingly enough, they did not follow courses or training programmes which would give them any formal competence in the form of diplomas, etc.

Whether the motivation for education is career-oriented or dominated by professional curiosity cannot be ascertained from our material. It does show, however, that many craft workers eventually fill high positions in the firm's hierarchy after ongoing education, different kinds of job experience, or an engineering degree. Our findings are insufficient, in that this question has not been systematically examined, but we know that the administrative directors of two firms, the technical directors of six, and the production managers of seven firms did advance from the rank and file of skilled workers. In addition, a considerable number of production technicians and almost all the foremen had started out as craft workers and 'rose in the ranks'. The same holds for the operations managers of the three firms that were studied in depth. One operations manager had a background in warehousing; another had previously been a machine technician.

Whereas recruitment for higher levels in French firms aims at university graduates or people with other professional educations (Maurice et al., 1982), in Denmark, as in Germany, it takes place largely among skilled blue-collar workers. This recruiting of management among the rank and file seldom occurs in one and the same firm. The technical and administrative directors we interviewed had gone through many firms and many kinds of work on their way to their present positions. This was true for most of the production managers as well, but for some of them and for a large proportion of the owner/managers and production technicians, there had been gradual advancement in the same firm.

The higher levels in the hierarchy work together with craft workers who often have as high qualifications but in other fields (new technology, programming, drafting, technical school courses), and therefore it is no wonder that there exists an egalitarian cooperation between supervisors and their subordinates. This seems to be the case, especially in firms with a large proportion of skilled labour, whereas other firms with a large proportion of unskilled workers—company F, for example—appear to have problems in communicating.

The interaction between educational systems, career patterns and the organisation of work has, in several foreign analyses (Maurice et al., 1982; Sorge and Warner, 1986, for example) pointed out the importance of a country's production culture—for instance in the introduction of new technology or in the further development of work organisation. We have attempted to sketch the contours of a similar pattern for Denmark, but we could not go beyond contours, as our results are based on too few case studies. On the other hand, however, they have revealed one thought-provoking phenomenon: craft workers and foremen have apparently been allotted a high degree of autonomy in the arrangement and execution of their work, and will likely continue to do so in the future. In addition, the career patterns and perspectives of the old craftsman-like forms of production (from apprentice to journeyman to master craftsman) are not only represented in the many small firms in Denmark, they are also representative of career patterns in medium-sized firms, where a journeyman can see his peer in the highest positions.

This allocates to the skilled worker a central position in the firm and a role in its changes. It not only infers a considerable degree of flexibility, as many new and unsolved projects can be laid out on the 'floor', but also presents a number of characteristic problems.

In none of the firms, at least in our sample, did skilled workers allow unskilled workers to program CNC machines. Apparently, a strict line is drawn at precisely this point in the stratification of the firm. This is due to the fact that journeymen have been able to gather a fairly wide spectrum of job tasks under their jurisdiction such as planning, set-ups, programming production, repairs and maintenance. Unskilled workers functioned primarily as operators, inserting and removing blanks in processing, adjusting machines and programs as well as checking tolerances.

There is no doubt that skilled workers regard this delineation as important, in that it maintains a standard of education 'on the floor'. The unskilled workers appear at first glance to be the victims in this struggle, which is ostensibly being fought to preserve the occupational autonomy that the skilled workers associate with the standard of education. The question is: to what degree are unskilled workers victimised? Our case studies indicate that delineation is an important factor in the formal struggle for the organisation and distribution of work, but that this formality conceals another reality. Different unions have contracts to perform specific categories of work, but if an employee wants to change jobs, all else being equal, it can be accomplished by having the worker change unions. This change apparently goes both ways: a journeyman blacksmith had joined a semi-skilled labour union in order to be an operator on a CNC punch at company D; a caster at company F became an adult apprentice (being paid as a semi-skilled worker) to train as a toolmaker in order to work later with CNC; a newly hired machinist at company I had received his basic training in running CNC from the unskilled operator, whom he would later be programming and doing set-ups for. In a number of cases, it was mentioned that unskilled workers could get certain types of skilled jobs if they changed over to the metal workers' union, so that the firm could continue to pay skilled wages for the job in question.

The difference between *de jure* rigidity and *de facto* flexibility in the problem of delineating job areas raises extensive problems of interpretation, also in terms of determining the structure of the job market in Denmark. It is a well-known phenomenon that the two educational systems—vocational school/apprentice training and courses for semi-skilled workers—compete with each other. But there are no analyses of whether courses for semi-skilled workers are gradually being combined in a coherent syllabus, which subsequently provides the unskilled worker with the same type of knowledge and understanding as the formally trained craft workers. The assumption that courses for semi-skilled workers were only intended to sluice workers from one routine job to another after a short retraining period is, in all probability, no longer correct, as the courses are often combined by the individual, who is qualifying himself in a specific field, and can then skirt the *de jure* systems and upgrade himself from unskilled to skilled worker. Unfortunately, analyses of this alternative form of education are not available.

Our studies show that the formal complex of problems surrounding delineation become a real problem in firms that try to organise work in conflict with the journeymen's notion of expedience in the planning of work; where the employees are consulted in working this out, the problem is 'taken care of'.

Education and new technology

Nothing in our material indicates that there have been difficulties in introducing CNC technology and using it in a relevant manner in Danish firms. Skilled workers have apparently been able to learn to program machines in a relatively short period of time. All the firms have had enough skilled workers who were interested in programming and learned it either by self-study or at evening school. The generally high level of education in Denmark and the country's renowned faculty for organising education for people in general seem to be an important factor in explaining this phenomenon.

Training in the use of CNC machines has, as a rule, gone through two phases: first, participation in a course of one to two weeks' duration, arranged by the supplier; then the worker is turned loose on the machine to experiment with it. In this latter phase a slow, individual accumulation of experience is begun, that apparently requires that the individual worker becomes closely attached to working with one or two specific machines over a long time span. During this period, the worker gives and receives tips, solutions and experience to and from his colleagues in the factory, and a 'mini-commune' apparently arises among those who are working on CNC machines. This 'mini-commune' is characterised by competition as to who can get the machines to operate more 'smartly' than the others.

During the late 1970s and the early 1980s, a number of skilled workers in the various firms achieved an extensive education and experience in running

CNC machines. Our investigations indicate that they have become virtuosi in their area, that they master and develop new possibilities in CNC technology, such that they now have command over a tool that can be used for flexible and demanding assignments. In addition, they can plan their work expediently and have the ability to intervene in operations, programming, tools, etc. They exert pressure to implement new improvements. Of course, the effect of this is that the firms are reluctant to move these employees to other jobs. They also accept that skilled workers maintain a distance from operators, who are only permitted to insert and remove pieces, whereas machine maintenance, programming, etc., become the domain of these skilled workers. The results of this can be ominous. A division has grown up between those who command and those who have never tried to work with CNC machines. The firms' job market has thus been split in two: those who have gained access to the new machines, and those who have not.

This division is reinforced by the fact that vocational training courses for semi-skilled workers and technical schools in general lag behind in purchasing, use, and command of the new CNC technology. All of the apprentices who were interviewed, received a scant and merely theoretical introduction to CNC at vocational school. Most of the technical schools could not afford to buy their own CNC machines, or else the teachers were only able to run them on the most elementary tasks. In most of the firms, the apprentices would be working with a skilled worker on a CNC machine for a month, but this was, in the opinion of the apprentices interviewed, much too short a time to be able to control the technology.

The result is that CNC divided the internal and external job market in two, and the effects of this are not yet clear. The problem can, however, become overwhelming. One possibility is that the firms will allow these qualified craft workers to follow a traditional career pattern and advance them to white-collar status to ensure that they are not lured away to other companies by the promise of better positions and higher wages. Programming competency would in this case become increasingly alienated from the shop and become a stage in the hierarchical division of labour.

Another possibility—which can be difficult to separate from the first on a formal level—would be to give in to this group's requests for new challenges in the form of courses and training time on CAD/CAM systems, for example. They would thus become bridgeheads for an even stronger disintegration of the division of labour between white- and blue-collar technicians. This way they would gradually pass on the CNC jobs to new workers, who they would then train, as they went on themselves to new and more challenging tasks. This pattern was particularly discernible in company I.

The choice between these and other options is one for management as well as labour; it is a question of perspectives concerning life and career, but it is also a choice that can exert great influence on how flexibility and work organisation can be connected in the future. Vocational training can have a significant role in this decision. By mass producing CNC 'virtuosi', it can become economically feasible for firms to let programming take place on the 'floor' and offer even greater challenges to skilled and unskilled workers who possess the necessary qualifications. Even though certain groups of skilled labour have obvious advantages in keeping these new qualifications within a narrow circle, organised labour also has interests—at local, regional and national levels—not only in spreading the mastery of this new technology to other skilled workers, but also in initiating semi-skilled workers in the 'art'. This eventuality would amount to a struggle against two evils at once: 'dualisation' of the labour market as a whole, and hierarchical stratification of work organisation in the individual firms.

Top management versus intermediate management

Whereas the transition to CNC technology and the conversion of factories toward group production and more autonomous workshops has taken place with a remarkable lack of drama and turmoil as far as the production workers are concerned, foremen seem to have become a virtual 'parking-lot' for problems.

It was predominantly administrative and technical directors and production managers who introduced 'just-in-time' (JIT) ideology into Danish firms. These executives brought with them extensive professional links, varied career backgrounds and perhaps even a degree in engineering. It is from this group that the initiative to reorganise production toward flexibility and introduce workshop-programmed CNC machines, as well as to give the employees more responsibility in the planning and execution of their work, has come. When these managers have been able to establish direct communication and cooperation with workers on the floor, reorganisation has been effected without difficulty, especially when the proportion of skilled to unskilled labour has been high. But this reorganisation has subsequently sidetracked the group of internally recruited foremen and even some production managers. When reorganisation has been relegated to these internally recruited managers, things have apparently gone haywire. This happened, for example, at company D, where the production manager neglected to involve the workers in planning the layout of production, and maintained his faith in a Fordist solution. At company F the foremen's power to grant privileges places them in direct opposition to change—in a firm that is in dire need of reform.

There can be many reasons for internally recruited foremen and production managers to oppose changes. One is certainly that they used to maintain specific efficiency norms in their own functionally divided shops, and through this ability have been able to win the respect of their superiors. Another is that they have become experts in the kind of processing that they have specialised in, and have been able to exploit this experience, in relations with both white- and blue-collar workers. In the 'schizophrenia' of the 1950s and 1960s between Fordist-oriented management on the one hand, and a form of work-organisation that was based more on craftsmanship than on Taylorism on the other, this intermediate group of managers were able to hold their own against top level management as well as the worker on the shop floor. Their deep knowledge of production won them the respect of management, while the workers were kept in line by the use of time and method studies, and by granting or withholding privileges, i.e. good piece rates to those they worked well with, and bad ones to those they wanted to get rid of. They were able to distribute assignments in such a way that those who wanted variety and change could have it, and those who preferred routine work were given the steady jobs. They seem to have been good at creating this kind of balance in their shops, as we have heard few, if any, critical comments about them from the workers.

The combination of craftsmanlike authority on the one hand, and the application of Fordist discipline and efficiency-promoting policies on the other, have made it relatively easy to live with this dichotomy between craft organisation on the floor and Fordist rationality and philosophy upstairs in the office. It is presumably due to this balancing act that foremen have managed to maintain a flexibility in their work organisation based on crafts-manship in spite of Taylorist attacks from higher levels of technical and administrative directors during the 1960s. As such, they presumably deserve a good deal of the credit for Danish firms being able to maintain production forms based on craftsmanship in the face of Fordist institutions in the job market and the vogue of Fordism among management. Changes in work organisation, production philosophy, the purchase of new technology and the implementation of computers in administration, have, however, radically altered things for these foremen and production managers.

The foremen are now put in charge of a group of employees representing several crafts, of which the foremen only know one or a few; the workers work with CNC technologies of which the foremen only have a superficial knowledge, and therefore foremen find themselves in a situation where they have lost the professional and technical foundations of their authority. If the firm also changes the wage systems (an extreme example would be to fixed, undifferentiated hourly wages), and if the workers are allowed to plan their own daily and weekly production with the aid of an administrative computer system, then foremen lose the 'whip' of rate fixing and job allotment. They will have difficulty in seeing the role of their jobs at all.

The administrative and technical directors and production managers who have initiated the changes have, on the contrary, a point they want to get across about the need for a challenge in the foreman role, which they themselves experienced a need for when they were on the shop floor. They have been able to transform this message through a role, wherein they create new projects and change the flow of work and the structure of cooperation in direct cooperation with the employees. In this role, they have pushed aside the group of intermediate managers: foremen, and even production managers, who have not been able to change their ways.

Many managers responsible for the changes expressed a desire to employ former school teachers as foremen. The new qualifications for these positions include ability to understand people, and a capacity for motivation and interaction within the framework of the administrative and managerial systems. Is this also a confrontation with the remnants of hierarchy that was established in connection with the 'concealed' organisation of labour? The problem with foremen is an important signal that the traditional stratification, which has survived since production was based on craftsmanship, and which has gained a new meaning in modern industrial society, is no longer viable. The question is whether foremen can maintain their formal position by finding new roles through education, or whether their position as 'middlemen' will disappear. No matter what the outcome, the organisation of labour will have changed.

To determine whether the solution to this problem relies on education via specially designed courses and examinations would require an extensive review of the possibilities that already exist within the educational system. A technically oriented education, such as in Germany, would merely magnify existing problems. The problem is that it is usually skilled workers who have a distinct interest in their craft, who rise in the ranks to become foremen. Very few are interested in psychology, education, administration, computerised administrative systems, or management. Some may hold honorary offices in their spare time, giving the kind of experience that is useful, but the majority are primarily highly qualified craftsmen without any particular qualities for leadership. The advancement to foremen, therefore, is often connected with a loss of job satisfaction.

In contrast to those who rise to foremen, workers becoming active in the labour movement often display an interest in education, leadership, psychology and motivation—but because of the nature of their preoccupation with the labour movement, they are often in direct opposition to foremen.

CONCLUDING REMARKS

Given the wish to increase workers' basic understanding of what they are engaged in and their ability to relate their part to the whole production process, the companies encourage educational ambitions, which fall in line with the skilled workers' work-relation. However, the new managerial types see little or no response to their desires for job rotation, aimed at creating a workforce which is flexible enough to be put on new jobs when the sale of products and their variants vary. Much resistance to job rotation is explained by institutional barriers such as agreements over borders between unions, by the companies' own organisational sins such as good and bad piecework, irrational division between blue- and white-collar jobs, but this is not the whole explanation. When a person wishes to change jobs within a company, these barriers can be overcome.

To be able to understand why a large number of employees wish to remain 'at their post', to 'keep their nose to the grindstone', involves a thorough understanding of the human psyche. But the question is whether or not the desire to stick with a specific job is a consequence of old Fordist styles of management and concepts of efficiency in the post-war period. The workers were trained to be efficient at a specific routine and could easily lose money and prestige by changing to new jobs.

The Fordist work rhythm has created a 'routine-aiming personality', which is in conflict with the new and varying job structures which follow from the new management's desires for a change in production organisation. It is hardly surprising that the companies in our study are running into a cascade of problems, which they can only answer by 'education'. The ever increasing demand for flexibility is creating, for everyone involved, new situations, where old roles and existing routines are not sufficient. Education has become the codeword to cover all these situations—education in new technology, education in basic understanding, education for responsibility, education to be able to understand the totality through its parts, ability to motivate, work together, to plan and complete a project, education to job rotation, and so on.

Norbert Weiner (1967), made the observation a long time ago that with the Taylorisation of mass production, humanity risked losing within a single century the enormous capacity for adjustment, change, variation and new possibilities which it had taken nature millions of years to create:

> Those who would organize us according to permanent individual functions and permanent individual restrictions condemn the human race to move at much less than half-steam. They throw away nearly all our human possibilities and by limiting the modes in which we may adapt ourselve to future contingencies, they reduce our chances for a reasonable long existence on this earth (Weiner, 1967, p. 52).

The problem for an industry moving toward flexible specialisation is that they are in need of people working at full capacity, while what they inherit from the Fordist factories are personalities tuned to half-steam. No wonder our studies show that many problems are involved in finding an assertive, self-conscious form of flexible specialisation, when factories themselves create people who resist change. But factories are not alone in this reluctance. Within Danish society, people who are 'forced to work in factories' expect jobs to be specialised, monotonous and meaningless. And though primary schools have changed radically within past decades, they still socialise students to discipline. So society equips those who are to become factory workers, with expectations and desires that are mediocre, and in industries moving toward flexible specialisation, many members of management are disappointed with the human resources they employ.

Apprentices beginning their education at a vocational school see their education more as a sentence than as a challenging possibility. Behind them is an educational path paved with failures, classifying them as stupid. According to the workers we interviewed, apprentices' vocational schools treat them as fools; the instruction level at these schools demands so little that it is necessary for them to act up or to sleep just to pass the time. And this encourages teachers to continue, with a good conscience, in the boring, routine, which inspires neither apprentice nor teacher. This mutual reinforcing behaviour strengthens teachers' conviction in the need for more discipline and to concentrate on single assignments, instead of an understanding of total work processes. If there is anything that a student at a vocational school learns it is how to 'file' a piece of metal.

On the other hand, what the student does not learn anything about at all, is how the divisions of a complete production process are interrelated, and how it might be possible to rationalise his work according to the whole. And as was mentioned previously, there is no possibility of satisfying his curiosity about CNC machines. Digging deeper it gets even worse: What do apprentices in the metal industry learn about metallurgy, atomic structures, etc.? What do they learn about the vicious circles in cooperation with their colleagues? Do they learn anything about learning?

To change these conditions requires more than new courses at vocational schools. But new institutional buildings are not necessary. What is needed is quality. It is necessary to change the mode of learning, to create higher expectations for jobs in factories, and to let these expectations blossom into demands that continue the direction that some of the companies we visited have only begun.

Address for correspondence:

Institute of Economic Planning, Roskilde University Centre, PO Box 260, DK-4000 Roskilde, Denmark.

REFERENCES

Hofstede, G. (1984) *Culture's Consequences. International Differences in Work-related Values*. Beverly Hills: Sage.

Maurice, M., Sellier, F., and Silvestre, J. J. (1982) *Politique d'Éducation et Organisation Industrielle en France et Allemagne*. Paris: PUF.

Noble, D. F. (1979) Social choice in machine design: The case of automatically controlled machine tools. In Zimbalist, A. (ed.), *Case Studies in the Labour Process*. New York: Monthly Review Press.

Piore, M. J., and Sabel, C. F. (1981) Italian Small Business Development: Lessons for US Industrial Policy. MIT Paper No. 288, Dept of Economics, Cambridge, Mass.

Piore, M. J., and Sabel, C. F. (1984) *The Second Industrial Divide*. New York: Basic Books.

Sabel, C. F. (1982) *Work and Politics*. Cambridge: CUP.

Sorge, A., and Warner, M. (1986) *Comparative Factory Organization*. Aldershot: Gower.

Wiener, N. (1967) *The Human Use of Human Beings*. Boston (Mass.): Houghton Mifflin.

13. Flexible Manufacturing Systems and Cells in the Federal Republic of Germany

Jutta Fix-Sterz[1], Gunter Lay[1], Rainer Schultz-Wild[2] and Jürgen Wengel[1]

[1]*Fraunhofer Institut für Systemtechnik und Innovationsforschung (ISI), Karlsruhe and* [2]*Institut für Sozialwissenschaftliche Forschung eV (ISF), Munich*

SUMMARY

The rapid development of microelectronics and the associated development of the information technologies is bringing about changes in an increasing number of fields of application. Thus, in the field of industrial production, we can expect to see fundamental changes in organisational structure on the basis of the new technologies, such as computer aided design (CAD) and manufacturing (CAM), together with the interlinking of these functions in the next few decades. These ideas are currently being discussed extensively under the heading of 'the factory of the future' or 'the factory of 2000'. The effects of these technologies on profitability, work organisation, work qualification and vocational training, together with the forms they can be given and alternative concepts are—especially in international comparisons—still largely undetermined. Various lines of technical/organisational development in these new technologies are beginning to emerge. Alternative effects can be expected from these systems, and are described in this chapter.

INTRODUCTION

The concept of 'flexible manufacturing systems' was introduced in 1967. The term was understood to cover a series of manufacturing devices interlinked by a common control and transport system in such a way that it was possible, on the one hand, to achieve automatic manufacturing and, on the other hand, to carry out various processing tasks on different workpieces within a given area (Dolezalek and Ropohl, 1970). Since it is not possible in the short term, because of technological and economic problems, to completely meet the requirement of automating the components of the system, the definition given must be interpreted as constituting an objective, which is achieved to differ-

New Technology and Manufacturing Management   Edited by M. Warner, W. Wobbe and P. Brödner
Published 1990 by John Wiley & Sons Ltd

ent degrees by the utilisation of flexible automation systems. Consequently, the present investigation is based on a definition which comprises both flexible manufacturing systems in the full sense of the term, i.e. multi-machine systems, and flexible manufacturing cells (single-machine systems).

This is the background against which the Fraunhofer Institut für System-technik und Innovationsforschung (ISI) and the Institut für Sozialwissen-schaftliche Forschung (ISF), on behalf of the Commission of the European Communities and additionally supported by the Ministry for Research and Technology of the Federal Republic of Germany, carried out a study which could also be used in an international comparison of the dissemination and the economic and social effects of flexible manufacturing systems.

Within the framework of the task description given above, we carried out in Autumn 1985 an investigation into the current state of utilisation of flexible manufacturing systems and cells in the Federal Republic of Germany, the results of which are presented in this chapter. The enquiry concentrated on the metal cutting branch, since this type of manufacturing process can be considered as a pilot sector for the utilisation of FMS. It has been augmented and substantiated by case studies of companies operating FMS.

DEVELOPMENT OF FLEXIBLE MANUFACTURING SYSTEMS AND CELLS IN THE FEDERAL REPUBLIC OF GERMANY

Type and extent of utilisation of flexible manufacturing systems and cells (FMS/FMC)

Intensive examination of technical literature and references given by machine-tool manufacturers showed that in Autumn 1985 there were 278 FMS/FMC installations in 144 firms in the Federal Republic of Germany. Of these, 195 were flexible manufacturing cells and 83 multi-machine systems. The companies concerned were predominantly (68.9%) in the machine building industry. Other sectors, which were less strongly represented, are automobile industry (8.4%), aircraft and aerospace (3.4%), electrical equipment (5.9%), precision engineering and optical industry (3.4%) and iron, lead and tin products (3.4%).

An analysis of the firms according to the number of employees clearly shows that utilisation occurs particularly in fairly large organisations with more than 1000 employees (over 60% of the installations), and shows generally that there is increasingly frequent utilisation with an increase in company size. Consequently, flexible manufacturing systems and cells cur-rently constitute a technology which is of little significance for the large majority of small and medium-sized companies.

The great majority of the installations are flexible manufacturing cells

(70.1%). The categories of two-machine and three-to-five machine systems represent approximately equal shares (11%) while large-scale systems (more than five machines) constitute only 7% of the total. This distribution is in striking contrast to the distribution of system size recorded in an early phase of FMS/FMC deployment: at that time, over 70% of the FMS installations were large-scale systems. Thus there has been a definite trend towards the use of flexible manufacturing cells and smaller systems comprising up to five machines.

Analysis of the sizes of system installed in relation to the size of the organisation (number of employees) shows that the number of large enterprises (more than 1000 employees) in the total number of user companies falls off as the size of the system decreases. The large-scale enterprises—with systems having more than five machines—represent a share of almost 90%, while those with cell installations total only 56%. The more frequent installation of cells and smaller systems is thus closely associated with the increasing involvement of small and medium-sized companies in flexible manufacturing technology. With this overall picture of FMS/FMC installations in Germany as a background, the written questionnaire in the investigation mentioned above gave us details concerning 93 installations: 35 flexible manufacturing cells, 22 two-machine systems, 21 systems comprising three to five machines and 15 systems with more than five machines. Comparison of the user firms for these 93 installations with all FMS/FMC users in Germany on the basis of the manufacturing sector and the size of the firm (number of employees) showed no significant differences in sectoral distribution; on the basis of the distribution of firm size, smaller companies with fewer than 200 employees are somewhat under-represented.

More marked deviations occurred in the comparison of distribution of system size. Whereas with multi-machine systems some 70% of all groups were covered by the written questionnaire, the proportion of cells was only 18%. This deviation is due to two principal reasons:

— As was shown by the comparison of the firm size categories, answers were received less frequently from the smaller firms. However, smaller companies had principally installed only flexible manufacturing cells.
— Relatively large firms with several installations often filled in the questionnaire only in respect of their larger (i.e. multi-machine) installations and gave no information about the cells they had installed.

The result is that in the following quantitative assessments the data broken down by system size are representative, whereas average values for all installations are distorted by the differing responses given. These data must, therefore, not be considered as absolute values, if significant deviations do arise between the individual system size categories.

If we analyse the FMS/FMC in service in the German companies from which information was obtained by the questionnaire according to the year of installation, it will be seen that the first utilisation dated roughly from the year 1972. This first installation was an FMS used to manufacture large parts for printing machines in a system of 10 interlinked machine tools. In other countries, too, FMS were first used in the early 1970s; up to around 1980 deployment was slow. In 1980, the number first reached 14; Warnecke (1985) speaks of 25 systems in service in 1983. This was due partly to the poor market availability of FMS. The first systems installed were built according to the specific operational requirements of each particular user firm, and these conditions were normally not reproducible. A further hindrance to rapid introduction of FMS/FMC was the heavy expenditure in time and money for planning and introduction which resulted from the lack of existing examples. The high risk attached to these investments frightened off many potential users of FMS in the early years. The slow distribution of FMS during the 1970s is also attributable to the 'system philosophy' existing at that time: there was a preference for large-scale FMS (with more than five interlinked machines), with a view to achieving the 'manless' factory by means of these automated systems. From 1980 onwards dissemination of the systems speeded up and in 1984 and 1985 the total number had reached twice the figure for 1983.

A further stimulus to the use of FMS/FMC was the change which occurred in the required level of investment. Standardisation of the planning process and of the system components brought about considerable reductions in the investment costs required per interlinked machine. In addition, it became clear that the proportion of investment required for processing and material flow systems had shifted. Whereas in the early stages of FMS deployment some 30% of the costs were required for the material flow system—which is not truly a productive system—this proportion had meanwhile fallen to some 20% and the economics of the overall system had consequently improved. Nevertheless, there are still considerable difficulties in demonstrating the economic advantages of an FMS/FMC using conventional methods of profitability calculation.

If we now make a differentiated analysis of the number of installations on the basis of system size categories and periods of installation, we see that the initial stages of the development are marked by the use of flexible manufacturing cells and large-scale FMS (more than five machines). Smaller FMS (between two and five machines) were first installed in appreciable numbers between 1980 and 1983. In this period, the installation figures in the four size categories were still roughly in step. In recent years, however, the trend has changed markedly. Flexible cells have increased rapidly, small FMS (two to five machines) are also on the increase (but less markedly so than the cells), while the increase of installations of large-scale FMS (more than five machines) is stagnating. It would, therefore, appear that in the future flexible cells and small-scale FMS will grow in importance.

It can even be said that it is the installation of smaller, less complex systems and cells—which also involve less risk—that has brought about the major increase in FMS/FMC in the last two years. The initial philosophy of the large-scale systems could therefore not justify itself for general use.

In specialised literature, discussion on the introduction of flexible systems/cells frequently goes under the heading of 'flexibilisation'. FMS are intended to provide an economic means of producing the shortened production series which result from shorter product cycles, increased number of variants, smaller series, etc. Thus, for instance, Schultz and Arnold (1983) argue that 'manufacturing technology is increasingly subjected to rapidly changing market requirements: increasing number of variants, shorter duration of product life, decreasing size of batches or more frequent changes of product. The answer to this is flexible manufacture "insular" manufacturing units, manufacturing cells, flexible manufacturing systems are all keywords which cover the whole range of manufacturing technologies'. Warnecke (1985, p. 269) shares this opinion:

> The market for many industrial goods has changed to a buyer's market. The profitability of a given company is no longer governed solely by quantity production and sales, but the survival of many firms is dependent on acting more flexibly on the market. For the company this means having to cope with an increase in the range of products and component parts, meet higher quality requirements and achieve shorter product-development and delivery times. And this also means that the efforts to achieve higher productivity which still exist today must be supplemented by the efforts to achieve higher flexibility. One means of achieving this is the introduction of highly automated flexible manufacturing systems for parts production.

This argument is based on the assumption that the users of flexible manufacturing systems and cells have hitherto been highly productive in manufacturing large series on transfer lines, but that they have manufactured less flexibly.

The typical field of application of FMS/FMC lies between the two extremes of highly productive but inflexible manufacturing of large series of the same parts on transfer lines and the highly flexible but less productive manufacture of many different parts in small and medium-sized batches, using universal machines.

There can thus exist two completely different basic situations in the use of FMS. If we analyse the type of manufacturing process replaced by FMS/FMC it is clear that FMS/FMC installations are used in only 11% of cases due to decreasing batch size and increasing number of variants to replace transfer-line manufacturing, i.e. to increase flexibility.

In most cases of FMS utilisation, it is non-linked conventional or NC/CNC machines that are being replaced, these machines having previously been used very flexibly but with reduced productivity on small or medium-sized batches. This type of FMS/FMC utilisation serves to increase productivity by raising the degree of automation of the manufacturing of small and medium-sized batches, for which the rigid automation of the previous systems was not suitable.

This relationship is, however, dependent on the size of the systems installed. Whereas about one-third of the large-scale FMS (more than five machines) are still being used to replace transfer lines, this proportion is falling off continuously with decreasing system size. In FMS with between three and five machines the proportion is still just 20%, with two-machine systems some 5%, while flexible manufacturing cells in no case replace transfer lines. However, since the growth area is precisely with cells and small-scale FMS, in the future the aspect of productivity increase will grow in importance compared with the flexibilisation aspect.

An FMS consists of three sub-systems: the machining system, the material flow sytem, the information system. These can vary in terms of complexity and automation (see Chapters 6, 12 and 14 for comparisons).

The machining system is basically characterised by the types of machine tool used. For the 93 FMS/FMC on which information was obtained from the written questionnaire, the distribution of the types of machine indicated in the systems is as follows: there was a clear predominance of machining centres, with a figure of 56%. Under the reply heading 'sundry' covering special machines and formings, each of these categories had a share of some 16% in the systems or cells.

The proportion of machining centres decreases with increasing system size and the other types of machine grow in importance. It is above all the special machines which are to a greater extent represented in the larger systems. Fairly large-scale systems thus frequently constitute a complement to the manufacturing process, whereas the smaller systems (above all the two-machine systems) replace earlier types of manufacture. The flexible manufacturing cells installed nowadays are 70% based on the use of machining centres. Lathe cells represent only 23%.

An analysis of the machine-tool manufacturers shows that there is a broad range of firms offering FMS/FMC and there is no very clear instance of a dominant manufacturer. Matters are different in the numerical control sector, where there is a very clear predominance of two manufacturers, namely Siemens and Bosch.

The types of linking equipment used to automate the material flow differ widely as a function of the system size. Flexible manufacturing cells based on a machining centre are predominantly (64%) linked via a pallet changing device to a pallet pool generally comprising six, eight or 12 pallet points. On a lesser scale (20%), rail-guided vehicles are used for transport. This makes it easy to extend the cell to a two-machine or multi-machine system.

With flexible lathe cells, the workpiece transport is largely (40%) carried out by a belt conveyor. Other possible technical solutions are roller conveyors or gantry loaders (20% each). As the ranges on offer at the relevant trade fairs show, one can expect in the future that there will be a trend to gantry loaders as a means of linking for flexible lathe cells.

The most frequently used linking device with two-machine systems is the rail-guided vehicle (41%). The proportion of automated guided, which means wire-guided, vehicles (AGVs) is still relatively low (9%) with two-machine systems. With three-to-five-machine systems the rail-guided vehicle is also the most frequently used linking device (38%). Here, however, the scale of use of AGV is increasing (14%). The conveyor belt is also a suitable linking device (19%). With systems comprising more than five machines, it is the AGV which is used most frequently as the linking system, and the scale of use of rail-guided vehicles falls off. Of almost equal importance with the AGV, however, are the roller conveyors and belt conveyors (20% each).

We can sum up by saying that overhead trolleys and industrial robots are seldom used as a linking device for FMS/FMC. The use of AGV increases with increasing system size and is therefore not likely to spread further, since the main growth is in the category of cells and small-scale FMS.

An essential prerequisite for the degree of automation of the information system of FMS/FMC is the presence of a central computer system. Such a central computer is an integrated element in just under half (46%) of all the systems we have recorded in detail. A differentiated analysis of the FMS/FMC solutions applied shows that the existence of a central computer depends very much on the size of the system. Whereas flexible cells based on machining centres have a central computer in only 32% of cases and flexible lathe cells in no case at all, 80% of the systems with more than five machines are fitted with a central computer.

Thus, there is an increasing trend towards the use of central computers as system size increases. A deviation from this trend can, however, be noted in the case of two-machine systems. They more often had a central computer than the three-to-five machine systems. One explanation for this is that the two-machine systems are frequently provided as a 'ready-for-use' system including a central computer by the manufacturers, whereas relatively larger FMS integrate machines from several manufacturers, so that the control software must be developed specifically.

If we now consider the functions performed by the system computer (if present) it becomes clear that the operating sequencing is carried out by computer in only 46% of cases. Most frequently the computer is used for DNC operating (83%) and transport control (74%). However, here again there is a clear dependence on the system size. There is a rising trend in computer control with increasing system size in terms of data recording, transport control and operating sequencing. On the other hand, the frequency with which the administration of the tools is computer controlled falls off with increasing system size.

If we consider the development in time of the use of central computers, we are struck by the fact that the earliest systems/cells up to 1978 were not provided with a central computer—with the exception of a large-scale FMS in the year 1972. Computer utilisation was strong from 1979 to 1981, died off between 1982 and 1984 and is now—in the most recent development—thriving again in 1985 and 1986 as far as present knowledge of plans goes. An analysis by system size and year of installation shows that this increase can be attributed to the more frequent utilisation of a central computer in cells and two-machine systems. Since these are the two groups which are growing most rapidly, it can be expected that further increases in the use of central computers will occur in the future.

Work organisation in flexible manufacturing systems and cells

Flexible manufacturing systems and cells involve comparable high levels of investment for firms. It is frequently considered that economic employment of these capital-intensive installations is possible only with multi-shift working. The questionnaire sent to the users of FMS/FMC produced the following finding: almost all systems, independently of size, are worked at least on a two-shift basis. The frequency of use of a third shift exhibits slight variations according to system size, but cells and two-machine systems are used even more frequently in the third shift than larger systems. On average more than one-half of all systems are worked on three shifts. Consequently, the trend towards smaller systems and cells in no way hinders the application of multi-shift working.

If we consider the number of staff employed per shift per machine, we find that the staffing in the second shift is lower than in the first shift, and the manning is even lower in the third shift. In the third shift, cells and two-machine systems are manned to about one-third of the level in the first shift; in the case of three-to-five machine systems the figure is 45% and with large-scale FMS it comes to 57%. The three-to-five machine system group exhibits the lowest manning levels per machine in all three shifts, which leads us to conclude that this size of system makes it possible to achieve exceptionally effective utilisation of the machine operating staff. In comparison, large-scale FMS are more heavily manned and in particular the manning level in the third shift does not fall by so much. This is probably attributable to the fact that, with these complex installations, the risk of machine problems and the associated costs are felt more strongly than the higher labour costs for the supervisory staff employed.

Analysis of the organisation of work with FMS/FMC refers, among other things, to the question of what kinds of different jobs are established, what tasks are performed in the individual jobs and what form the division of labour consequently assumes.

The degree of division of labour in FMS/FMC depends on which and how many functions are brought together in one or several workplaces. In order to be able to classify the systems and cells recorded in respect of the division of labour carried out in each of them, two basic types of work organisation were selected from the many options available; the features of these two categories are outlined below.

Basic type I (low degree of division of labour)

(a) The system operators are responsible for carrying out the following tasks in the system either on a permanent basis or in job rotation:

— testing and correcting of programmes;
— making tools available, charging magazines;
— palletising workpieces;
— monitoring the processing operation;
— changing the fixtures;

unless these activities are automated or are not required.

(b) The system operators are in addition responsible for two out of three of the following activities:

— responsibility for trouble-free operation of the system;
— elimination of minor faults;
— monitoring function(s) (during manufacture and/or final checking).

(c) In addition to this, it is characteristic of a low degree of division of labour that there are no other jobs directly in the system which have a restricted range of tasks (except in the case of job rotation).

On the basis of this classification of work organisation in FMS/FMC we can now describe, as follows, the range of tasks performed by the operators in systems with a low degree of division of labour (basic type I).

Almost always (in more than 80% of all cases) the operator carries out the following tasks:

— testing and correcting programmes;
— responsibility for trouble-free operation of the system;
— making tools available, charging magazines;
— palletising workpieces;
— setting/re-setting of fixtures;
— monitoring the processing operation, removing cuttings, etc.

Frequently (in more than 60% of the cases) the following tasks are performed in addition:

— eliminating minor faults;
— checking dimensions during the processing operation.

The activities:

— programming;
— manufacturing control tasks;
— major maintenance/repairs

are on the other hand included in the system either in upstream or down-stream areas. The system operator takes on these tasks, if at all, only as an extra helper to a specialist from a department outside the system proper. This form of work organisation corresponds to a large extent with the organisation of work, for example, in the FMS of the gear factory at Friedrichshafen, in a pilot project carried out with parallel studies of work and social science aspects as an alternative to the traditional division of labour (cf. Schultz-Wild *et al.*, 1986).

Basic type II (high degree of division of labour)

A good half of all systems (56%) operate with a high degree of division of labour. Variations from this average occur with cells and two-machine systems. Whereas cells lie slightly below the average in respect to division of labour (50%), some 70% of the two-machine systems operate with a high degree of division of labour. Since it is precisely these system size categories which are in full growth, it is important to examine the reasons for the specific choice of division of labour in further investigations.

In general, from the division of the systems recorded into two categories of virtually equal size, i.e. with low and high degrees respectively of division of labour, governing manpower utilisation, it may be supposed that the type of work organisation is determined less by technical constraints associated with the manufacturing technology than by the predominant forms of manpower utilisation encountered in the different manufacturing sectors of works (Fix-Sterz and Lay, 1986; Schultz-Wild, 1986).

The tasks of the operators in systems with a low degree of division of labour are assigned to several jobs in the systems with pronounced division of labour (basic type II), for example:

— machine operators;
— pre-setters
— pallet operators;
— foremen/shift leaders/control-station staff;
— tool-setters;
— fixture setters.

Two main groups of workplace combination can be distinguished in this area.

(a) Basic type IIa: machine setter. In this case, the following functions are carried out by the pre-setter instead of the machine operator:

— testing and correcting programmes;
— responsibility for trouble-free operation of the system;
— making tools available, charging magazines; and
— minor repairs.

The machine operator is thus trusted with a restricted range of tasks rather like that of a palletiser.

(b) Basic type IIb: machine operator and palletiser. In this case, the machine operator is responsible for tasks rather like those of a pre-setter, whereas the following tasks are principally removed from his responsibility and transferred to the palletiser:

— fixing/palletising workpieces;
— monitoring the processing operation.

In some instances there is an even greater division of labour: pre-setter, machine operator and palletiser.

Skill requirements and training

The survey's findings demonstrate clearly that the installation of flexible manufacturing systems and manufacturing cells creates in most firms a demand for additional skills. The personnel operating the system and to a certain extent other persons involved with the newly installed system such as programmers and maintenance personnel will, in almost all cases, be confronted with initial on-the-job training periods of varying duration. This on-the-job training period usually coincides with the running-in phase of the new system, during which full manufacturing output often cannot be expected for technical reasons; the duration of this period is usually proportionate to the size and complexity of the new systems installed, while the training effects are naturally by no means uniform.

Moreover, explicit training programmes are carried out (often in connection with the actual on-the-job training) in the form of off-the-job training courses offered by the manufacturers of machines, controlling equipment and software, or also by the training department of the user companies themselves. The nature and scope of these training programmes and their participants are determined by a number of factors, such as basic skill level of employees, degree of innovation of the manufacturing technology installed, the type of work organisation and its similarity or dissimilarity to the accustomed form of manpower utilisation in the particular company.

In 78 of the 82 recorded cases (95%), at least one functional group within a given company received special training in the operation of the new system. With the system using a low degree of division of labour, there was only one case in which no further training was given; with the system having a higher degree of division of labour this was true in three cases.

Corresponding with the different job structures, the groups of people involved in the training courses differ with the degree of division of labour involved in the application of the system. Where there is a low degree of division of labour, the system operators—who clearly have a multiplicity of different functions to carry out—are almost always (in 95% of cases) given further training. Where the degree of division of labour is high, training for machine operators was given in only 75% of cases; on the other hand, in these instances machine pre-setters are trained nearly as frequently for the new tasks. It is far more usual to find the foremen, shift-leaders or control-station personnel included in the training when division of labour is high than when it was low (42%, versus 11% of cases).

Whether the programmers and maintenance personnel receive training obviously depends less on the degree of division of labour; in about 50% of cases programmers were trained, and about 20% of maintenance specialists. Only rarely (in 10% of cases), are pallet operators and tool pre-setters given special training in systems with a high degree of division of labour.

If a company provides training for a particular functional group, this does not necessarily mean that all the workers in this group actually receive training. Very different procedures are possible: at one extreme, only a few individual workers are instructed during the initial phase of system utilisation and then pass on their knowledge to other colleagues (e.g. when shiftwork is extended), while at the other extreme the entire workforce is trained for the system, even possibly including workers who are not currently, but may later be, involved in system operations.

An important indicator of the outlay necessary to provide the skills is the number of man-days devoted to training courses. This figure is naturally governed by the size of the systems and by the varying requirements and conditions of application.

Taking the average over all systems and all groups of workers we get a figure of 15.7 training days per machine tool integrated into the systems. This average outlay on training is only slightly lower in the systems with a high degree of division of labour than it is in those with a low degree of division of labour (15.6 and 15.8 training days, respectively). However, the time devoted to training in individual cases varies very widely with the system size and also with the type of manufacturing process replaced by the flexible production installations:

— With those few systems which have replaced transfer lines, the duration of training per machine tool is more than twice the overall average: with systems with a high degree of division of labour 38 days of training were provided; with systems with a low degree of division of labour 27 days per machine tool.

— The average time devoted to training was correspondingly lower in the much larger number of flexible manufacturing cells or systems which had replaced stand-alone conventional or NC/CNC machines; where the degree of division of labour was high there were 12 days of training; where there was a low degree of division of labour 14 days of training per machine tool.

— The lowest amount of further training in the systems which were introduced to replace individual machines is found with the two-machine systems (average of nine training days), while the highest figure was found with the flexible manufacturing cells (average of 15 training days).

— Apart from the flexible manufacturing cells, the amount of training per machine tool is a little higher with systems with a low degree of division of labour than with a high degree. The differences are, however, only of the order of one to two days, i.e. some 10%.

The total amount of further training in man-days is the product of the number of workers given training and the duration of training for each worker. The overall average shows that about 1.5 workers were trained in 11.5 days per machine tool. It is almost the general rule that with all system sizes, where the utilisation involved a high degree of division of labour fewer workers were given training than where the degree of division of labour was low, but that the duration of training per worker was higher with a high degree of division of labour than with a low degree. On an overall average, with a low division of labour 1.6 workers were trained for 10 days, and with a high degree of division of labour 1.2 workers for just under 13 days of training. With more than two specially trained workers per machine tool, the number of workers involved was particularly large in the case of flexible manufacturing cells, but the duration of training per man was particularly low. There is an especially long period of training per worker (30 days with low division of labour, 33 days with high division of labour) for those systems which were introduced to replace transfer lines.

There are naturally considerable differences in the training outlay even between the different groups of workers or functions, which are affected by system utilisation to different extents. Such differences in the scope of the training process and the persons involved therein reflect the structure of manpower utilisation, which varies very widely with system size and work organisation.

With systems having a low degree of division of labour the training is above all directed at the system operators. On average, more than three workers were trained per system, each for just under 11 days. Even when the degree of division of labour is high, the operating staff (i.e. machine operators, machine pre-setters and, in rare cases also, palletiser and tool pre-setters) as a whole constitute the largest group given training; the number of workers trained on average per system is, however, lower with a high degree of division of labour. In addition, where the division of labour is high more workers of the other functional groups (such as foremen, shift-leaders, control-station and maintenance personnel) are included in the training.

Where the degree of division of labour is low the duration of training per worker is higher for the operating personnel than where the degree of division of labour is high, while the relationship is generally the converse for most of the other groups of workers. The highest amount of training—more than 50 days of training per man—was given to the control-station personnel in systems with a high degree of division of labour; however, this occurred in comparatively few cases.

The average values referred to for all the cases examined inevitably conceal some part of the variations in the training policy procedure of the user companies when they introduce flexible manufacturing technology. Nevertheless, the close relationship between the choice of certain work organisation options and the scope of the training programmes can be clearly seen.

Skills and vocational training policy

From the point of view of vocational training and labour policy, it is of particular interest that a lower degree of division of labour on the shop floor (which has been strongly advocated in recent discussions about the future of the factory, see Brödner, 1985), does not generally require increased training expenditures by the user companies. The number of man-days devoted to training per newly installed flexible system is actually markedly higher with applications involving a high degree of division of labour than with a low degree (60 days to 44 days of training). If consideration is given to the number of machine tools employed, then—as already stated—the duration of training is only a little higher with a low degree of division of labour than with a high degree. Among other things, such differences can naturally be connected with the varying initial qualifications of the personnel available and also with whether or not the introduction of flexible manufacturing technology is at the same time associated with a change in the normal in-plant forms of manpower utilisation.

It can be assumed—and was confirmed in the case studies—that in many cases the staff from the corresponding conventional or replaced manufacturing process are not simply taken over, but that a broader selection process in terms of creaming off took place. A policy of this kind is quite frequently practised, specially at the time of the first introduction of new manufacturing technologies, since this reduces the training expenditures required in connection with the technological change; it can, however, soon come up against the problem of an inadequate supply of workers able and willing to become involved in new jobs and training, where there is a large-scale introduction of new manufacturing technologies. Consequently, the question of the availability of relevant skills and qualifications is of considerable importance for the further dissemination of computer aided, flexible manufacturing technologies.

The information summarised in the job profiles and relating to the task or function areas covered by various groups of workers seems broadly compatible with the content of the vocational training approved in Germany at the end of 1984 within the framework of the new regulations for the trades in the metal industry. The vocational training of both the industrial mechanic (production technology branch) and the machine operator for lathes, milling machines and grinding machines seems likely to meet the modified qualification requirements in connection with the application of flexible manufacturing installations.

Since the administrative implementation of the new approved trades is not yet complete and the vocational training under the new arrangements requires a period of 3.5 years, the firms will not actually receive young skilled workers qualified to this extent until the end of the 1980s/early 1990s.

However, it can be expected that even now there will be some adaptation of the training of young people to the recognisable new requirements on the basis of the increased utilisation of computer aided manufacturing technologies. This is also possible, to a certain extent, within the framework of the traditional vocational training schemes and has been achieved in the past by individual firms and training centres on a more or less broad basis. It may be asked to what extent such anticipatory action in respect of the future training schemes will be incorporated in the ongoing vocational training of young people in connection with the introduction of new types of manufacturing equipment.

For many reasons—not least the rapid development of technology—it seems evident that increased importance will attach to further training of adults as a result of technical innovation. This is by no means only a matter of dealing with the bottlenecks which will occur until qualified skilled workers are available from the updated apprenticeship programmes. It is much more the case that re-training of adults can also provide a major contribution towards avoiding cutting the link between the existing operational workforces and the new technical developments; otherwise they would be exposed to the risk that in the short or long run they would be pushed out of their jobs, so that there would be a greatly increased risk of employment and labour-market problems for them.

From the point of view of vocational training policy, it is of considerable importance to determine the content, the form and the objectives of such procedures for enabling adults to obtain higher qualifications. In general this area, compared with the apprenticeship training within the so-called 'dual system', is in Germany much less subject to legal regulation or standardised in a way that guarantees the transferability from one company to another of the qualifications acquired. In principle there always exists the risk of too narrow an approach to qualification, e.g. towards the specific requirements of the particular technical equipment in a plant, which raises problems in respect of the longer-term potential of the acquired skills both for the worker and for the firm.

It is in this context of particular interest to see what role is played by the training measures run by the suppliers of modern computer aided manufacturing equipment. It is precisely in connection with the introduction of technical innovations that so-called customer training courses run by the manufacturers have become of great importance in recent years.

More-or-less systematic instruction and training customers' staff have for a long time been usual in connection with fairly complex machines and installations. Now, however, some machine-tool producers offer not only the product itself but also the so-called 'teach-ware', i.e. a systematic training of the customers' staff, frequently as a separate paid arrangement.

In connection with the export of the machines and FMS, such training packages are offered not only on the national market. Particularly from an international point of view, it would be interesting to find out how far such forms of adult training have begun to be accepted beyond the relevant national vocational training systems, in the context of the introduction of new technologies, accompanied perhaps by a certain international standardisation in this field of skills and qualifications.

To sum up, the principal results obtained from the survey questionnaire sent to companies using flexible manufacturing systems and cells can be listed as follows:

(a) FMS/FMC are utilised mainly in the machine building industries in larger firms (more than 500 employees).
(b) Utilisation has risen steeply in recent years: between 1983 and 1985/86 the total number of installations has doubled.
(c) Flexible manufacturing cells and small-scale FMS (maximum five machines) exhibit the greatest rate of increase; large-scale FMS are stagnating or even falling off.
(d) FMS/FMC are principally (85%) installed to raise productivity by increasing the degree of automation; only 11% of the installations were mainly intended to increase the flexibility of the manufacturing process.
(e) Machining centres—56% of all integrated machine tools—represent the most important type of machine; in fairly large systems the importance of lathes and special machines is increasing.
(f) The choice of the automatic transport and linking equipment used in FMS/FMC depends greatly on the size of the system and on the types of machine tool integrated; it is not possible to indicate average trends.
(g) Just over 50% of the systems installed operate without a central computer. In the future, however, increased use of central computers is to be expected.
(h) Almost all FMS/FMC are operated on at least two shifts; approximately 50% of all the installations are run on three shifts.
(i) The degree of automation of FMS/FMC allows the use of considerably less personnel in the second and third shifts compared to the day-shift.
(j) The choice of the type of work organisation, and in particular the degree of division of labour in the system, is governed less by the constraints of the manufacturing technology than by the traditional structures in the firm; this is shown by the fact that the ratio between systems with low division of labour and systems with high division of labour is about 50 : 50.
(k) The choice of work organisation also affects the duration of the training given upon introduction of the system and the group(s) of workers involved. The type of work organisation does not, however, seem to have any significant influence on the overall duration of the training measures.

TOWARDS THE FUTURE

The investigation has shown that flexible manufacturing systems and flexible manufacturing cells have gained considerable significance compared to their state of development a few years ago. The dissemination process of flexible manufacturing cells is more dynamic than that of systems comprising several machines. In those systems comprising several machine tools and possibly other aggregates, a certain trend towards smaller system units is notable. Where at present very large systems with 20 or more machines are still being planned, these are divided up into smaller subsystems (3–7 machines) which are mostly autonomous and tend to be loosely interlinked as far as material and information flow is concerned.

With regard to information systems the utilisation of a central system computer is now frequently dispensed with in favour of a less elaborate, more decentralised design of the information and control system. Future systems consisting of several machines will usually be equipped with a system computer; however, a more strongly hierarchical computer configuration with decentralised computer intelligence is planned so that it becomes technically possible for the system operators to make decisions 'decentrally' (concerning the planning of machine utilisation, for example) by means of interactive communication.

The majority of machine tools integrated by the systems are machining centres; lathes and special machines play an important part in larger systems. The choice of linking equipment for workpiece and tool transport as well as their handling depends mainly on system size and machine configurations; therefore general developmental trends are not very apparent in this area.

The majority of the systems (85%) take over production tasks which were previously handled by stand-alone conventional machines or NC machines; only 11% of the systems replace transfer lines, i.e. highly automated, but rigid manufacturing systems. Thus the innovation objectives of increasing productivity and reducing throughput times were of greater significance than increasing flexibility to cope with a larger number of variations in the manufacturing area.

Medium- and large-scale enterprises (with 500 employees and more) in engineering industries are the main field of FMS utilisation. For most companies system utilisation (still) has the character of a pilot project. Nevertheless it can safely be assumed that flexible manufacturing systems and cells are an important technological line of development, namely one of the components of the increasing computer aided integration with which the companies are trying to realise or expand manufacturing concepts which have been termed 'the factory of the future'. Apart from this, other possibilities of technical innovation are being pursued, partly as a parallel strategy, in other cases as a complementary course. These come under the heading of computer integrated manufacturing (CIM), such as computer aided design and computer aided manufacturing (CAD/CAM), extended DNC utilisation, as well as new systems of production planning and production control (CAPM) etc.

While flexible manufacturing systems and cells had spread rather slowly up until the beginning of the 1980s, they are now undoubtedly an important line of technical development and their effects on work organisation and manpower policy require closer analysis. At present, however, it is difficult to judge future developments on the grounds of the experience gained so far, due to this specific period of transition and the fact that many companies are still experimenting with these new manufacturing technology components.

The findings presented here demonstrate clearly that there are no deterministic connections between the systems' technical design, the solution chosen for work organisation and manpower utilisation and the type and extent of training measures subsequently resulting from these technical innovations. It is apparent that individual companies make different use of similar manufacturing equipment. This shows that it is possible to adapt and design technology according to different company and employee requirements (particularly the information system's control software, but also in terms of operator convenience). But a systematic improvement of working conditions by introducing forms of work organisation based on less division of labour, for example, has been attempted by relatively few companies so far.

The form of work organisation opted for is in reality not so much determined by imperatives of the manufacturing technology but more by the traditional structures within the companies themselves. In many companies, this means an orientation towards forms of work organisation and manpower utilisation based on a high degree of division of labour. Particularly when the issue of division of labour between system team and the areas of planning, control and supervision is to be determined, then existing structures of company organisation with separate departments for work planning, maintenance and quality assurance will tend to favour system external performance of functions such as programming and optimisation, production control, correction of system failures or the quality inspection of manufactured workpieces. Also the proportion of flexible manufacturing systems and cells with a strong internal division of labour, i.e. where several specialised jobs have been defined for workers with different qualifications, is greater (although only marginally) than that of systems organised on a lesser degree of division of labour.

The case study findings, however, do point towards an increasing recognition of the advantages of more comprehensive forms of work and the utilisation of skilled workers in connection with new manufacturing technologies installed in the companies.

— In view of the still comparatively high costs of flexible manufacturing technology, the argument of reducing wages and labour costs plays a relatively minor role. The differences in wage costs between specialised semi-skilled workers on the one hand and comprehensively qualified skilled workers on the other are negligible when compared to the high machine rates per hour.

— In a number of cases it was found that problems concerning insufficient availability of complex manufacturing systems were only seemingly of a solely technical nature and proved also to be connected with the forms of manpower utilisation opted for. Larger system operating teams with comprehensive training can prevent system failure and breakdown periods by expert and timely intervention.

— Vacancies are easier to compensate for when all system operators are capable of performing all required tasks and can therefore take each other's places if need be.

— Finally, due to the altered labour market situation in the past years, many companies have fewer difficulties in recruiting skilled workers, particularly younger skilled workers who are often more familiar with modern manufacturing technologies, provided that reasonable working conditions and wages are given. This even holds true in cases where more shift work must be accepted.

The limits and stability of such forms of work organisation and manpower utilisation cannot be clearly defined at the moment. While their dissemination is furthered by their obvious advantages for the company and employees, the persistence of traditional structures and principles of manpower policy which in many companies are oriented to a strong division of labour and a strong supervision of job performance, must not be underestimated.

This is an area which requires further research. A substantiation of the above points would be an important task, particularly during this present early phase of dissemination of flexible manufacturing systems and cells, in order to prove to the companies that the 'investment' in more human job structures and the retention of skills and qualifications in the immediate vicinity of the manufacturing process is indeed a 'profitable' one. Moreover, it must not be forgotten that the conditions presently observed within the companies are often strongly influenced by the special situation arising during the introduction of new technologies in which uncertainties are evident and which is characterised by company experimentation.

CONCLUDING REMARKS

A definite trend in work design in the area of flexible manufacturing systems and flexible manufacturing cells, we may conclude, is not yet discernible. Within the entire field of companies having experience of new manufacturing technology the forms of work organisation and manpower utilisation differ widely and in individual cases several revisions of organisational principles have occurred.

Moreover, in many cases in which new systems have been installed there have been no definite improvements in working conditions for the personnel immediately affected. Apart from the previously noted trend towards increased shift work and new forms of work burdens and stress factors in a more open work situation, this also has to do with the specific forms of recruiting personnel for the new jobs. In almost all cases, a strategy of 'creaming off' has been pursued, in which workers are recruited from the internal labour market who appear to be particularly well qualified and suited and who have gathered experience in similar work situations in other parts of the company. The need for additional training is recognised by many companies. In most cases, however, this remains restricted to comparatively short training courses offered by the companies supplying machines or control systems and to the process of 'learning by doing'. Comprehensive and compensatory training of manufacturing workers for their new jobs and tasks is very rarely undertaken. In almost all cases the flexible manufacturing systems so far installed form small 'islands' within the companies' manufacturing apparatus and therefore the policy of minimising training expenditure has been quite successful so far, as it has not yet exhausted the existing qualification reserves. This issue will gain another dimension in the near future, however, when flexible manufacturing systems lose their pilot character and, in conjunction with other computer aided technologies, find widespread use.

Addresses for correspondence:

Jutta Fix-Sterz, Gunter Lay and Jürgen Wengel: Fraunhofer Institut für Systemtechnik und Innovationsforschung (ISI), Breslauer Strasse 48, D-7500 Karlsruhe 1, FRG.

Rainer Schultz-Wild: Institut für Sozialwissenschaftliche Forschung eV (ISF), Jakob-Klar-Strasse 9, D-8000, Munich 40, FRG.

REFERENCES

Brödner, P. (1985) *Fabrik 2000. Alternative Entwicklungspfade in die Zukunft der Fabrik*. Berlin: Sigma.

Dolezalek, C., and Ropohl, G. (1970) Flexible Fertigungssysteme, die Zukunft der Fertigungstechnik. *Werkstattechnik*, **60**, 446–51.

Fix-Sterz, J., and Lay, G. (1986) The role of flexible manufacturing systems in the framework of new developments in production engineering. Paper prepared for the EC Symposium 'New Production Systems', 2–4 July, Turin, Italy—Working Party No. 3.

Milberg, J. (1985) Entwicklungstendenzen in der automatischen Produktion. *Fachberichte für Metallbearbeitung*, **62**, 357–65.

Schultz-Wild, R. (1986) New production technologies and their implications for manpower and training policies. Paper prepared for the EC Symposium 'New Production Systems', 2–4 July, Turin, Italy—Working Party No. 3.

Schultz-Wild, R., Asendorf, I., Behr, M. V., Kohler, Ch., Lutz, B., and Nuber, C. (1986) *Flexible Fertigung und Industriearbeit. Die Einführung eines flexiblen Fertigungssystems in einem Maschinenbaubetrieb*. München/Frankfurt: Campus Verlag.

Schultz, H., and Arnold, W. (1983) Stand und Tendenzen beim Einsatz flexibler Fertigungssysteme. *Werkstatt und Betrieb*, **116**, 61–5.
Warnecke, H. J. (1985) Flexible Fertigungssysteme—Einsatzperspektiven in der Bundesrepublik Deutschland. *Fortschrittliche Betriebsführung und Industrial Engineering*, **34**, 269–76.

14. The Diffusion of Programmable Automated Systems and its Work and Training Implications in the Netherlands

Rob Bilderbeek

Centre for Technology and Policy Studies TNO, Apeldoorn

SUMMARY

An overview of empirical research on programmable automated systems in the Netherlands is presented, focusing on technological and organisational alternatives in the process of introducing and implementing computer applications in industry. The diffusion of programmable automated systems is discussed. Three major trends in advanced manufacturing technology are identified, each of which has its organisation and work-related counterpart. Considering the limitations of a high qualification recruitment strategy, priority should be given to a retraining strategy, aiming at the constructive use of available staff and its innovation skills.

INTRODUCTION

For some time now, development in manufacturing technology has been receiving wide and almost unlimited interest, partly resulting from fundamental changes expected to be of great importance for the future development of industrial production structure as well as of industrial employment. In accordance with the US Office of Technology Assessment terminology, we will refer to this development as 'programmable automation' (OTA, 1984).

There is still a great deal of uncertainty concerning the nature of the development of programmable automation, and the direction it is taking—uncertainty, among other things, about development potential, diffusion rate, adequate application and introduction, as well as implications for employment and organisation. Given this uncertainty, there is considerable need for structuring the problem area and in particular for identifying available management and policy alternatives.

New Technology and Manufacturing Management   Edited by M. Warner, W. Wobbe and P. Brödner
Published 1990 by John Wiley & Sons Ltd

It is against this background that the Centre for Technology and Policy Studies TNO (CTPS-TNO) in the Netherlands undertook a three-year, national government-sponsored research programme called 'Programmable Automation', focusing on discrete production automation in Dutch industrial firms. Discrete production consists of production processes in which raw materials to be processed undergo a change of form, as opposed to process industry, in which raw materials undergo a change of condition. The central theme in this research programme is the existence of organisational alternatives in the introduction of computer applications in industrial production. Using an integrated approach, economic as well as sociological aspects of computerisation have been analysed in their mutual interdependence. In particular, the interrelatedness of these different aspects has been emphasised. The efforts within CTPS-TNO in this field (see Bilderbeek *et al.*, 1985) resulted in some useful insights into the policy and management-related aspects of manufacturing automation (in the firm, branch of industry, as well as the societal level). Some of these will be dealt with later in the chapter.

Until recently, a general view in the field has been that many of the most important issues are related to the *process of introducing* new technology into firms. Organisational choices are considered a major important intermediary variable between new technology and its eventual economic and social implications. Therefore, the research focuses on the interaction between technology and organisation, rather than on technology–workplace or man–machine relations, although inevitably the latter enter into the analysis at some point. As a result the research primarily aims at identification of choices that can be made—with or without the intervention of consultants—in adapting technology to organisation and vice versa.

Before discussing three major trends underlying programmable automation, an overview will be given of the rate of penetration of programmable automated equipment in Dutch industry. After that, the concepts of *technological and organisational choice* will be discussed. Next, some attention will be given to *technological and social trajectories* of computer integrated manufacturing, followed by an exposition of possible manpower policy and training implications of advanced manufacturing technology.

DIFFUSION OF PROGRAMMABLE AUTOMATION IN DUTCH INDUSTRY

Programmable automation in the Netherlands at this stage of development mainly consists of industrial robots and CNC machines. The utilisation of highly advanced production systems, in which the control of *several* production process functions has been integrated and linked to some extent within a computer process control unit, is still in its infancy. These highly advanced production systems are referred to as flexible manufacturing systems (FMS).

Other computer technology application areas in manufacturing, like CAD and production planning systems, will not be considered here.

In general, the availability of penetration data on programmable automation in Dutch industry is limited. In particular, data about FMS utilisation are hardly available. It is known, however, that advanced production systems have been installed in a limited number of firms that are often involved in experimentation with new production techniques. The introduction of advanced manufacturing technology has been stimulated by means of government programmes, subsidising part of the investment in a number of so-called demonstration projects and covering the costs of external technical and organisational expertise and advice. Nonetheless, the number of 'frontier technology' firms is very limited, and thus far there are no signs that indicate application of advanced production systems in a broader range of firms.

The available material suggests a rather modest rate of utilisation of 'common practice' programmable automation (i.e. industrial robots and CNC machines) in Dutch industry, compared with other industrialised countries. An explanation for this general picture, characterised by a somewhat hesitant approach to programmable automation, can be partly found in the national industrial structure. Dutch industry consists of a relatively high proportion of small firms, and a small proportion of big firms. Only 2.5% of industrial firms have more than 500 employees, while a major proportion have less than 10 employees. Moreover, branches of industry that are generally considered a major application area for programmable automation (e.g. the automotive industry), seem to be relatively underrepresented in Dutch industry.

Robotics

As far as robotics is concerned, registration of industrial robot utilisation in Dutch industry is severely handicapped by the lack of standardised measurement: a broad range of industrial robot definitions is being used, leading to a rather vague overall picture of the robotics diffusion pattern.

In order to facilitate technological knowledge transfer, a three-year joint robot training project was established in 1985, between a major industrial robot producer and a number of higher technical schools. The project involves teacher training in the robot producer's training facilities with external advisory assistance. The Dutch Ministry of Education is subsidising the project in order to overcome the lack of expertise in higher technical education. For the robot producer, this training project generates a vehicle for stimulating industrial robot introduction in small and medium-sized firms.

CNC machining

Whereas the general picture of programmable automated equipment penetration in Dutch industry is characterised by inaccurate, and insufficiently standardised data, diffusion data on CNC machines are more readily available. These data have mostly been drawn from an extensive survey of Dutch mechanical engineering and process industrial firms. This project focuses on the introduction of programmable automation in relationship to skill and recruitment patterns (Alders *et al.*, 1988).

Focusing on CNC machining in the Dutch mechanical engineering industry, the empirical material available suggests a relatively moderate diffusion rate of programmable automation. In 1988 about 48% of Dutch mechanical engineering firms operate at least one CNC machine. In 1984 the penetration rate was 44%. Substantial differences occur between firms depending on size. Clearly, the penetration rate of programmable automation in terms of CNC utilisation has reached a higher level in 'medium-plus' employment size firms. In 1988, about 41% of Dutch mechanical engineering firms in the 20–49 employee range utilised CNC technology, against about 81% of firms in the 200+ range.

Considering the diffusion pattern, however, the assumption seems justified that smaller firms are involved in a process of catching up with the larger ones. In the period 1984–87, the penetration rate of CNC machining was greater in firms with 100–199 employees than in firms with more employees (⩾ 200). CNC penetration in bigger firms seems to be slowing down, possibly indicating the approach of a saturation level in this size category.

Comparison with another branch of industry that can be considered a major potential application field of programmable automation, the chemical industry, shows no major differences in the diffusion pattern. The overall penetration rate of computer process control in this sector (varying from the utilisation of programmable logic controllers to process computers) reaches roughly the same level as in mechanical engineering. Both sectors show a pattern of gradual introduction of programmable automation. The data suggest a somewhat slower penetration of programmable automation in small (less than 100 employees) chemical plants than in mechanical engineering firms in the same size range.

Next to the question whether or not CNC equipment is in operation (irrespective of the number of CNC machines or the proportion of CNC machines in total plant machinery), the *degree* of CNC utilisation can also be considered an indicator of CNC penetration, taking into account the absolute or relative degree of CNC utilisation within a firm.

First, in terms of the *number* of CNC machines in a firm, in 1987 more than two-thirds of Dutch mechanical engineering firms had less than five CNC machines in operation. Apparently, at this stage there is no massive CNC substitution of conventional equipment. Empirically, there appears to be a positive relationship between firm size (in terms of the numbers of employees in a firm) and the degree of CNC utilisation. Larger firms appear to have more CNC machines in operation than smaller firms. Considering, however, the *proportion* of CNC machines in total plant machining equipment as an indicator of the rate of penetration of programmable automation, the relationship between rate of penetration and firm size appears to be only weakly positive.

The data presented above refer to a specific application area of CNC machinery, the mechanical engineering industry. Although major differences in the rate of penetration between branches of industry are most likely to occur, probably these conclusions give to some extent a valid indication of CNC penetration in the Dutch metal industry as a whole.

Summarising this empirical material, CNC technology (as a major element of programmable automation) in Dutch mechanical engineering firms is approaching a penetration rate of approximately 50%. The diffusion pattern indicates a moderate and gradual expansion rate, possibly slowing down in the larger firms, while smaller firms seem to be catching up with the larger ones. The available data suggest that, at least for the time being, there is no massive CNC substitution of conventional equipment and that conventional machining equipment will remain in operation next to CNC machines.

Parallel to the higher rate of penetration of CNC machining compared with the degree of robot introduction in Dutch industry, CNC-related education and training has been somewhat more institutionalised. Several medium and higher level technical schools offer CNC training facilities. Moreover, several governmental training institutes operating as an interface between the educational system and labour market, have developed courses for CNC operators-to-be in cooperation with firms dealing with CNC machining.

MAJOR TRENDS IN PROGRAMMABLE AUTOMATION

In the development of production technology and its practical application three major trends can be identified. First of all, the development is characterised by the growing importance of 'informatisation': the increasing tendency to fully and unambiguously record human operations of procedures in a language that can be 'understood' directly or indirectly by a machine (e.g. a computer). In the present stage of development, methods of automation are usually based on quantifying product characteristics and product operations in such a way that information processing systems are capable of functioning as control units in the production process.

The result of this approach may be that the translation into a machine readable language remains restricted to those aspects of human (production) operations, that lend themselves to informatisation, thereby abstracting from non-quantifiable, intuitive and 'skill' aspects. In the end, this process could result in a reduction of reality to those aspects that are accessible to objective measurement. Within production processes, informatisation could lead to marginalisation of the human worker—skilled or not—making it even more difficult or even impossible for him to independently and adequately process production-relevant information and control the production system.

Secondly, the production technological development is believed to make possible a growing flexibility: 'flexibilisation'. This belief has probably attributed to a considerable degree to the popularity of the term 'flexible automation'. Strictly speaking, this emphasis on flexibility has not yet been justified, considering the as yet limited degree of flexibility that can be attributed realistically to industrial production systems until now. According to a survey (see Prakke, 1985) of 610 Dutch industrial firms involved in discrete product manufacturing, flexibilisation does not appear to be a predominant motive for investing in automation. Motives like cost price and labour cost reduction are considered more important than flexibility-related motives like quicker product adaptation (considered by 34.9% of the respondents as no motive at all). Reducing set-up and throughput times in order to reduce delivery time, however, is considered a slightly less important motive than cost-reduction-related motives. Although the available programmable automated production systems make flexibilisation (e.g. with respect to product volumes, product variability, product routing, etc.) attainable, it would seem that in Dutch industrial *practice* the flexibilisation potential is not fully used.

Parallel with this technological flexibilisation trend, a tendency can be identified towards flexibilisation with respect to work and organisation. Indicative of this tendency is an increasing receptivity to new forms of organisation, which offer a better capability to react to external changes than traditional Taylorist organisation types (see Bilderbeek *et al.*, 1985), as well as the growing interest in flexible labour contracts, enabling employers to make more flexible use of employees. In particular, the increasing use of flexible manning, sub-contracting and putting out, resulting in growing numbers of temporary and part-time workers with a weak labour market position, along with the increasing importance of functional flexibility, embodied in so-called multi-skilled craftsmen, are illustrative of the flexibilisation of work.

Given the as yet limited degree of technical flexibility that has been attained, this tendency to use more flexible forms of organisation and work, may be interpreted as an attempt to compensate for the lack of technical flexibility. After all, the human factor is and probably continues to be an outstanding example of flexibility.

The third major trend associated with the development of programmable automation is that of *integration*. In strategic thinking about industry's future competitiveness, a growing need can be observed for understanding the integration of manufacturing automation with automation in other parts or functions within a firm. Adequate application of new production technology is considered of crucial importance for future competitiveness. These application areas relate amongst others to computer systems for product and process design, for production planning, for production control, logistics, product testing, and for supplying management and personnel information.

The integration of these computer applications—often referred to as computer integrated manufacturing (CIM)—is expected to be of crucial importance. In fact, integration of all production-related activities can be considered to be the underlying philosophy for all present and future efforts aimed at production automation, be it of discrete products or continuous (bulk) products. This integration trend may be applicable to the internal organisation of production facilities as well as to the external suppliers of goods and services, and customers. However, there is some reason for moderating expectations concerning the integration trend, as well. Until now, there seems to be more integration on paper and seminar sheets than in practice.

As a counterpart of this technical integration trend there is a tendency to create high level jobs in which various tasks are integrated and for which a broad variety of skills is required. At this stage, however, it is by no means clear whether this tendency towards multi-skilling will turn out to be dominant.

TECHNOLOGICAL AND ORGANISATIONAL CHOICES

The 'operationalisation' of these trends—informatisation, flexibilisation and in particular integration—is and will be achieved by means of all the tools provided by modern information technology: it is information technology that is becoming more and more the centre of gravity in the production environment, gradually replacing to some extent traditionally important production factors like craftsmanship and mechanised machinery.

Applying informatisation and integration as a philosophy, and information technology as an instrument, to the internal and external organisation of production, management until now seems to have been aiming at complete controllability of production, of which flexibility is one important aspect. This controllability is directly related to organisational objectives like overall cost reduction, product quality improvement, and enhanced flexibility towards customers.

Within this context integration may be seen as an essentially organisational problem, within which human factors play a major role. Integration problems in designing advanced production systems, for instance, can be traced back to cultural–disciplinary differences between mechanical or production engineers on the one hand and information engineers on the other. Imperfect communication between these categories of specialists may impede an integrated perspective even on a technically defined automation problem.

Finding the right technology, or determining what technology we need (which is more important than finding out how to make technology work), should therefore be deduced from an organisational diagnosis. First, it should be clear in what direction and in what sense the organisation will have to change before considering the question by what means (technological tools and manpower) this organisational change can be accomplished. Technology is no more than a means. Deducing from an overview of what is considered technologically and organisationally conceivable, all feasible combinations of technological and organisational options can be compared. A confrontation of possibilities and desirabilities may eventually result in choosing an optimal combination of 'machinery and people'. Supposing that this choice will be based on rational considerations in particular and not so much on intuition, several appropriate criteria can be identified that are relevant in the decision-making process. The viability of this supposition is supported by German research (e.g. Schultz-Wild, 1986), indicating the absence of deterministic connections between the technical system design, the solution chosen for work organisation and manpower utilisation, and the type and extent of training measures subsequently resulting from these technical innovations. The form of work organisation opted for is in reality more determined by traditional structures within firms. Therefore, in the decision-making process concerning organisational change, intuitive and 'non-rational' factors appear to play a major role.

Criteria with respect to work and training aspects of programmable auto-mated systems should take into account the following factors:

— The degree to which available manpower is to be used in a new production system. The use of available manpower will to some extent be determined by the qualification potential of personnel on the one hand, and the qualification (skill) requirements consequent from a new production system on the other.
— The views concerning the role that can be attributed to the production factor of labour in controlling advanced production systems; and related to that:
— The degree to which the organisation concept opted for (a specific combination of people and machinery) is offering real opportunities for controlling the production system. How vulnerable is a specific production system, given a specific organisation concept?
— The degree to which—in technical terms—technical skills can be objectified, formalised and informatised (made accessible to informatisation). This factor is related to the question of how to incorporate technical knowledge into a computer program so that there will be no essential difference, in terms of performance, from an advanced production system that is basically controlled by skilled, relatively highly qualified workers.

What could be the role of the human worker, especially the 'Facharbeiter' (the German-style craftsman) in such a system?

TRAJECTORIES

Future-oriented research into work-related implications of advanced manufacturing technology requires an insight into the lines of development in production technology *and* its related organisational aspects. Identifying so-called technological and social trajectories of computer integrated manufacturing (CIM) is therefore an essential step. We are interpreting the term trajectory, here, as the main lines of development such as have evolved up until now, within which technological and organisational choices can be identified. These choices may be important determinants of further courses of development.

A description of technological trajectories in, for instance, manufacturing automation, takes account of the evolution of all relevant types of machinery (the application of numerical control in varying degrees of sophistication (NC, CNC, DNC), the development of industrial robots in several generations, the use of flexible machining cells or systems, transport systems, etc.). Research into technological trajectories concentrates on mechanisms playing a part in the selection of these parallel and/or successive kinds and generations of technology. Techno-economic arguments dominate this selection mechanism, but there will be some interaction with human factors as well. Analogous to the concept of technological trajectory, we introduce the concept of social trajectory, representing in this context the main lines in production organisational development.

Since the organisational choices with respect to the introduction and application of programmable automated systems are—as indicated above—considered to be a crucial intermediary variable between new technology and the eventual economic and social implications, making prognostic judgements about work and training implications of new production systems is hard to justify, *without* making assumptions about the organisational choices involved.

It is probably for this reason that in research on the implications of the 'factory of the future', assumptions have often been made about the characteristics of this future factory, resulting in scenario-like models or dichotomies.

For instance, Manske (1983) identified two opposing trends in the application of CNC machines and manufacturing control systems, offering ample decision latitude in the organisation of work. In the 'partialised central control work organisation' the skilled worker loses particularly those functions which determine his high qualification requirements and his independence. His job is 'Taylorised', is subject to decreasing quality, and becomes rigidly controlled. On the other hand, in the 'integrated self-regulated work organisation' the worker preserves numerous work functions and may even be given further tasks. More recently, Brödner (1985) distinguished between a 'technocentric' and an 'anthropocentric' production concept in the future factory, the former based on continuing Taylorist rationalisation, the latter advocating a more labour oriented approach to production technological development and its organisational use (see Chapter 8).

It is tempting to use such opposing trajectories as a point of reference in making predictions about the implications of programmable automated production systems for work and training. At one extreme is the basically Taylorist rationalised organisation model, characterised by bureaucratisation tendencies, standardisation, 'hierarchisation', specialisation and centralised control. The currently dominant model of industrial production organisation bears a rather strong resemblance to this classical Taylorist organisation model. In this model there is a strong tendency towards technical solutions for essentially organisational problems, an ongoing process of labour division, elimination of skilled labour, restriction of decision authority and worker autonomy, and concentration of knowledge and control in management positions. Eventually, this model is likely to result in a strongly polarised labour organisation, with some highly qualified workers who are involved in work preparation, planning and development, and some 'jedermanns' (everybody's) jobs, with a low skill profile, involved with simple unskilled work. At the other extreme is a more labour friendly organisation model, basically aiming at development of productive and creative human potential, and productively uniting the opposed characteristics of man and machine. By using job (task) integration and job enrichment, this model is offering more qualified jobs, better opportunities to use available innovative resources, and results in an improved capability to adapt to internal and external changes.

IMPLICATIONS FOR MANPOWER POLICY AND TRAINING

Presently available information about programmable automation in the Netherlands gives some indication about the direction of development. The CTPS-TNO survey mentioned earlier indicates that in about a third of the firms involved in automation of production, planning or design, introductory problems have occurred. About a third of these problems appear to be directly related to adapting and retraining older skilled employees. About two-thirds are related to internal, organisational factors.

In the same survey employers were asked to what extent shortages of certain categories of personnel were perceived. Shortages of personnel appear to be not overwhelmingly high: between about 55% and 82% (varying with category of personnel) of the consulted firms appear to have no shortage at all. Shortages arise mainly in the categories of medium (20.9%) and higher

(27.5%) technically educated employees, employees with an informatics background (24.7%) and in particular skilled craftsmen (31%).

These findings can be considered as supporting the often predicted shift in the composition of industrial employment, with a tendency towards higher education of a predominantly technical nature. However, judging from these data, the shift does not seem to be very dramatic as yet. The shortage of skilled craftsmen and medium or higher educated technical staff could at first glance be interpreted as a corroboration of the flexible specialisation thesis. Considering the relatively high proportion of shortages there is, however, reason for careful interpretation.

In this context there are two further interrelated aspects to this perceived shortage of medium and higher skilled personnel. In the first place, the perception of a shortage of a certain category of personnel could be a misleading reflection of the kind of qualifications that are objectively necessary for handling new technology equipment. Recent empirical research in the Dutch discrete products industry is giving support to this view (Alders *et al.*, 1988). Many firms appear to be inclined to use a high qualification recruitment strategy as a means of reducing uncertainty resulting from high paced technological change. More highly educated personnel are believed to be more flexible. Traditionally this strategy coincides with recruitment of these employees on the external labour market. The Dutch survey results show, however, that many firms are confronted with severe labour market problems.

No less than 38% of firms turn to a strategy of retraining, because employees with the desired qualifications are insufficiently available on the external labour market. At the same time these figures demonstrate that there is no absolute need for recruitment of personnel more highly qualified than already employed staff. The retraining strategy implies that training less qualified personnel for tasks on advanced CNC machinery is perfectly possible. This even includes the rather complex task of programming the CNC machinery. Obviously there are firms trying to recruit more highly qualified personnel because they overestimate formal education and underestimate tacit skills, day-to-day technological knowhow, and material, organisational and workplace expertise.

Another reason why firms might adhere to the high qualification recruitment strategy is that highly qualified staff are perceived to be rapidly employable. In other words, the need for long-term training within the firm is believed to be diminished. Apart from the already mentioned labour market problems, more highly qualified personnel are usually reluctant to accept shop-floor jobs, the more so if these jobs include less preferable working conditions like shift-work. Taking into consideration their solid labour market position, these well-qualified employees apply for more appealing jobs in planning or management departments. Medium and higher level technical staff appear to be especially hard to recruit in the external labour market, but—once taken into employment—still harder to keep.

These labour market related considerations indicate why recruitment of highly qualified personnel might turn out to be a 'dead end street' policy.

The other aspect of the perceived shortage of highly qualified personnel is the discarding of older staff. Embracing a high qualification recruitment strategy may implicitly lead to adoption of the 'garbage' strategy: getting rid of old staff on grounds of reputed inflexibility, inability or unwillingness to adapt to quickly changing circumstances and to undergo another retraining cycle.

However, the 'garbage' approach denies the presence of innovative skills, i.e. the ability to bring about or to contribute to innovation processes on the basis of practical experience and workplace expertise (so-called 'innovatorische Kwalifikationen', see Fricke, 1983). By discarding older, experienced staff, these skills, which can play an essential constructive role in embedding new production technology into the organisational context, will no longer be at the firm's disposal.

Both the high qualification recruitment strategy and the strategy aiming at retraining available staff can be qualified as *educational trajectories*. As with technological trajectories, within these educational trajectories technological and organisational options can be identified. The choice of a specific educational trajectory has implications for the feasibility of technological and organisational options.

Given the swift technological developments that are to be expected, it seems evident that the regular education system will not be able to keep pace with the resulting shifts in labour market demand. As, for instance, experiences in the printing industry (see Beyddorff *et al.*, 1982) show, discrepancies between the regular education system (especially vocational training) and occupational practice tend to be compensated by in-firm, tailor-made training programmes. The regular education system can, in the first instance, suffice with providing an adequate basic educational programme, and in the longer term, as the structural implications for work and training have crystallised, absorb elements from in-firm training programmes into their curricula.

In-firm training seems to be largely dependent on the training arrangements of producers or suppliers of new machinery, especially in small and medium-sized firms. These training arrangements, however, tend to concentrate on handling the new equipment. It is probably the case that often these arrangements are not sufficient for enabling employees to handle equipment adequately. As a result an additional experimentation period with on the job training is necessary. Needless to say, this often leads to costly production losses. Retraining of older staff, as pointed out before, may lead in many cases to serious problems. In particular older staff who seem to have reached their intellectual ceiling in subsequent retraining cycles, are a problematic category. In addition, older staff tend to get weary of constant retraining.

In practice, the ultimate 'solution' often appears to be discharging older staff. There is a tendency to select available staff with a high qualification potential, a good sense of responsibility and strong motivation, for positions at advanced production systems, resulting in a category of 'Olympiareife Belegschaften' (first division personnel). As indicated before, high qualification recruitment policies carry the risk, on the one hand, of underutilisation of highly skilled employees, whose capacities are being fully used only in the process of introducing and implementing new production systems and, on the other, of losing innovative skills because of discarding experienced, older staff.

CONCLUDING REMARKS

In conclusion, the educational trajectories identified above should be considered as alternatives offering manpower strategies to be implemented. Having indicated the risks involved in the high qualification recruitment strategy (or the 'garbage' model), it is clear that in our view the retraining strategy offers a better opportunity for knowledge development within the firm. In this respect it is closely allied to the anthropocentric organisation model, aiming at development of productive and creative human potential and offering better opportunities to use available innovative potential. However, in practice a combination of this strategy with external recruitment of highly qualified personnel seems to be the case. Wherever possible, the 'knowledge development' model should be favoured above the external recruitment model. Whenever recruiting highly qualified staff on the external labour market is inevitable, the risks attached to this approach should be carefully avoided.

Address for correspondence:

Centre for Technology and Policy Studies TNO, PO Box 541, NL-7300 AM Apeldoorn, The Netherlands.

REFERENCES

Alders, B. C. M., Christis, J., and Bilderbeek, R. H. (1988) Technological change and employment structure. Programmable automation and qualification, training and recruitment options. A survey report from Dutch industry. The Hague (NL): Ministry of Social Affairs and Employment.

Beydorff, R. O., Bilderbeek, R. H., Davies, D. R., Schwarz, J. J., Kalff, P. J., and Kloppers, M. J. M. (1982) Research into the relation between technological developments and labour market relations on the basis of a pilot study in the printing industry. Apeldoorn/Amsterdam (NL): Centre for Technology and Policy Studies TNO, Institut voor Grafische Techniek TNO & Adviesgroep Mens en Organisatie NV (in Dutch).

Bilderbeek, R. H., Kalff, P. J., and Prakke, F. (1985) Manufacturing automation: an exploration of technological, economic and organizational aspects. Deventer/Apeldoorn (NL): Kluwer/Centre for Technology and Policy Studies TNO (in Dutch).

Brödner, P. (1985) *Fabrik 2000. Alternative Entwicklungspfade in die Zukunft der Fabrik*. Berlin: Sigma.

Fricke, W. (1983) Participatory research and the enhancement of workers' innovative qualifications. *Journal of Occupational Behavior*, **4**, 73–87.

Manske, F. (1983) Social and economic aspects of alternative computer aided production systems in small and medium batch runs. Preprints IFAC workshop 'Design of work in automated manufacturing systems'. Karlsruhe, November.

Office of Technology Assessment (OTA) (1984) Computerized manufacturing automation—employment, education and the workplace. Washington DC: US Congress.

Prakke, F. (1985) Flexible automation in the Netherlands: some facts and figures. Paper prepared for CAPE conference on CAD/CAM. Apeldoorn: Centre for Technology and Policy Studies TNO, May (in Dutch).

Schultz-Wild, R. (1986) New production technologies and their implications for manpower and training policies. Proceedings of EC Symposium on 'New production systems, implications for work and training in the factory of the future', Turin, July 2–4, Brussels: EC-FAST.

15. A European View of Advanced Manufacturing in the United States

Werner Wobbe

Commission of the European Communities, Brussels

SUMMARY

The author argues that the American pattern of automation should not be copied by Europe. An alternative human-centred approach would be preferable. The chapter is based on visits to advanced technology establishments. The limitations of the purely technology-based approach are analysed, and suggestions for policy are set out.

This chapter sets out to assess, from a critical European viewpoint, the specificities of the new American way of manufacturing. The main direction taken is to understand why the US is trying to accelerate its manufacturing activities towards computer integrated manufacturing (CIM) in order to stay competitive. The author argues that the reasons for doing so do not apply to Europe, and that human-centred and skill-based concepts would better enable Europe to develop its full manufacturing potential.

The focal point of the author's field investigation, organised in 1987 by the US Information Agency, was the so-called Rust Belt in the old industrial heartland (from Pittsburgh to Detroit). This is now known as 'Automation Avenue' as a result of the revival that has occurred there in recent years, particularly in the field of automation technology. Discussions were held with more than 70 experts in some 30 establishments and a total of 12 inspection visits covering advanced technology applications were undertaken. All remarks are based on data from the visits. The subsequent assessment is made in the light of the author's empirical research in German manufacturing activities and European Community research programmes (Wobbe, 1986).

Although the study was planned to include the most advanced examples of CIM, such as Boeing, Everett, Cincinnati Milacron, Ohio, the National Bureau of Standards, the Center for Manufacturing and Engineering, Maryland,

New Technology and Manufacturing Management   Edited by M. Warner, W. Wobbe and P. Brödner
Published 1990 by John Wiley & Sons Ltd

Industrial Technology Institute, Michigan, Carnegie-Mellon University, Pittsburgh, the Centre for Research in Integrated Manufacturing, University of Michigan, and despite the fact that numerous newspaper articles create the impression that the CIM factory of the future will shortly come into operation or is already an investment option, no really integrated completed project was evident to the author. Of course, there are building blocks of automation technologies, and more importantly, the strong will of important political, economic and scientific actors (for example, the National Research Council, the Bureau of Economic Affairs and the Department of Defense) exists to support this integrated concept. However, the assessment of the state of the art could be more appropriately designated 'advanced manufacturing' than 'computer integrated manufacturing—CIM', since, as one of the European experts pertinently remarked, the status of CIM should be understood by analogy with the 'United States of Europe'. That is, both are distant objectives shaping measures which, at present, are few and far between.

The reason why the US tries to get the leading edge in CIM by heavy State support seems to be founded in the moves towards the reindustrialisation of its economy prompted by the US budget deficit and trade imbalance. Americans are now asking whether their country can achieve long-term competitiveness in the manufacturing sector and what measures need to be taken to ensure that it does. For the most part, CIM is seen as providing the optimum solution in the form of *fully automated production* backed up by the country's undoubted data-processing resources.

THE CRISIS OF MANUFACTURING IN THE US

In no country in Europe is industrial activity so strongly orientated towards a sophisticated form of *mass production* as in the US. This has economic, historical and cultural roots: the big internal North American market, the rapid process of industrialisation at the end of the last century. The fact that mass production fitted in well with the workforce available, itself has social roots. An influx of European engineers and skilled workers to supply the machine-tool factories, as well as the mass of black, unskilled labourers and other migrants from the South provided ideal human resources for a system based on a sharp division of labour and managerial control over the work process. Taylorist mass production did not come up against craft traditions as it did in Europe.

However, this inherent 'American production pattern' has now become a restraint. The requirement of flexibility and the importance of 'economies of scope' in manufacturing, that is, the variety of products that can be made, might replace the 'economies of scale' and require new socio-economic patterns of production as well as new organisation cultures. (See Piore and Sabel, 1984.)

Also, the accounting-oriented view on cost reduction and quarterly reporting has been detrimental to long-term strategic manufacturing aims. Externalisation of sub-assemblies, outsourcing of engineering expertise, changing production sites to the most profitable locations in the short term, are measures decided for mainly financial reasons. Management often seems to be more dedicated to financial acquisition than to improving manufacturing.

Contrary to American manufacturing, which produces twice as much 'garbage' as any other major industrial nation, the Japanese do not like wasting anything. Their development of sophisticated manufacturing installations which turn out well-designed high quality goods can be seen as a result of their attempts to reduce waste. That they have to import expensive energy and raw materials has had an important influence on their production methods and has, for instance, stimulated them to find ways of operating with low inventories.

In the pursuit of short-term goals based primarily on the financial aspect, quality considerations, product replacement and after sales service have been neglected. (Analysts such as Dr Wozny of the Brookings Institution, the BRIE project at Berkeley, Dr Merchant of Metcut and Professor Hancock of Ann Arbor agree on this point.) Mass markets in such sectors as motor vehicles, consumer electronics and semi-conductors have been surrendered to the Japanese and this has resulted in an identity crisis, since no new direction has as yet been established to replace the philosophy of mass production.

Suppliers have also suffered from this loss of mass markets, particularly in the modules and components sector and in the capital goods industry. At present, Japanese investment in the motor vehicles sector is causing particular concern in the supply and capital goods industries, since the Japanese firms concerned are expected to bring with them their own suppliers who, in the long term, would also serve American automobile companies. In the Detroit area, there are some 450 machine-tool and mechanical engineering firms which probably could not compete on the world market because of the obsolete manufacturing structure which they have retained under the protection of their privileged relationship with the major motor vehicle companies.

SOCIAL ATTITUDES OF AMERICAN MANUFACTURING: ENGINEERING VERSUS MANUFACTURING

In many areas, such as space, military, aircraft, chemical and material engineering, computer science based application, the US still has advanced engineering expertise. But, to stay competitive on the world market, the manufacturing of a broad range of sophisticated quality products cannot just be carried out by excellent engineers and scientists in centres of excellence.

The design of products (mainly called engineering) demands a different kind of expertise from the kind of engineering competence required to organise the manufacturing of complex products.

The US has the disadvantage that although it possesses a strong tradition of engineering (focusing on the design end), this applies less to the other end of manufacturing. Because of this engineering tradition, the practical problems of manufacturing have not so far been prominent in university education. The CIM strategy, understood as a movement towards full automation, is a typical example of this engineering bias. There is relatively little understanding of the human factor in production, which is seen more as a source of interference. Until two years ago, the National Science Foundation had never offered a programme in the manufacturing sector, with the result that university research in this field was almost non-existent.

On the other hand, the defence sector funded research in institutes and universities with a view to developing engineering techniques requiring no human intervention in the advanced manufacturing technology sector. The research funds made available by the Department of Defense helped to increase engineering knowledge and this has ultimately benefited the information technology sector. Manufacturing know-how, however, has remained inadequate in comparison to Japan or the Federal Republic of Germany.

Analysts qualified to make comparisons on an international level regard the Fraunhofer Institute in Germany as the leaders in the development of manufacturing knowledge. The best-known German centres in the US are the WZL in Aachen, the IPA/IAO in Stuttgart and the IPK in Berlin.

The low valuation of manufacturing activities constitutes a cultural attitude. As in England, blue-collar workers and their skills are not very highly esteemed *vis-à-vis* Germany. This prejudice is transmitted to the manufacturing engineer, leading him to change his role to business management or 'white-collar engineering' where he will not have to 'get his hands dirty' alongside production staff. In comparison to Germany or Japan, shop-floor workers are less trained and less adaptable. Flexibility is achieved by hiring and firing rather than by further training and a systematic staff policy. Since costs and profit are the dominating criteria, companies buy large proportions of individual products so as to maintain a low manufacturing depth. As critics point out, there is relatively no long-term investment in manufacturing equipment (by contrast to Japan, which has consequently taken over the mass markets by continuing with activities even when over certain critical periods they make no profits and even incur losses). The attitude of management is to get rid of firms facing short-term problems, as the concern with costs precludes longer-term strategic decision-making with regard to production.

The implementation of company training schemes for production workers scarcely seems feasible because of the obstacles created by the seniority system. In unionised plants, job security, employment and wage levels are all determined by seniority and remain unaffected by the acquisition of additional qualifications. Employees who undertake further training can expect to receive a bonus for their additional qualification or be promoted only if they change companies. Similarly, firms which provide further training for their staff must expect to lose them to their competitors.

University research is also marked by the unfavourable attitude to production staff. It is assumed that the latter are unreliable and poorly qualified and that they should therefore be replaced by appropriate technology, such as artificial intelligence (AI) systems. This attitude to research is supported by Department of Defense funding, since the military takes a similar view of operatives and put their trust in automatic weapons systems.

The whole complex, starting from the engineers' education, the tradition of using workers for their manual labour and not as experienced 'artisans' with their tacit knowledge, the prejudice against blue-collar work, the short-term financial operations, constitutes a pattern and approach towards manufacturing which could be called 'technocentrism'. This means favouring a form of manufacturing that deploys technology as far as possible to displace and control shop-floor work.

This engineering pattern finds its counterpart in Europe at the level of shop-floor practitioners and experienced manufacturing engineers in 'anthropocentrism'—the solving of manufacturing problems by exploiting the human potential. This involves applying adequate and specifically developed technologies, and creating a factory organisation which is less hierarchical and has an organic structure of cooperation. The latter is particularly successful with skilled workers in small and medium-sized production units, batch production and rapidly changing products and production demands. It can be found particularly in the European machine-tool industry or similar types of manufacturing units.

IS COMPUTER INTEGRATED MANUFACTURING A US CULTURAL BIAS?

Thus, as a result of the existing 'cultural conditions' and the strength of the information technology sector, the forward strategy for manufacturing in the US would appear to centre exclusively on CIM. The Manufacturing Studies Board of the National Research Council (National Research Council, 1986) has provided the following breakdown of the economic *advantages* offered by CIM on the basis of data provided by five companies (John Deere, Ingersol

Engineers, McDonnell-Douglas, Boeing and Caterpillar):

— Reduction in engineering design cost	15–30%
— Reduction in overall lead time	30–60%
— Increase in product quality	2–5 times
— Increase in capability of engineers	3–35 times
— Increase in productivity of production operations	40–70%
— Increase in productivity of capital equipment	2–3 times
— Reduction in work-in-process	30–60%
— Reduction in personnel costs	5–20%

It should be noted, however, that these figures, which are repeatedly quoted in one form or another, do not relate to a fully technically integrated system—since none yet exists—but to individual component applications.

The most important conclusion to be drawn from the above figures is that the crucial cost advantage derives not from staff reductions, but from company reorganisation. This poses problems for companies in calculating the economic consequences of investment in technical systems in the US, since *traditional accounting*, which seeks to minimise the number of blue-collar workers, is of no assistance here.

A number of versions of CIM have been described in the investigation. The most impressive was provided by Boeing, which presented CIM as a *philosophy or strategic concept* for the organisation of investment planning on the basis of computerised integration. It involves the interlinking of all the important commercial and production departments of a company. Each of the four following major divisions,

— business (purchase, sales, etc.)
— engineering (design, construction, technical drawing, etc.)
— plant operation (planning, control)
— manufacturing (parts production and assembly)

is equipped with a complex computer sub-system for both intra- and inter-divisional communication.

So far only the engineering and manufacturing divisions have been linked up and there have already been problems with connections in the latter.

In this context, *flexible manufacturing systems* (FMS) represent the most advanced form of integrated manufacturing. One of the largest machine-tool producers, Cincinnati Milacron, demonstrated an extremely impressive system in the form of a facility for its own use. Other systems, such as that developed by Westinghouse, were created for armaments production.

Even FMS, however, can only cover small branches of manufacturing. *Robot* manufacturers of American origin have nearly gone out of business because to produce them highly skilled manufacturing engineering has to be applied. Only Unimation, now owned by Westinghouse and Cincinnati Milacron, produce the outcome of their own developments. GMF, the biggest producer, is an American/Japanese firm (Fanuc/GM) buying Japanese mechanical parts and providing controller and software of American origin. However, its success seems to be dependent on the investment strategies of General Motors (GM). Investments dropped sharply, for example, in 1986/87 because of GM cutbacks.

Future strengths of American equipment might be found in the production of *vision systems* as this is a very software intensive business in which the US could excel. Vision systems could have a considerable impact on automation by replacing human inspection, monitoring and control. According to Dataquest, the share of sensors and machine vision in the market for manufacturing automation systems in the US will increase from about 3.5% in 1986 to 5% in 1991.

Artificial intelligence or (to put it more moderately) *expert systems* are being developed to incorporate shop-floor knowledge of processing into machines. There are great aspirations by American engineers that this development will become independent from human labour in shop floors and will assure continuous production flows. The military budget in particular has fostered this development.

In addition to the specific development of matching equipment *regulation and standardisation* of communication interfaces are of crucial strategic importance for CIM. In this connection, reference can be made to General Motors' Manufacturing Automaton Protocol (MAP), which is exclusively concerned with manufacturing, and Boeing's Technical and Office Protocol (TOP), which essentially covers the non-manufacturing sector (office and engineering systems). Valuable work has been carried out by EEC funded research to standardise open systems in Europe. The success of these standardisation measures is essential for effective CIM integration based on the use of systems and equipment supplied by more than one manufacturer.

The interconnection of various machines and systems (e.g. a robot, a transport supply, a vision system and an NC machine) produced by different firms creates an immediate need for *systems engineering*. Thus the connection of any two machines necessitates the installation of an interface to provide 'translation' between the two systems involved. An interface alone, however, costs around $20 000. Although a higher degree of standardisation would enable such a device to be dispensed with, the control units of machines, robots and similar equipment would have to be designed to provide the function in question. Systems engineering would still be required, being important both for mechanical engineering firms and for the training of technicians and engineers.

THE ROLE OF 'LEAD USERS' OF AUTOMATION EQUIPMENT

The BRIE research team in Berkeley, California used the term 'lead users' to describe industries which exercise a decisive influence on capital goods industries by virtue of their demand. Their requirements determine the development of production equipment and production programmes. Lead users are crucial for the evolution of a particular industrial sector into a field for the application of advanced manufacturing technologies. For a long time, the motor vehicles industry was a lead user in the advanced manufacturing sector, although as early as the 1960s the defence industries began to take over this role in the US because of the growth of areas of computer development and its applications, and aeronautics and aerospace applications. Along with optoelectronics, the processing and industrial application of new materials are becoming increasingly important for defence (e.g. Strategic Defence Initiative—SDI) and could develop into the new lead user sector.

This puts some pressure on Europe in continuing the application of advanced production technologies. In the interests of its own production base, Europe must constantly monitor, and itself be actively involved in, the leading industrial sectors (lead user fields) or ensure satisfactory transfer to the capital goods industries in the case of the aeronautics, space, new materials/chemistry, optoelectronics/light technology sectors. In the case of both R & D and science and technology policy, America's SDI programme can be expected to give rise to a coherent and industrially strategic national support programme in the manufacturing and engineering sectors which will affect the fields of computing, engineering, precision instruments and new materials and chemistry, and might change the direction of the advanced manufacturing scene.

However, the direction taken might in the long term have counter-productive effects and lead to a deterioration in the broad industrial manufacturing base. The reason is that the Department of Defense has established a dominant position with regard to the *promotion of research* in the field of advanced manufacturing technologies. To a large extent, therefore, it has determined the development of these technologies as regards design, research capacity, the acquisition of state-of-the-art systems and indirect support involving defence sector industries and the creation of special markets.

An earlier data source supplied by the Office of Technology Assessment (OTA, 1984), which nevertheless remains structurally valid, clearly reveals the predominance of defence-related research. Thus in 1984, federal funding of research and development in programmable automation amounted to $63.60 million for military agencies as against only $16.65–18.95 million for civilian ones. The dominant influence of defence on manufacturing technology has inevitably resulted in a certain degree of bias. Concentration on the exclusion of the human element has greatly favoured 'technocentrism' and the trend towards engineering solutions, contributing, in the author's view, to America's 'manufacturing knowledge gap'.

CONCLUDING REMARKS

The information acquired from the American field investigation highlights the importance of the research results of the FAST (Forecasting and Assessment in Science and Technology) Programme of the European Community with regard to longer-term industrial innovation in Europe. The FAST recommendations try to emphasise (backed up by R & D) the manufacturing potential in Europe, by developing anthropocentric concepts of technology for Europe, which can provide fertile ground for such an approach, if it is accompanied by education and training measures (Schultz-Wild, 1986). In addition, the combination of new materials, light technologies and information technology will have far-reaching consequences, particularly for the capital goods industry, and should be carefully monitored. Finally, the concept of computer and human integrated manufacturing (CHIM) is important from the standpoint of manufacturing knowledge, and can remedy the shortcomings of an engineering-based strategy. The technology-centred approach of computer integrated manufacturing (CIM) has yet to be proven.

Address for correspondence:

Commission of the European Communities, DG XII–MONITOR Programme–FAST, 200 rue de la Loi, B-1049 Brussels, Belgium.

REFERENCES

National Research Council (1986) *Towards a New Era in U.S. Manufacturing—The Need for a National Vision.* Washington DC: NRC—National Academy Press.
Office of Technology Assessment (OTA) (1984) *Computerised Manufacturing Automation: Employment, Education and the Workplace.* Washington DC.
Piore, M., and Sabel, C. F. (1984) *The Second Industrial Divide. Possibilities for Prosperity.* New York: Basic Books.
Schultz-Wild, R. (1986) New production technologies and their implications for manpower and training policies. EC Symposium on 'New production systems', 2–4 July, 1986, Turin.
Wobbe, W. (1986) *Menschen und Chips: Arbeitspolitik und Arbeitsgestaltung in der Fabrik der Zukunft.* Göttingen: SOVEC.

CONCLUDING REMARKS

REFERENCES

Section 4

Strategic Management Applications

16. The Factors behind Successful Technology Innovation

Martin Lockett

Oxford Institute of Information Management, Templeton College, Oxford

SUMMARY

This chapter analyses the factors behind success and failure in new (information) technology innovation in a major UK manufacturing company. The research covered 29 projects, mainly in the fields of expert systems, production management and sales and marketing. Organisational issues were much more important than technological ones. Major factors behind successful projects were: (1) a project champion in a business function; (2) late formalisation of the project; (3) a development team bridging the gap between the information systems function and users; (4) prototyping in the early stages of a project; and (5) transition from a development to an implementation phase with different management requirements. The chapter concludes that successful information technology innovation requires an 'R & D approach' together with a changed climate towards risk-taking.

INTRODUCTION

Information technology is becoming increasingly recognised as an important weapon in business competitiveness. As well as traditional data processing applications designed to increase business efficiency through cost-reduction, information technology is being used to improve effectiveness, for example through improved information for decision-making and speed of response. Further, there are a range of examples where the use of information technology can give sustainable competitive advantage to a business, for example in airline reservation systems and flexible manufacturing systems. While opportunities for straightforward cost-reduction still exist, their importance relative to opportunities for business effectiveness and gaining competitive advantage is declining.

It can also be argued that the availability and cost of information technology are not the major constraints on its effective application in business. Today, the potential applications of information technology which can be

New Technology and Manufacturing Management   Edited by M. Warner, W. Wobbe and P. Brödner
Published 1990 by John Wiley & Sons Ltd

cost-justified and which are technically feasible exceed the capability of organisations to exploit these opportunities. But while this potential is large, there are many cases of projects which fail to meet their objectives and produce business benefits, as well as exceeding budgets by large margins. These problems have become more acute with the growth of new forms of information technology such as personal computers and expert systems, as well as the integration of information technology with information processes.

Therefore the capability of information technology has become less of a limiting factor than the recognition and exploitation of business opportunities for information technology applications. Given this context, determining the factors behind success (and failure) in innovations making use of information technology is an important precondition for effective use of information technology for competitive advantage and for organisational learning about how to achieve this goal. This chapter reports on a project to identify the factors behind successful innovation in information systems projects in a large British manufacturing company. The research was based in the Oxford Institute of Information Management at Templeton College, Oxford.

THE INNOVATION FRAMEWORK

Industrial innovation

The research started from the hypothesis that the factors behind success and failure in information technology innovation would be similar to those previously identified for product and process innovation in industry. These studies include Science Policy Research Unit (1972), Rothwell (1977), Roussel (1983), Shanklin and Ryans (1984), Kanter (1985), Cooper and Kleinschmidt (1986), and Fischer et al. (1986). Innovation is defined as the commercial application of new technology—as opposed to invention of new ideas (Freeman, 1974). These studies have shown a number of factors to be particularly important in successful industrial innovation:

(a) Good understanding of customer and end-user needs by those involved in development.
(b) The use of external information, skills and contacts by system developers and customers.
(c) Senior management sponsorship, commitment and involvement (by both developers and customers).
(d) The existence, and relatively senior position, of an internal champion.
(e) Effective, but not necessarily fast, technical development of the system.

Based on this background of industrial innovation studies, this research took an information systems project as the unit of analysis. Projects were viewed as similar to other technical innovations, which to be successful must combine technological development with a market opportunity, whether internal (process) in the sense of changing business processes or external (product) by providing new marketable products or services. It was hypothesised that the organisational process of innovation would explain much of the variation in success between projects. Similar processes would apply in the cases described in this volume.

Research design

In order to limit some of the variations in technology and to concentrate on applications designed to increase effectiveness and gain competitive advantage, three areas were chosen:

— expert systems,
— production and research management systems,
— sales and marketing systems.

Within these areas a total of 27 projects were selected to give (i) varying degrees of success and failure; (ii) wherever possible matched pairs of projects which used similar technology but had different degrees of success; (iii) a range of operating divisions and locations within the company. Two further projects in decision support and manpower planning had been used to pilot the research instruments, making a total of 29 projects. For each project the aim was to interview (i) *system developers*, usually from the information systems function; (ii) internal *customers*, a manager responsible for the commissioning and/or use of the system; (iii) *users* of the system, where applicable. This approach was used to obtain the often differing perspectives of information systems professionals and those in business functions using the systems. It also allowed cross-checking of the data.

For each project the following areas were examined:

(a) *Problem recognition*: the process of recognition and definition of a problem.
(b) *Problem characteristics*: the characteristics of the problem tackled.
(c) *People characteristics*: the developers, customers and end-users of the project.
(d) *Innovation process*: the management of the innovation process.
(e) *Success or failure*: the degree of success or failure of the project.

Defining success and failure

The success of a project was assessed in terms of:

— *achievement of goals* of these involved,
— *extent of use* by ultimate end-users,

— impact on business *efficiency*,
— impact on business *effectiveness*,
— *strategic impact* of system.

In the case of projects which were not yet working commercial systems, an assessment of the prospects for the system was obtained from those interviewed. For projects which were not implemented or stopped after implementation, the reasons for stopping the project were explored. The results presented here are based on an initial analysis of the data and hence detailed figures are not given.

IS TECHNOLOGY THE CONSTRAINT?

The results confirmed the starting point of the study that the availability and cost of information technology are not the major constraints on business. In 70% of the projects, cost was not a significant constraint. Only in a 15% minority of the projects was the availability of technology a significant problem delaying its application in the past. As expected, technical problems during systems development were higher with projects for which technology availability was an obstacle.

But while the availability and cost of information technology were not a major constraint, the projects certainly were innovative and used new technology for the users and/or the system developers. As rated by those involved in the projects, the technology used was either significantly or completely new to users, while on average having significant new elements for system developers. The majority of these new elements were in the software and user interface area, as well as in applying information technology to the particular application area. Thus the projects were cases of innovation at least at the business unit level—and in some cases are seen more widely as innovative examples of the business application of information technology.

New technology from the viewpoint of users and system developers was associated with technical problems in the project and greater time taken and higher cost over-runs. However, overall, the newness of the technology in itself had a small positive association with project success. Thus there is little evidence that the newness of technology itself has a major impact on overall success and failure of information technology innovation. While there can be no doubt that cost-justification of information technology investment is important, the cost of the technology itself is not a major constraint on successful innovation. Rather it appears that the benefits from projects which pay off are substantial relative to the technology costs, but that the risks are also significant and must be managed.

CHAMPIONS AND SPONSORS

If technology does not explain the success and failure of information technology innovations, what does? The clearest factor to emerge from the research was the existence of a project *champion* in the relevant function within the business. In almost every project, the lack of a champion was associated with failure. The moving of a project champion to a new role in the business was also directly linked to the subsequent failure of the project in cases where the new incumbent did not take over the champion role. But why are champions so important?

A champion in the user rather than the information systems function is able to coordinate the project and guide it towards relevant business goals. This increases the chances of success for two reasons: (i) by influencing the design of the system to make it meet user and business needs more closely, and (ii) by providing impetus for the implementation of the project. Such a champion therefore manages the project in a way more likely to achieve business objectives than one which either is championed from within the information systems function or has no clear leadership.

In the event of problems during the development of the project, a champion is able to gather support for the project if he or she believes it to be viable. However, some champions are not at a sufficient level in the organisation to be able to allocate adequate resources on their own initiative. A second role of *sponsor* is important here—a senior manager who takes an interest in the project, makes some commitment to it, and reviews its progress. Two patterns emerged which were associated with successful project development: first a relatively senior champion, and second a more junior or less enthusiastic champion backed by a more senior sponsor. So while sponsors were important, they were not a substitute for a champion actively involved in the project.

Thus the existence of a champion, combined with a sponsor where appropriate, was the single most important factor for success. This broadly confirms the findings in technical innovation research—and also shows something of the dynamics of the roles of champion and sponsor, which are sometimes not distinguished.

PROBLEMS OF FORMALISATION

In recent years there has been great stress placed on the need for formal controls over information systems projects—starting with formal approval and using structured development methods and a formal project structure. This has been intended to avoid the problems of cost and time over-run. However, this research showed such formalisation to be positively associated with both costs and elapsed time exceeding budgets and expectations. This was particularly true of projects using formal project management structures. Further, there was little association between these formal structures and success or failure. Thus at first sight, formal management processes appear to have done little good.

A detailed examination revealed a more complex pattern in which formalisation in the later stages of a project was associated with success while early formalisation had the opposite effect (cf. Kanter, 1985, on technical innovation). Qualitatively this was confirmed by cases of success which took place outside the 'proper' channels for approval and systems development. In these a champion often worked informally with the information systems function to produce a prototype or initial working system. In a number of cases corporate rather than divisional resources were used—again to some degree outside normal procedures. On the other hand, in two of the projects with earliest formal approval and highest visibility, there were serious problems and the systems were implemented late and were rejected by users after development.

The best explanation is in the costs of exit from projects which are not meeting business objectives. Early formalisation tends to freeze a project in a particular form and to make it more difficult for those involved to stop as this involves 'public' admission of failure. Also real checkpoints tend to be months apart on larger projects. In contrast, unapproved projects using discretionary resources have to gain continual approval from those involved. Thus commitment is built on both sides over time and deciding not to pursue the idea does not count as a 'failure' as it is less visible. In such projects, it is also easier to change approach: for example the focus of the project or the information technology tools used. Such changing of approach was associated with project success.

Underlying these problems of formalisation is the nature of systems aimed at effectiveness through faster and better decision-making or aimed at gaining competitive advantage. In these it is difficult to define precisely in advance what will meet business needs, especially where the technology or the application—or both—are new to those in the business. Early formalisation tends to make it more difficult to change approach, for example as a result of better understanding of user needs or market opportunities. It also makes stopping a problematic project more difficult. However at later stages, formalisation becomes important as in broader project implementation, lack of formal approval and integration into the planning and operations of the business function concerned tends to substantially reduce the impact of the project on business results.

Thus the problems and management requirements for successful information technology projects differ during their development. Two broad phases can be distinguished: a *development* phase lasting from the initial idea generation to the development of an initial working system, and an *implemen-*

tation phase in which a system is implemented fully within the business. These two phases will now be discussed in more detail.

THE DEVELOPMENT PHASE

In the development phase of a project, four main areas are of interest. The first is the *origin of ideas* for projects; the second the *nature of the problem* tackled; the third the nature of the *development team*; and the fourth the use of *prototyping* methods—which were found to be associated with project success.

Origins of ideas

Taking the origins of the projects, there was a small positive relationship between success and ideas coming from users rather than the information systems function. What was clearer was a positive association with championing of the project and ideas coming from the user side. Also there was a predominance of projects in which there was some form of joint initiative in formulating ideas. In this, organisational structures facilitating discussion and initial investigation of such ideas from both business and information systems viewpoints seemed to be beneficial. One such structure was through an information systems professional responsible for liaison with a business function, in effect in an 'account manager' role.

Problem characteristics

In the area of problem characteristics, it was not surprisingly found that the more a problem involved quantification, the more likely it was to succeed. The opposite was true of problems involving substantial judgement. Generally, the better the understanding of the problem structure involved in the project, the higher the level of success. The same was true of expert systems—refuting the view that expert systems are able to tackle unstructured problems. Rather expert systems were most applicable for structured problems involving relatively routine judgement, often combined with some quantification. More generally, understanding of the business processes involved in the area tackled was an important factor in success.

The user/information systems gap

The ability to understand business problems and hence develop information technology based solutions depended on the nature of the development team. In particular, success depended on bridging the gap between (i) users who often knew little about information systems and had not been involved in previous projects, and (ii) information systems professionals often unaware of detailed business needs. In successful projects, this gap was bridged within the development team—there had to be no significant gap in understanding and communication between those involved. The most critical area was converting business needs into functional specifications of information systems requirements, for example a production manager specifying the information needed to analyse plant performance.

Here past experience of a project champion was useful in some of the projects, though they were regarded as tough customers to please by the information systems function. Where this was not the case, someone had to fulfil this role—typically either by someone from the business area being moved into information systems in mid-career, or by an information systems professional with a long working relationship in the business area. This also implies that in the early stages of a project the quality of the staff in the development team is more important than the quantity.

Prototyping and its problems

The use of prototyping methods was associated with project success. Prototyping in this context is the development of small systems of restricted scope and/or functionality which users can test for themselves. The system design develops through an iterative process of evaluation followed by a further prototype system. Particular gains come from enabling users unfamiliar with information systems to see what can be done and thus to refine the specification of the functions of a desired system. Prototyping also enabled user interfaces to be tested before they were finalised, thus meeting user needs better. Using prototypes enabled changes of approach to be made at an earlier stage in a project. This meant the cost of change was lower as the technical design of the system was still undecided. It also enabled users to see if information technology could produce benefits without the cost of trying to specify and produce a full system, thus making it easier to stop a project which turned out not to be as promising as expected. However, analysis of the research results indicated that while a certain amount of prototyping gave positive results, a high level of prototyping gave no more benefits—and probably gave less. Why was this?

There were two main problems which arose from prototyping, both connected with the transition between the development and implementation stages of a project. The first was the nature of prototyping tools which are intended to permit rapid development (within days) of prototype systems. While these tools (e.g. *Lotus 123* and '4th generation languages') were highly productive at the early stages of projects, they were often inappropriate for future commercial working systems. For example, prototyping tools tended to be inefficient in the use of computer hardware leading to higher costs and response time problems. Also they were usually not the best tools for future maintenance of the system.

The second problem of prototyping was that associated with the 'freezing' of a specification at an appropriate stage. Having had the freedom to make changes quickly and easily in the early stages, there was a problem in moving towards a working system which would be more stable. This was necessary not only for the technical reasons outlined above but also for other reasons such as needing a final design to train users. In very few cases was it appropriate to continue prototyping methods into the implementation of the project. Thus while prototyping was a useful tool in the early stages of a project, there was a need to move away from this approach later on. This represents part of the shift from the development to the implementation phase of a project.

THE IMPLEMENTATION PHASE

The analysis above suggests that for successful development of an information technology project from an initial idea to a working system, a prototyping approach with a small high quality team probably works best. In addition, there is a need to be prepared to stop or change approach towards projects in which initial ideas do not work out. However, in the study there were a number of cases in which projects reached an initial working system but did not achieve the commercial use or business benefits foreseen by their initiators.

Project ownership

A major reason for this was the lack of management support and commitment among those who would be using the system. Again the roles of champions and sponsors are important. For while a champion from the information systems area or one in a boundary-spanning role could push an idea forward into an initial working system, wider implementation relied on commitment from the business function itself. Thus either a reasonably senior champion or a lower level champion combined with a high level sponsor had a much better chance of success. In particular it was necessary for the implementation of the system to become part of the planning and operations of the business function. In short, ownership of the project had to be in the business rather than the information systems function.

Managing the transition

The management and technical requirements in the implementation phase differ from those in the development one. On the management side, the marketing of the project becomes critical in ensuring that it will actually be used both internally and sometimes externally, especially for projects in the sales and marketing area. Technically, the requirements of the system change to include reliability and its delivery to users in a suitable form. This internal marketing is important for both technical and organisational changes associated with new computer and manufacturing systems.

Delivering the system

The delivery issue was a major one in some projects as prototypes had been developed on hardware to which most potential users did not have access. For example, customer access to viewdata was lower than predicted at the start of one project—meaning either a limited customer base or the need for a new method of delivery, for example on a personal computer. More generally, part of the marketing of a project could include persuading users that it was worthwhile to buy additional hardware. An established information technology infrastructure obviously helps provide a base for delivery as well as making it clearer when new hardware and system software will be needed. Software licensing conditions could pose problems, especially if use on a personal computer meant buying full licences for software which would not be used regularly.

As a result, it was easier for projects to succeed when they built on existing systems rather than requiring major new investment, especially when use of the system was not continuous—as was the case in most projects directed at improving management effectiveness and gaining competitive advantage. Sometimes this was impeded by the difficulty of linking new systems to existing ones, especially in the expert systems area. Another area of linkage, which has still to be exploited in many cases, is that between automated production technologies and business information processing.

User interface

This also meant that the user interface was an important aspect of success. With irregular use, often by managers with other competing priorities, it was necessary to ensure that the system fitted in with their methods of working. In cases where other systems were used, a common user interface was popular. For example, one project used an interface similar to Lotus 123, with which many users were familiar, although it was written in a standard computer language. In another, local sales offices had problems with a system for one product line which did not use the same interface as the system for others.

Maintenance

Maintenance of systems was another issue. In some expert systems projects, prototypes were abandoned after an assessment of the maintenance needs for a full system. This problem was particularly acute as maintenance of an expert system involves not only data but also rules. It was found that the best expert system and other prototyping tools often provided poor maintenance capabilities. Responsibility for maintenance was a potential organisational difficulty while the need to rekey data from other manual or computer systems was another obstacle. Other organisational issues posed problems in some projects, for example whether to give customers a copy of a marketing system or whether to keep it under the control of sales representatives and other internal staff. Perhaps the most serious was the loss of a champion through moving jobs before a project had been implemented and gained acceptance.

Many but by no means all of these problems can be foreseen in the development phase, e.g. user interface, delivery, maintenance and some organisational problems. In other cases it is the integration of the innovative information technology project into the business function which is critical. While linked to the development phase, the management needs in this implementation phase differ significantly. However, projects which were implemented fully often gave much higher benefits than originally envisaged, though taking longer to implement and sometimes costing more than expected.

MANAGING INNOVATION

Comparison with technical innovation

The results from the research broadly confirm that the factors identified for other forms of technical innovation such as advanced manufacturing technology also apply in the case of information systems projects. In particular, the existence of a strong project champion in a business (rather than information systems) area is critical to success. Good understanding of end-user needs by system developers is another important factor, as are mechanisms for communication with the users of the system. Senior management sponsorship and commitment was another factor behind success, but dependent on the existence of a champion. Use of external sources of information and contacts was not a major factor in success, though less successful projects were associated with low use. Effective development was essential, and in successful projects this often involved a relatively small project team working over an extended period of time.

An R & D approach?

This analysis of information technology innovations has concentrated primarily but not exclusively on those designed to increase effectiveness and gain competitive advantage, as with many flexible manufacturing systems (FMS).

This is in contrast to many earlier information systems geared mainly to efficiency gains through cost-reduction and automation of existing manual systems. This research suggests that these information technology innovations have both higher risks and higher benefits than are widely recognised—and that this trend is likely to continue. But while innovative projects are likely to be risky to various degrees, the management structures and processes related to information technology have become increasingly formalised and tend to make assumptions of a relative certainty of benefits. Further, there has often been budget pressure on the information systems function reducing the 'slack' resources available for discretionary use. This combination of factors has serious implications for future success in information technology innovation.

The analysis presented above implies that information technology innovation should be seen as essentially similar to research and development (R & D). It is particularly necessary when the focus of effort is on improving effectiveness and gaining competitive advantage. This means that a relatively large number of ideas wll be generated, of which some will be selected for further investigation. Then, using prototyping or similar methods, these ideas can be tested out and those with greatest potential selected for implementation. This process of continual selection and rejection of potential projects contrasts strongly with the tendency in many companies towards early formal approval of projects whose costs and benefits are assumed to be certain.

In the management of information technology innovation, such an 'R & D approach' means that two processes are important: (i) the recognition of opportunities for significant potential business gains; and (ii) the rejection as early as feasible of those which will not realise these gains. It is also important to recognise that if more risky projects are to be tackled, those considered must have higher potential gains than less risky ones; there is no point in aiming for high risk, low benefit projects.

This implies that formal approval procedures will need to be changed such that there are discretionary resources for the development of potential projects at early stages, followed by an increasing formalisation of approval processes. A checklist of factors likely to be behind project success could be used, including the following:

— Is there a champion/sponsor?
— What are the business gains and how risky?
— How can the project be stopped?
— Is prototyping being used?
— Are technology risks limited unless necessary for business goals?
— Are there gaps of understanding within the development team?
— How will it be delivered to users?
— Who will be responsible for maintenance and how?

The risk climate

Even if such changes were made to formal procedures, there are still substantial organisational obstacles to more successful information technology innovation. Probably most important is that of the climate of attitudes towards risk-taking. In many organisations, risky projects are avoided because of the costs to those involved of failure—in terms of prestige and career advancement. Stopping a project is often seen as an admission of failure, rather than a good management decision after investigation. Thus for effective innovation, there must be a tolerance of failure for risky projects and a climate which favours risk-taking when the benefits can be high. So while involvement in successful projects should be rewarded, failure up to a certain level should be accepted. These findings should be borne in mind when considering the advanced technology innovations in this volume.

Developing organisational capability

Even if the changes in organisational processes recommended above are implemented, there is still a need to develop an organisation's capability for information technology innovation. This involves two aspects: the first within the information systems function, and the second within the business as a whole.

Within the information systems function, there is obviously a need to ensure that some discretionary resources are available for the early development of project ideas. This could be done by reserving a proportion of the information systems function budget for such development work. Those involved in such areas will need a high level of business awareness, probably gained through either coming from or working closely with a business function. This also implies that many existing information systems professionals will need education in areas such as marketing. In addition they will need high productivity prototyping tools to use in the early phases of a project. Ideally, it should be possible to use these tools as a basis for commercial working systems in the future—with perhaps a proportion of the system needing rewriting if performance is an issue. It may also pay to use hardware inefficiently in order to reduce the lead times in implementing projects and increase the utilisation of scarce staff resources.

CONCLUDING REMARKS

More generally within the business, there is a need to spread awareness of the potential uses of information technology for effectiveness and competitive advantage. Education is one method, but its pay-off is likely to be greatest if it can be concentrated on senior management (potential sponsors) and also on potential champions. In the longer term, substantial benefits are likely if management development involves some time in the information systems function. Also staff could be recruited into the information systems function from user areas and then trained in the use of prototyping and other tools. In all these mechanisms, the pay-off will not be quick and will require commitment from both business and information systems functions. Training is of primordial importance in increasing organisational effectiveness. Such commitment is particularly true when linking manufacturing innovation with information technology.

Address for correspondence:

Oxford Institute of Information Management, Templeton College, Oxford OX11 5NY, UK.

REFERENCES

Cooper, R. G., and Kleinschmidt, E. J. (1986) An investigation into the new product process: steps, deficiencies, and impact. *Journal of Product Innovation Management*, **3**, 71–85.

Fischer, W. A., Hamilton, W., McLaughlin, C. P., and Zmud, R. W. (1986) The elusive product champion. *Research Management*, May/June, 13–16.

Freeman, C. (1974) *The Economics of Industrial Innovation*. Harmondsworth: Penguin.

Kanter, R. M. (1985) *The Change Masters: Corporate Entrepreneurs at Work*. London: Unwin.

Rothwell, R. (1977) The characteristics of successful innovators and technically progressive firms. *R & D Management*, **1**(3), 191–206.

Roussel, P. A. (1983) Cutting down the guesswork in R & D. *Harvard Business Review*, September/October, 154–60.

Science Policy Research Unit (1972) *Success and Failure in Industrial Innovation*. London: Centre for Study of Industrial Innovation.

Shanklin, W. L., and Ryans, J. K. (1984) Organising for high-tech marketing. *Harvard Business Review*, November/December, 164–71.

17. Managing Advanced Manufacturing Technology

Adrian Campbell[1] and Malcolm Warner[2]

[1]*School of Public Policy, University of Birmingham and* [2]*Department of Engineering, University of Cambridge*

SUMMARY

Traditional forms of organisation, characterised by fixed functional boundaries and hierarchical communication, may be inappropriate for computer integrated manufacturing and associated innovations. The difficulty involved in finding appropriate structures and practices for new technologies and manufacturing philosophies, and the acceleration of the change-cycle leads to a need for a 'culture of permanent implementation'. It may only be brought about within a highly adaptive organisational framework, and expansion in the resources devoted to training in general and management training in particular.

INTRODUCTION

Technologies, philosophies, and interdependence

Innovations currently being implemented in manufacturing should cover both technological systems and organisational philosophies. The emphasis thus far has been on *integration* (see Haywood and Bessant, Chapter 6, for example) and as such the technological and organisational solutions have themselves become increasingly interdependent. In cases such as computer integrated manufacturing (CIM), the term implies for both a technological configuration and an organisational approach. Without the organisational 'effort' implied by the concept of CIM, the full benefits of the relevant systems such as CAD/CAM (computer aided design/computer aided manufacturing) and MRP2 manufacturing resources planning) are unlikely to be forthcoming. Implementation has to be accompanied (and preceded by) *strategic* reappraisal of organisational aims, structures, practices and attitudes (Campbell, 1989). In

New Technology and Manufacturing Management   Edited by M. Warner, W. Wobbe and P. Brödner
Published 1990 by John Wiley & Sons Ltd

parallel, it may be said that the currently popular notions of 'just-in-time' (JIT) and 'total quality control' (TQC) are unlikely to be effectively applied in the absence of some form of information technology based system, which is likely to contain at least some of the elements associated with CIM (see Bullinger, Chapter 2 and Lay, Chapter 10, for example).

The epoch of the simple technological or organisational 'fix', whereby specific innovations could be applied successfully in isolation from each other, is now remote, if indeed it ever existed. In this chapter we attempt to explore the implications of these changes for *management roles*, *skills* and *structures*, and to link these to the central theme of the volume, as represented by specific chapter contributors.

Priorities and outcomes

Several questions come to mind. Will managers fulfil more or less flexible roles, will they have more, or less, discretion in decision-making? Will management become more participative, or less? Will there be more, or less, centralisation of organisational hierarchies? The answers to such questions depend, in the first place, on why new technologies are being introduced. Different managerial groups are likely to have a mixture of different goals regarding technology, which may be related to different perceptions of the organisational environment and what its implications are for strategy. Markets and the changes taking place within them provide one explanation for the extent of the interest in new technology:

> In order to remain competitive, many firms are investing in new technology incorporating microelectronics because markets are becoming more complex and (possibly more differentiated) where the environment in which firms operate has become more variable and uncertain. Even if the technological state-of-the-art is often ahead of the market, new manufacturing technologies are opening many marketing directors' eyes to new markets (Warner, 1986, p. 280).

Markets and technologies

Markets provide the first link in a causal chain, leading to responses involving new technology (although, as stated above, the process can work the other way round). Changes in markets and technologies, in turn, imply a variety of organisational effects. Before examining these, we should first summarise how technologies and their market-related rationales have themselves been undergoing changes given that: 'the previous logic of socio-technical design has been geared to specialised homogeneous mass markets, based on inflexible automation, an erosion of craft worker skills, and increased emphasis on separate planning activities' (Sorge *et al.*, 1983, p. 158), and several chapters in this volume have concentrated on this development.

In recent years, this picture has become fragmented, with more differentiated markets, smaller batches and greater customisation (Campbell and Warner, 1988a). Overall, the scene has been one of industrial 'demassification', with (in some countries and regions) the potential for 'flexible specialisation', whereby skill-intensive small-batch production across complex networks of small and medium-sized producers could become the dominant form for many industrial sectors (see Slack, Chapter 3; Kristensen, Chapter 12, for example).

In practice, however, it is still likely that the 'giant company' will continue to provide the context within which the activities of smaller firms operate. However, increased 'hiving off' and sub-contracting to smaller firms represents one of the major organisational changes taking place in the large firm sector, a process in which developments in microcomputer technology may play a facilitating role, as it has with 'teleworking' and organisational decentralisation in an (as yet) limited number of cases.

There are thus a number of discernible trends towards decentralisation (although this may mean a strengthening of the organisational operating-core), re-integration of skills, smaller batch production and increased customisation (linked to higher expectations from customers regarding quality). The phenomenon of CAD/CAM and CIM may be seen as particularly suited to the last stages of this sequence, where the technology is flexible, and a product either relatively or wholly customised, in differentiated or changing markets.

Management attitudes, not market forces

We may go on to argue that CAD/CAM and related technologies therefore make strategic sense. If organisations operated as they are believed to do according to classical free market theory, whereby firms are guided by 'market forces' to make appropriate decisions, there would be no organisational problem. However, as Senker (1988) has pointed out, the actions of management and of 'market forces' are not the same thing. Managements always have the discretion whether or not to innovate in a particular fashion (see Lockett, Chapter 16) and the consequences of their not doing so, or doing so badly, may not immediately become apparent. Such choice is a significant factor even where new technology is introduced as part of an integrated strategic approach, in relation to product and markets (and this is frequently not the case). The potential for success may still be constrained by managements' inability or refusal to innovate progressively in the area of organisation. Senker cites the example of training in Britain, where years of neglect by managements have resulted in skills shortages which in turn place constraints on the range of strategic options open to management regarding new technologies and products (see Campbell and Warner, 1987).

As Lane (1988) notes, firms in the Federal Republic of Germany have been more consistent in their pursuit of flexible specialisation strategies than their

British counterparts, despite the latter's aspirations in the same direction. In part, this discrepancy arises because 'British management is unwilling to make the long-term investment of resources which a sustained programme of training and retraining requires' (Lane, 1988, p. 161). Furthermore, she goes on to point out that:

> Whereas in Germany the new strategy is very much technology-led and inspired, in Britain the impetus has come more strongly from the relaxation of the constraints previously exerted by labour market conditions and the industrial relations systems (Lane, 1988, p. 165).

British management strategy has tended to emphasise control of labour as a yardstick of organisational effectiveness (see Sorge and Warner, 1986; Campbell *et al.*, 1989). The renaissance of interest in *management culture* in recent years has signalled a move away from this approach. Nonetheless, managements will still too often seize upon a concept such as 'flexibility' as a virtue in itself in the time-honoured tradition of management 'flavour of the month' initiatives, rather than embark on the more systematic reappraisal of organisational priorities and practices that the current situation demands (cf. Slack, Chapter 3).

IMPACT OF ADVANCED MANUFACTURING TECHNOLOGIES ON MANAGEMENT STRUCTURE

Vertical versus horizontal

Management structures in the 'flexible production system' we focus on, may emphasise either the *vertical* or the *horizontal*. If the former is emphasised, roles and tasks are clear-cut and communication (in theory) is rooted in the lines of hierarchical authority. If the latter is emphasised, there is more delegation of responsibility. In addition, the flow of information is more open, and there is a blurring of organisational barriers. Organisations of the latter type tend to be generally more adaptive, and it is such organisations which are more likely to be successful in periods of rapid change.

At the present time, organisations are being pushed in the direction of a more horizontally oriented structure, not only by the pace of change generally (including the speed with which technical innovations are diffused and product life-cycles shortened), but also, according to some commentators, by the intrinsic qualities of the technologies involved (in particular the current shift from mainframe-based systems to micro-based networks).

This process is likely to be accelerated (and complicated) by the expanded networks of informal links that occur where task-groups and project or matrix structures are involved (Campbell and Warner, 1989). These forms of 'team work' are likely to become an enduring feature of organisation where new technology is concerned (see Section 3 of this volume).

Removal of hierarchical levels

Such trends confirm the findings of Rothwell (1984), regarding new technology and the elimination of the supervisory level. If such elimination occurs, it would very likely amplify the role played by middle managers, along with the latter's need, in present circumstances, to liaise more closely with customers and suppliers regarding design, deliveries, quality and service. A different scenario is of course possible; the potential microtechnology provided for closer monitoring by senior management could be used by the latter as a 'protective cloak' under which they would have few reservations about delegating more responsibility to supervisory level. Middle management, therefore, deprived of both its authority-enforcing and information-passing roles, could be rendered increasingly redundant.

Development on these lines may depend on how the term 'middle management' is defined. If, for example, decentralisation of functional or business units is increased, and this decentralisation takes place on account of senior management's increased ability to monitor performance from a remote point, are the managers who head up such satellite units 'senior managers', or does their increased day-to-day accountability to the organisational 'core' of senior managers mean that their status is lower than it would have been considered in the past?

Technical complexity and organisational adaptation

A variety of structural adaptations, we would argue, are possible to a given technological challenge, particularly in the European context (see Wobbe, Chapter 15). Perhaps more important than the intrinsic qualities of this challenge, therefore, are the *speed* and *complexity* with which technological developments succeed one another (whether the trajectory of development is driven from within the organisation or from outside, and then introduced into the organisation). With each advancement, the network of technical and therefore also organisational interdependencies becomes more complex (see Kristensen, Chapter 12; Lockett, Chapter 16, for example).

Too often it has been assumed that organisational responses are able to keep pace with technology, and that an appropriate response emerges relatively easily. In practice, managers tend to underestimate the implications of technology for structure, or, more dangerously, expect the new technologies to fit in with the very structures, practices and (above all) assumptions which they have the potential to render obsolete, and make their selections and implementation decisions on that basis. In other words, organisations install technologies with *ex ante* structures which they believe will cope and provide a predicted level of performance. Indeed, managements would be unlikely to install new systems if they did not believe they could manage them. However, the *ex post* control structures which emerge may be somewhat different.

Where organisational complexity is concerned, what we are really referring to is organisational or managerial interdependency. In most situations we may say that greater technical complexity leads to greater organisational interdependency. Greater organisational interdependency potentially means greater difficulty in terms of managing the system as a whole. The question that occurs then is: does this potential for managerial breakdown actually result in a loss of control, or does the potential for systems integration offered by complex systems facilitate greater control than we have implied? With information technology systems we appear to encounter something of a 'dialectic paradox'. By this we mean that with each successive development, the greater the potential for organisational decentralisation, the greater the potential for re-centralisation.

In part, this 'paradox' derives from the earlier appearance of the mainframe computer, which is more inherently a tool of centralisation, to which end its successor, the microcomputer, may also be harnessed, if that is what senior management wishes. Had the microcomputer appeared first it is unlikely that it would serve so often as part of centralisation strategies.

The paradox of CIM

With CIM, the scenario may, however, be more complex than the picture outlined so far suggests (see Haywood and Bessant, Chapter 6). We referred above to the *information technology paradox* whereby the potential for its opposite also occurs. This paradox is founded on the trend whereby more complex systems generate greater possibilities for integration at a higher level, if this is desired.

We would argue that with each group of process innovations there are organisational forms which are appropriate to the demands of the technology in terms of optimal utilisation. Greater use of project and matrix forms represents one example of the trend whereby more flexible and integrated technologies have encouraged the spread of more flexible forms of organisation. Such developments have proceeded further where high-technology product development is concerned—where sophisticated microelectronics-based systems involving a need for more interdisciplinary communication, project and matrix structures have been maximised (often crossing the boundaries between firms as well as disciplines), and traditional line hierarchies have been minimised (Campbell and Warner, 1987).

With CIM in the full sense, however, the tension between the need for flexibility of organisation and the need for integration of disparate operations

functions and databases, already critical with CAD/CAM and flexible manufacturing systems (FMS), may be such that no optimal or even operable form
of management or work organisation can be suggested.

Its successful utilisation demands a clear break with the traditional characteristics of manufacturing businesses, particularly in the Anglo-Saxon world,
as the main emphasis of this volume argues. It is by no means clear, however,
that human organisations can effectively mirror the complex web of iterations
implied by computer-based integration and the associated disciplines of JIT
and TQC. It is, however, fairly clear what CIM would require in negative
terms; a shift away from the short-term business perspective generated by the
priorities of financial investors, a shift towards planning as an operation to be
undertaken by the organisation as a whole, not merely by isolated planning
staffs and elite groups of senior managers (excluding manufacturing managers, traditionally). It would also require an *upgrading* of the manufacturing
function itself (see Wobbe, Chapter 15, for example). Herein lies another of
the paradoxes of new technology. Hitherto the disorganised, expediting-
oriented approach to manufacturing meant that, for manufacturing managers
per se, low status was compensated for by a relatively high level of day-to-day
autonomy in the running of the plant. With innovations such as CIM, or with
CAD/CAM, MRP2, JIT and TQC for that matter, the renewed strategic
focus on manufacturing strategy could well lead to an intrusion of hitherto
distant senior managers into the manufacturing arena, against which traditional manufacturing (as opposed to production engineering), with little tradition of strategic planning, would have no effective response. The two scenarios in this case therefore are either:

(a) a *confirmation* of the subordinate position of the manufacturing manager,
    as other more 'strategically inclined' functions become involved with the
    manufacturing process as a whole, or
(b) an *upgrading* of the manufacturing role itself, whereby manufacturing
    managers will become the key coordinators of business operations—a
    role for which they would need a higher level of understanding of the
    potential of computer-based systems, as well as new skills and experience
    in the areas of marketing and customer liaison.

We should note here the extent to which the process of computer-based
integration in the factory has been accompanied by increased customer
contact in areas traditionally remote, such as stores, production, order-
processing, scheduling. Particularly where manufacturing resource planning
(MRP2) is present, we may find a greater emphasis on the relatively new
functions of 'customer development' and 'supplier development', and an
increase in the emphasis on boundary-spanning roles in general. There seems
to be a further paradox regarding information technology in manufacturing,

namely that the greater the emphasis on integration between functions within the enterprise, the greater the level of involvement with outside firms needs to be if the benefits of integration and cooperation within the firm are to be achieved.

The culture of permanent implementation

Another problem with CIM and related technologies is that, in contrast to earlier technological changes, there is not likely to be a clear break between successive stages of innovation (see Lockett, Chapter 16). System development, accompanied by shortening product life-cycles (as well as tighter competition generally) will continue more or less permanently, and in more than one direction simultaneously. In the long run, this will clearly have a number of consequences:

(a) An increase in the power of whichever agency within the organisation has the most control over (and awareness of) systems development, and the strategies and options available in that area.
(b) The more or less perpetual operation of project teams concerned with the design, selection and implementation of systems, although individual teams will appear and disappear with each designated project, during which there may also be many changes in the actual composition of the team.
(c) In smaller firms, or in firms without sufficient resources in terms of technical (or strategic) knowledge, there will perhaps be a greater role for consultants or persons seconded from systems suppliers. This move comes at a time when the market for consultancy in new technology has grown more competitive, and consultants (and systems suppliers) are looking to rely more heavily on repeat-business and possibly long-term relationships with particular firms. Tensions may arise with this expanded role for outside agencies, as consultants' perceptions of the need to place the implementation of new technology within an appropriate strategic context may clash with clients' conceptions of their own 'right to manage' (Campbell, 1989).

Susceptibility to environmental instability

In the preceding discussion, we have noted the extent to which integration within the firms depends for its success on a strengthening of links beyond the confines of the organisation, with customers, suppliers (of materials), suppliers (of systems) and external consultants. These 'voluntary' contacts form only part of the picture regarding new technology and external factors. There is also the question of environmental stability.

FMS and similar technologies may, we argue, result in higher levels of technically interdependent relations, technological uncertainty and environmental fluidity. Greater employee autonomy and sub-system self-regulation thus seem to be called for (see Schumann, Chapter 4; and d'Iribarne, Chapter 5).

DECISION-MAKING AND PARTICIPATION

Greater employee involvement at lower levels may not only be made more desirable with new technology, but may also be facilitated by it. A great deal depends on how technology is responded to in terms of changing the organisational structure of the enterprise. Our own research has found evidence that there will be a preponderance of graduates and skilled workers and technicians, vis-à-vis unskilled or semi-skilled labour, although gains in the numbers of skilled personnel will not offset the employment losses (at firm level) caused by shedding less skilled labour (Campbell et al., 1989). The changed composition of the workforce will render traditional management styles even less appropriate than they were in periods characterised by lower average skill levels in the workplace (see Brödner, Chapter 8; and Fix-Sterz et al., Chapter 13).

If decision-making on innovation selection is anything to go by, however, the outlook for greater participation is not as promising as some might have wished. Rothwell (1985) found that decisions on technology were 'top-down' in character, to the extent that supervisors and users were often the last group to know what was occurring. The key factor in determining this was apparently the management style of the project managers involved, depending on whether they were 'technically, hierarchically, or people-oriented'. The situation where even managerial users know nothing of the technology until it is dropped on their desk contrasts with the position in a number of US firms studied by Walton and Susman (1987), where trade union representatives participated in every stage of the process of introducing new technology, from visiting vendor companies onwards. Although, it is now fashionable for managers to speak of the need to win commitment from the workforce regarding new technology, there are few examples in Britain of unions being brought so early into the process of introducing technology. British trade unions are as yet unlikely to be allowed to participate in the selection of new equipment; their involvement is usually confined to implementation once the equipment has been purchased.

IMPACT ON MANAGEMENT STYLES AND SKILLS

What new skills will technology managers in a European context need? First, they will have to be more technically aware, if not technically qualified.

German firms have an existing advantage as a greater number of their managers have technical or engineering degrees; Japanese managers too, have technical qualifications of a high order. Second, they need specific management training to acquire the appropriate 'interpersonal skills' needed for operating within more complex, less hierarchical organisational structures (in addition to the likelihood of more external contacts). The nature of managerial work and therefore the skill requirements also, will change, right from first-line supervisor to top management. Managers need to be able to manage the process of change, and, as we have already implied, *communication* plays a very significant part in this, whether in particular projects, or in the 'adaptive organisation', where change becomes a permanent feature of the organisational culture (see Schultz-Wild, Chapter 7; Corbett, Chapter 9, for example).

MANAGEMENT EDUCATION, TRAINING AND DEVELOPMENT

Management education, external to the organisation, will need to be geared to the principles of technology and manufacturing strategy, in addition to the principles associated with technology management in the more routine sense. Implementation, increasingly recognised as an area of difficulty, will also need to be addressed by specific courses.

Management training will be required to present change in human-based systems as an organisational feature, rather than an occasional activity carried out within organisations. Students need to be encouraged in the direction of investigating the accelerated interdependence associated with new technological systems, rather than the more traditional approach geared to the management of discrete projects. Recent technological developments and the resulting need for a more 'holistic' approach to change have also led to demands for different approaches to accounting and project evaluation techniques. We believe that management training in this area would require more emphasis on recent alternatives in accounting, which have been developed with this broader approach to technology in mind.

In addition to the communication skills mentioned above, there is also the need for changes in traditional styles of management which may obstruct change: Adaptive behaviour may thus be developed and encouraged through appraisal systems and in-house courses.

We do not of course suggest that change is not problematic. It may frequently be the case that sweeping changes are put into effect on someone's initiative high up in the organisation, on the basis of half-baked principles, or straightforward self-interest. Those forcing the change may even employ the rhetoric of the 'adaptive and flexible organisation', whilst presenting an unadaptive and inflexible face to opponents of any part of the strategy, who are deemed to be 'resistant to change'. Such initiatives are misconceived not least in that they regard change strategies as exclusively top-down in nature. The point is that the more attitudes are encouraged which are open to change, the less one particular person or group's view of change is likely to dominate unconditionally or undeservedly. Scenarios of the type referred to immediately above may well be what results from a prior period of stagnation.

Finally, we should briefly mention the change occurring in the role of the training function. With the decline of union influence the traditional personnel function has also declined in influence. In Britain, our own findings have found many instances of a more strategic role being played (discreetly) by revitalised training functions within larger organisations (Campbell and Warner, 1988b). As awareness increases of skills and adaptiveness as a factor in gaining competitive advantage, the strategic scope and influence of the training function may well increase markedly. Training may provide some of the momentum for change in organisations where the line management is either weak or conservative, or where there is a growing body of opinion that the hierarchically oriented approach is *not* proving either proactive or responsive enough (see Sorge, Chapter 11; Bilderbeek, Chapter 14, for example).

CONCLUDING REMARKS

Organisational responses need to be open-ended where new technologies are concerned. We would strongly argue that what is true of the shop floor may also be appropriate where managerial personnel are concerned. Managerial organisation must now emphasise the complementary relationships between the user and the technology, as well as the interdependence of the different organisational and technical elements of the system as a whole. To sum up, the human-based systems emphasised throughout this volume must accompany the onset of the 'flexible factory', at all levels.

Addresses for correspondence:

Adrian Campbell: School of Public Policy, University of Birmingham, Birmingham B15 2TT, UK.

Malcolm Warner: Department of Engineering, Management Studies Group, University of Cambridge, Mill Lane, Cambridge CB2 1RX, UK.

REFERENCES

Campbell, A. (1989) Innovation and organisation: A consultancy perspective. IDOM (Innovation, Design and Operations Management), Working Paper, Aston Business School.

Campbell, A., and Warner, M. (1987) New technology, innovation and training. *New Technology, Work and Employment*, 2(2), 86–99.

Campbell, A., and Warner, M. (1988a) Workplace relations, skills-training and technological change at plant-level. *Relations Industrielles*, **43**(1), 115–30.

Campbell, A., and Warner, M. (1988b) Strategic choice, organisational change, and training policies: Case studies in high technology firms. Management Studies Research Paper, No. 8/88, University Engineering Department, Cambridge.

Campbell, A., and Warner, M. (1989) Organisation for new forms of manufacturing operations. In R. Wild (ed.), *International Handbook of Production and Operations Management*, London: Cassell.

Campbell, A., Sorge, A., and Warner, M. (1989) *Microelectronic Product Applications in Great Britain and West Germany: Product Strategies, Competence Requirements, Training and Personnel Policies*. Aldershot: Gower.

Lane, C. (1988) Industrial change in Europe: The pursuit of flexible specialisation in Britain and West Germany. *Work, Employment and Society*, **2**(2), 141–68.

Rothwell, S. G. (1984) Supervisors and new technology. *Employment Gazette*, January, 21–5.

Rothwell, S. G. (1985) Supervisors and new technology. In E. Rhodes and D. Wield (eds), *Implementing New Technologies: Choice, Decision and Change in Manufacturing*, Oxford: Blackwell, pp. 374–83.

Senker, P. (1988) International competition, technical change and training. Science Policy Research Unit and Imperial College Papers in Science, Technology and Public Policy No. 17.

Sorge, A., Warner, M., Hartman, G., and Nicholas, I. (1983) *Microelectronics and Manpower in Britain and West Germany*. Aldershot: Gower.

Sorge, A., and Warner, M. (1986) *Comparative Factory Organisation*. Aldershot: Gower.

Walton, R. E., and Susman, G. I. (1987) People policies for the new machines. *Harvard Business Review*, March–April, 98–106.

Warner, M. (1986) Human-resources implications of new technology. *Human Systems Management*, **6**(4), 279–87.

Index